D1451489

THE NEW
NEGOTIATING
EDGE

The new business agenda of the '90s focuses on working with change and developing people's potential and performance. The *People Skills for Professionals* series brings this leading theme to life with a range of practical human resource guides for anyone who wants to get the best from their people in the world of the learning organization.

Other Titles in the Series

COACHING FOR PERFORMANCE
The New Edition of the
Practical Guide
John Whitmore

CONSTRUCTIVE CONFLICT
MANAGEMENT
Managing to Make a Difference
John Crawley

EMPOWERED!
A Practical Guide to Leadership in the
Liberated Organisation
Rob Brown and Margaret Brown

LEADING YOUR TEAM
How to Involve and Inspire Teams
*Andrew Leigh and
Michael Maynard*

LEARNING TO LEAD
A Workbook On Becoming a Leader
*Warren Bennis and
Patricia Ward Beiderman*

MANAGING TRANSITIONS
Making the Most of Change
William Bridges

NLP AT WORK
The Difference that Makes a
Difference in Business
Sue Knight

POSITIVE MANAGEMENT
Assertiveness for Managers
Paddy O'Brien

THE POWER OF INFLUENCE
Intensive Influencing Skills at Work
Tom E. Lambert

THE STRESS WORK BOOK
Eve Warren and Caroline Toll

THE TRUST EFFECT
Creating the High Trust,
High Performance Organization
Larry Reynolds

THE NEW NEGOTIATING EDGE

The behavioral approach for results and relationships

Gavin Kennedy

NICHOLAS BREALEY
PUBLISHING

LONDON

To Kim, Giorgo, Harry, and Angela

First published by
Nicholas Brealey Publishing Limited in 1998

36 John Street	17470 Sonoma Highway
London	Sonoma
WC1A 2AT, UK	California 95476, USA
Tel: +44 (0)171 430 0224	Tel: (707) 939 7570
Fax: +44 (0)171 404 8311	Fax: (707) 938 3515

http://www.nbrealey-books.com

Library of Congress Cataloging in Publication Data applied for

ISBN 1-85788-205-9 (PB)
ISBN 1-85788-200-8 (HB)

British Library Cataloguing in Publication Data
A catalogue record for this book is available from the British Library.

Printed in Finland by Werner Söderström Oy.

Contents

Preface   xi

1 **Executive Overview**   1

2 **Negotiation as a Universal Process**   **8**
   A behavioral definition of negotiation   10
   Negotiation as an alternative   12
   When should you negotiate?   14
   Negotiation as a universal process   17
   The four phases   19
   Negotiation and culture   22
   Are there red and blue phases?   24
   Summary   25
   Recommended reading   27

3 **Attitudes, Beliefs, and Behaviors of Negotiators**   **28**
   Self-assessment 1   28
   A simple behavioral model   29
   The red–blue continuum   32
   Red attitudes   34
   Blue attitudes   37

Prisoner's dilemma	38
Red–blue game	42
Common plays of red–blue	45
Tit-for-tat	47
Purple behavior	50
Summary	54
Recommended reading	56
Answers to Self-assessment 1	57
4 The Haggle	**62**
Self-assessment 2	62
First offers	65
Price haggling	68
Haggler's surplus	75
Distributive haggling	78
Summary	80
Recommended reading	81
Answers to Self-assessment 2	82
5 Red, Blue, and Purple Ways to Prepare	**84**
Self-assessment 3	84
The red preparer	86
Tactical pressures on attitudes	88
Red and blue responses to preparation	90
Strategic pressures	96
Purple responses	98
Summary	101
Answers to Self-assessment 3	102
6 Basic Purple Preparation	**104**
Self-assessment 4	104
Interests	106
Issues	108
Priorities	109
Trading ranges, not positional posturing	111
Frigo's purple preparation	113
More than one issue	118
Summary	120
Answers to Self-assessment 4	122

7 Fights, Arguments, and Discord   **124**
  Self-assessment 5   124
  Red fights   126
  Threats   129
  "No more Mr nice guy"   131
  Red argument   135
  Irritation   138
  Interruptions   139
  Attacking and blaming   140
  Summary   142
  Recommended reading   143
  Answers to Self-assessment 5   144

8 Debates, Signals, and Concord   **146**
  Self-assessment 6   146
  Managing movement   151
  The language of the signal   152
  The purple message of the signal   157
  The purple response to a signal   159
  Wallowing techniques   161
  Listen to Mrs Luigi   165
  Summary   168
  Recommended reading   169
  Answers to Self-assessment 6   170

9 Difficult Red Negotiators   **172**
  Self-assessment 7   172
  Match or contrast?   175
  Behaviors and outcomes   180
  Merits or trade   185
  Summary   186
  Answers to Self-assessment 7   189

10 The Color Purple   **190**
  Self-assessment 8   190
  Multiple-issue trades   193
  Red demands versus blue offers   194
  Purple conditionality   197
  Handling all behaviors   200

Summary   204
Answers to Self-assessment 8   207

11 Proposing   **208**
Self-assessment 9   208
Tentative proposals   214
Purple responses to a proposal   220
Purple packaging   223
Summary   226
Answers to Self-assessment 9   228

12 Purple Bargaining   **230**
Self-assessment 10   230
Negotiating a purple bargain   233
Bargaining leverage   235
Purple relationship bargaining   241
Closing the negotiation   245
Summary   250
Recommended reading   252
Answers to Self-assessment 10   253

13 Rational Problem Solving: An Alternative?   **254**
Self-assessment 11   254
Rationality and irrationality   256
Hard or soft?   256
A brief critique of principled negotiation   257
Recommended reading   261
Answers to Self-assessment 11   261

14 The New Negotiating Edge   **262**
Self-assessment 12   270

Appendix: Rules for the Red–Blue Dilemma Game   273

The New Negotiating Edge – Map of the book

Chapter 1:   Executive Overview

Chapter 2:   Negotiation as a Universal Process

Chapter 3:   Attitudes, Beliefs, and Behaviors of Negotiators

Chapter 4:   The Haggle

Chapter 5:   Red, Blue, and Purple Ways to Prepare

Chapter 6:   Basic Purple Preparation

Chapter 7:   Fights, Arguments, and Discord

Chapter 8:   Debates, Signals, and Concord

Chapter 9:   Difficult Red Negotiators

Chapter 10: The Color Purple

Chapter 11: Proposing

Chapter 12: Purple Bargaining

Chapter 13: Rational Problem Solving: an Alternative?

Chapter 14: The New Negotiating Edge

INTRODUCTION

↓

PREPARE

↓

DEBATE

↓

PROPOSE

↓

BARGAIN

↓

SUMMARY

Preface

"Why is it that Black, Brown, White, Grey and Green should
be so prevalent as surnames whereas, so far as I am aware,
Blue, Red, Yellow and Purple are not?"
G.A.A. Scriven, Letter to *The Times*, 3 February 1997

*T*HE *New Negotiating Edge* is a thoroughly practical learning
tool, making full use of my 28 years' experience in this field.
It can be read as a single text alone or alongside
recommendations for further reading for those who want to
consider the subject in more depth.

In most of the chapters there are self-assessments for you to
practice on. You can compare your answers with mine at the end
of the chapter. Examples of negotiating behaviors are illustrated
in "boxed inserts" (names have usually been changed to protect
confidentiality) and these can be dipped into at will or set aside
for later reference.

A short MBA-type examination in negotiation is also included
as the final self-assessment for you to try after you have read *The
New Negotiating Edge*. If you would like this to be assessed by me,
please send your answers to the address shown at the end of
the book and, if you pay for my postage, you will receive a set of
model answers!

My aim is for the text to be interesting as well as informative, with a light touch in commentary and explanation, behind which there is a heavyweight message. Sure, some ideas about negotiation require some hard (but not too hard) work to grasp first time round and I see my task as to make things as simple as I can (though not too simple). So I invite you to enjoy what you read as much as you enjoy the rewards from putting these methods to work, under whichever behavioral color you find relevant for the circumstances.

The New Negotiating Edge is for negotiators everywhere— including those who lead and train them. It is also for the people with whom you deal, for the sharper their perception of their behavior the better the deals you will get with them. So, in pursuit of self-interest, sell them a copy. As so often in life, by serving their interests you serve your own!

Over many years, many thousands of people have contributed to my understanding of the ubiquitous phenomenon of negotiation. To mention them all would be impossible, but among those to whom I owe a personal debt are: E. Taylor, Anthony Lambert, Geoff Knight, A. Perry and Dr Adrian Lander of the Shell Haven management team and W. Mullinder, R.A. Bellinger and C. Mansfield of the Shell Haven Joint Union Negotiating Committee. Their patient cooperation with a "youngish" lecturer during 1969–71 sparked my life-long interest in how people negotiate prices, as opposed to how I taught price determination from economic theory.

Also, no account of my work on negotiation would be complete without acknowledging the contribution of Colin Rose, of Rose & Barton Pty, Victoria, Australia. He will recognize what follows, but, more importantly, I hope he approves.

Ex bona fide negotiari.

Gavin Kennedy
Edinburgh and Langragnat, 1998

Executive Overview 1

THIS is the first book on negotiating to provide a clear language for handling the complexity and dilemmas of everyday bargaining. It uses vivid mind's-eye images of red, blue and purple to identify a whole range of negotiators' behaviors and links these to the four phases common to all negotiations—prepare, debate, propose and bargain.

Identifying the competing colors of the phases and practicing the behavioral skills appropriate to each color provides the **new negotiating edge**, long sought but seldom attained in negotiation practice.

Most authors present negotiating as a choice of mere "tactics" and ploys, delivered by so-called tough wiseguys, in what *The New Negotiating Edge* calls the **red** style.

THE RED STYLE

This obsession with red behaviors reflects the all too common perception among untrained negotiators of what negotiation is about. They believe that manipulation is normal and therefore they behave as they believe. It is more than wish-fulfillment—it is self-destructive, because in the real world, no matter how "tough" you try to be, waiting round the corner is a tougher guy.

Red behaviors are associated with aggressive, intimidatory and manipulative attitudes. You behave in a red manner when you fear exposing yourself to exploitation by the other negotiator, but in protecting yourself you provoke the very behavior you to seek to avoid.

You always behave red when you intend to exploit the other negotiator: the result you seek is based on what you believe is best for yourself alone because you feel no obligation to sustain a relationship.

Red behavior begets red behavior. You cannot assume that everybody with whom you negotiate sees the relationship in the way that you do. Their behavior can reveal, or mask, their intentions. The result they seek may be at your expense.

THE BLUE STYLE

Other authors believe that something softer, kinder and more open than manipulation is the necessary antidote to red posturing. They often assert that this is a "win–win" approach, but give little practical advice on how to achieve the results they seek. It is a great deal easier to sign up to win–win intentions than it is to practice win–win behaviors, particularly in a red bargaining environment. *The New Negotiating Edge* calls these behaviors the **blue** style.

Unfortunately, unilateral attempts at win–win behaviors have little scope in everyday commercial negotiations—in practice, for example, people bring with them to their negotiations a bag full of "tough" red and "soft" blue attitudes that drive their behavior when they are face to face with whomever they see as the obstacle, or the means, to their getting what they want.

Blue behaviors are associated with cooperative, trusting and conciliatory attitudes. The result you seek if you are a blue behaviorist is driven by what you believe is best for both of you, because you are seriously biased towards your relationships.

In the extreme, however, your assumed relationships

may be a mirage. If any of them are, your blue intentions will be frustrated and you will be disappointed with both your results and your relationships.

The main behavioral dilemma in negotiation is whether to **cooperate** (blue) or **defect** (red). This dilemma drives your behavior and, therefore, how you treat the other person and how they treat you.

The consequences of cooperation or defection are explored through prisoner's dilemma games, which address that ubiquitous concern of practicing negotiators: "To what extent, if any, can I trust them?"

Where there is trust, there is also risk. But being too trusting is naive; not trusting at all provokes untrustworthy behavior.

The key to solving the dilemmas of trust and risk is not to alternate between non-trusting red and too trusting blue, but to fuse them into **purple** conditional behavior.

This fusion neatly expresses the essence of the negotiation exchange: give me some of what I want (my red results side) and I will give you some of what you want (my blue relationship side). Red is taking behavior, blue is giving behavior and purple is trading behavior, taking while giving.

Purple behavior is a two-way exchange and not a one-way street.

Purple behavior deals with people as they are and not how you assume or want them to be. It is biased towards how negotiators behave and prefers the evidence of their behavior to affirmations of their good intentions, but it is not a rationale for cynicism.

Purple behavior responds to and nurtures purple behavior and plays strict tit-for-tat behavioral strategies that are open, learnable, certain and 'nice'.

Experiments show that young children can identify a tit-for-tat strategy after a few exchanges, but that educated adults find difficulty in identifying competing non-tit-for-tat strategies, even after long sequences of exchanges. What can be spotted quickly has a learning advantage over what remains unclear and controversial.

Negotiators know where they stand with purple behaviorists who apply a consistent set of behaviors in response to all other negotiators.

To a red behaviorist, the purple negotiator insists on the reciprocity of the proposed exchange: "You will get absolutely nothing from me unless and until I get something from you." This can be said in any tone of voice—it does not require so-called tough shouting (or phoney posturing) to have effect.

Real toughness

Real toughness comes from a resolute determination to resolve problems solely by the twin criteria of the merits of a case and/or the terms of a negotiated exchange. There is no need to waver between red and blue, nor to dither about trust or distrust. You set your terms for the deal and only move from them in direct exchange for movement by the other party. Whether the other person is trustworthy or otherwise depends solely on what they agree to do, not on their hidden and unknowable intentions.

Purple behavior brings people as they are, warts and all, right into the center of the negotiating process. With purple negotiating styles you can handle all possible behaviors from the other party without you losing the plot.

The purple negotiator has the same message for the devious red player and the submissive blue player: it's merits or trade! Purple behavior denies victory to either red- or blue-biased behavior, should either of them be tried, and eschews exploitation of others, whatever the color of their behavioral bias.

Purple behavior is the **new negotiating edge** you need when looking into the eyes of other negotiators who believe (but do not necessarily reveal) that they have got your measure.

THE FOUR PHASES

The New Negotiating Edge is not about what people ought to do, rationally or otherwise—it's about how they really do behave and what you can do about it. This authoritative text is written from the unique perspective of **negotiation as the purple fusion of red and blue behaviors within a universally common process**, practiced the world over.

That universal common process has four phases. Each phase identifies its minimal task. Hence:

Phase	Task
Prepare	What do we want?
Debate	What do they want?
Propose	What wants could we trade?
Bargain	What wants will we trade?

You negotiate about the ratio of what you want from them to what they want from you. This clarifies what negotiations are about and, for those who acquire that clarity, it is a distinct **negotiating edge**.

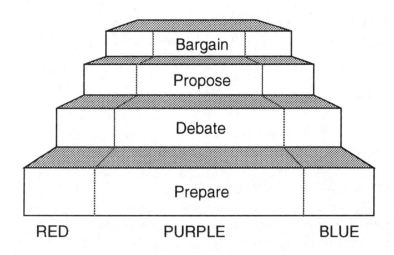

RED   PURPLE   BLUE

Changing previously poor red or soft blue **preparation** behavior generates substantial improvements in your performance. Out-preparing the other party is a **negotiating edge** that you can gain without indulging in

PREPARE

disreputable behavior towards other negotiators. How much time and effort you decide to expend in your preparation is completely within your own control and does not detract from the time and effort the other negotiator may decide to expend on their own behalf. Clearly, time and effort invested in purple preparation are well spent, while red or blue preparation on their own waste scarce resources of time and effort.

DEBATE

Constant exposure to how people negotiate demonstrates that much face-to-face behavior is misdirected. **Debate** can degenerate into red argumentative behavior (attacking, blaming and threatening) and, when it does, negotiators lose their edge along with their temper!

Debate can also be constructive (questioning, listening, summarizing and signaling) and, when it is, negotiators sharpen their purple edge. They control their emotions and, with the confidence that comes from thorough purple preparation, they enhance their performance, often quite dramatically.

PROPOSE AND BARGAIN

Proposing and **bargaining** behaviors distinguish negotiation from other decision-making techniques such as persuasion, instruction, and coercion. Negotiating is about getting what you want from somebody by exchanging with them some of what they want.

In proposing or bargaining you state the contents of potential purple exchanges. Proposals are tentative suggestions; bargains are specific conditional offers. Both can be assertively purple only if the negotiator chooses the appropriate conditional language.

Inadequate ways of proposing or bargaining blunt the negotiator's edge. They turn potential deals into confused rambles, or into unassertive statements of intention, and surrender the initiative to people who may not have your best interests among theirs.

KNOW WHAT YOU ARE DOING

All negotiators are four-phased negotiators, because the negotiation process is universal to all peoples in all cultures, but not all negotiators are purple players. Some (too many) are merely red takers and many of the rest are merely blue givers. Some (too few) are purple traders.

Those negotiators who become aware of which phase they are in and which color of behavior they are exhibiting (they know what they are doing) undoubtedly gain an edge over those who remain unaware of phases or behavioral styles. The unaware negotiator stumbles about in relative ignorance—sometimes they get it right by luck rather than judgment, but mainly they get it wrong without knowing why, nor do they know what they can do about it.

The New Negotiating Edge is not an academic treatise. It offers a behavioral perspective, not a theoretical one, and its prescriptive advice is founded on solid practice in the real world of deal making.

THE BEHAVIORAL
APPROACH

2 Negotiation as a Universal Process

ANIMALS do not negotiate. They use violence, or the threat of violence, and various forms of "dominance" and "display" to get what they want, be it food, mates or territory. Theirs is a red world: red in tooth, claw, instinct and intention, because nature is cruelly, not benignly, neutral.

It is true that nobody has ever seen two dogs negotiate over a bone. Animals (and some humans) who are cowed by red behavior do without; those who aren't, fight for what they want. In this way the bounties of nature have been distributed over the millennia.

Not everyone negotiates

Not all humans negotiate. Some also use violence, or the threat of violence, to get what they want. They are nature's red takers, not humankind's purple negotiators. They belong to the "Genghis Khan" school of wealth distribution. While what they want exists they take it. Once it has gone, they have to move on. They create a desert and call it peace.

But, while both the bounties of nature and the fruits of labor can be *distributed* by violence, they cannot be *created* by it. That is the fatal flaw in all societies based solely on red violence and coercion. They are, in consequence, always poorer than those based on voluntary exchange through purple negotiation.

That this is self-evident has not averted 10,000 years of futile attempts by our predecessors to defy it nor, unfortunately, does it help those who in recent years have suffered the social consequences of unbridled violence in the likes of Afghanistan, Liberia, Rwanda, Burundi, Congo and the Balkans.

It was humankind's proclivity for trade that eventually triumphed over violence. The change was initially almost imperceptible, but because it was cumulative (the law of compound interest) it did not require the sanction of human will.

The triumph of trade over violence

Trade is the foundation of human civilization. It is what makes humans different from animals. The triumph of trade over violence created the conditions for the sustainable creation and distribution of wealth, quantitatively and qualitatively, on scales beyond our predecessors' imaginations.

Inescapably, trade also created the very human phenomenon of negotiation.

Negotiation is anathema to tyrants, who usually want something for nothing and do not recognize a need for another person's voluntary consent before they get what they want.

This is not to say that the traders themselves were, or are, a band of brotherly saints. Far from it. Many, if not most, traders were no doubt devious and duplicitous in the extreme. As Tennyson said, "Who but a fool would have faith in a tradesman's ware or his word?" Many were knaves and they made an unedifying spectacle while conducting their business.

So-called noble savages were not superseded by even more improbable noble traders! Traders reflect the mores of their times and for many of them their trading activities were inextricably bound up with the violence of their societies. Early experiments with international trade were exposed to piracy, ambush, and confiscation, some of it probably conducted by the same people who pioneered trading.

If the road to hell is paved with good intentions, the road to mass affluence was pioneered by some very dubious characters who laid no claim to what today we call the "moral high ground". In popular consciousness, evidenced in surviving literature and probably with good reason, traders were hardly considered fit to walk in the company of those destined for a heavenly abode.

Keeping promises

For trading to develop into a self-sustaining social system, it required an ability for individual traders on both sides of the bargain to keep their promises by fulfilling their side of the bargain. Early traders learned that there were violent consequences if they broke their promises.

Today the law of contract and judicial remedies have replaced private vigilantism against promise breakers, but many of our trading predecessors suffered appallingly if they were caught cheating (and some still do in the retributive discipline of criminal drug gangs).

But the act of trading itself, when finally it was able to thrive over a long enough period and coincidentally with emerging technologies, eventually triumphed over the monopoly of decision making through red violence.

However, remnants, sometimes more than just remnants, of the red taker's philosophy, be it by coercion or by duplicity, are still found in today's Age of Negotiation, and they pose latent threats to its continuance.

A BEHAVIORAL DEFINITION OF NEGOTIATION

The negotiator says, in effect:

> "Give me some of what I want and I will give you some of what you want."

It is as simple and complex as that!

Exhibit 1   Negotiation defined behaviorally

> The process by which we search for the terms to obtain what we want from somebody who wants something from us.

The best negotiation is purple

Negotiation is conceived of as trading or exchanging something we have for something we want from another person. As we shall see throughout this book, for the most enduring effect trading is neither red coercive nor blue submissive—it is a purple exchange that gives up what we have (blue) in exchange for what we want (red).

Negotiation is the essential characteristic of a wealth-creating society because it makes possible the voluntary distribution of whatever, allied to nature, is created by human effort and serves human needs.

Without purple negotiation, humankind's future would be centuries of tyrannies and the kind of living standards not experienced for millennia.

Negotiation is an explicit voluntary traded exchange between people who want something from each other. Negotiators can veto the offered terms, whereas in violent red processes, common to animals and tyrants, there are unpleasant consequences from resisting them, hence blue submissives don't resist.

Ideally, negotiators are free to say "yes" when the terms are seen to be right and "no" when they are not.

Negotiators search because they do not know beforehand whether agreement is possible. You may search in good faith (and should do so—*ex bona fide negotiari*) and still not find a solution on terms that you are willing to accept.

In negotiation you are dependent on finding somebody else who wants something from you. If nobody wants anything at all from you, then you must do without what you wanted, or revert to violence or tyranny—the red inflict the violence and the blue suffer the tyranny.

Humans can choose to cooperate when they are in conflict (negotiation) or they can choose a "two dogs solution" (war). Negotiation, then, is about finding out if there are terms for cooperation that are mutually acceptable to both parties.

NEGOTIATION AS AN ALTERNATIVE

Negotiation is an alternative to several other decision methods, some of them closely associated with, and helpful to, negotiation processes, and others that are not.

Exhibit 2   Some ways we make decisions

Persuasion	"We deserve a break"
Giving in	"OK, you deserve a break"
Instruction	"Give me a break"
Coercion	"Give me a break—or else!"
Litigation	"I'll sue to get a break"
Problem solving	"How can we both get a break?"
Chance	"Heads I get a break"
Arbitration	"Which of us deserves a break?"

Source: *The Negotiate Trainer's Manual*, 1996, Negotiate Ltd, Edinburgh, p. 4.

Persuasion

Selling skills, for example, are based on **persuasion** techniques. Persuasion is usually the first method we choose when we want something. When it works, persuasion is fine.

People who have been persuaded are not usually angry with you (unless they find out that you lied). But when persuasion doesn't work it usually ends in tension and conflict: "I came here to be reasonable but you have chosen to be stubborn!"

Persuasion is also a powerful technique when used as part of a negotiation, but it is a less effective substitute for negotiation when interests or opinions differ markedly.

Giving in is not a wimp's choice.

Giving in

It is best to give in when the odds are overwhelming or the costs of doing otherwise are excessive. You give in when you buy anything for the price on the tag. It makes sense to do so if the cost is small and the time likely to be required to haggle for a better deal is excessive. (If it takes you 30 minutes to get 3 pence off a can of beans, you value your time at only 6 pence an hour!)

Giving in is *not* a helpful choice when it sends the wrong message to the other negotiator.

Instruction is appropriate when the person instructed is obliged to do what you tell them because you have the authority (as a manager or a parent) and they have the obligation (by contract, convention or law) to do so.

Instruction

Instruction is only efficient if the other person has the ability, the tools (including knowledge) and the time to carry out your instructions.

Instruction is not usually helpful in negotiation as it implies that the other person does it because they are obliged to, rather than them consenting to do it.

Coercion varies in degree from gentle reminders of unspecified consequences to threats of specific acts of violence. Even stating your options—"I can take my business elsewhere"—can be coercive.

Coercion

Threats and coercion are not normally helpful when you are negotiating as they sour the atmosphere and change the basis of the decision. Threat cycles explode into sanction battles where pressure replaces voluntary consent.

Most **litigation** (over 94 percent!) is settled by negotiation or lapses before it gets to court, which shows that there is great scope in the civil legal process for the resolution of disputes by negotiation.

Litigation

However, sometimes you have no other option other than to resort to litigation. Writs sometimes "bring the

Problem solving

Chance

Arbitration

other person to their senses" during a negotiation. In criminal law, "plea bargaining" is becoming common.

Problem solving requires a high degree of trust between the parties involved and the recognition that they share the problem. If the parties have built up a strong relationship, then problem solving is an appropriate choice.

Trying to problem solve in other circumstances (because somebody thinks it is "nice" or a "good idea") is mostly futile.

Leaving the decision to **chance** is OK if you are not too concerned about either of the competing decisions, otherwise it is not so clever. Tossing a coin can save you from an acrimonious argument or a great deal of wasted dithering.

Arbitration effectively hands the decision to a third party and, once the disputing parties make their final submissions, they have no further influence on the arbiter's compromise between the competing parties' positions.

Alternatively, in pendulum arbitration, the arbiter must choose outright one or other of the competing final positions, with no compromises allowed. This tends to pull the parties towards each other to avoid provoking the arbiter into rejecting their extremism which, it is alleged, sometimes removes the necessity for arbitration.

No single decision process is superior to its rivals and, in different circumstances, some processes are less appropriate than others. Should negotiation be judged to be appropriate, the conditions for negotiation may have to be created before its benefits can be enjoyed.

WHEN SHOULD YOU NEGOTIATE?

The most important motivation for negotiating is the necessity of securing the consent of those who have what you want. If their consent were not needed there would be no point in negotiating with them. You would simply take what you want and leave them to fend for themselves.

There has been a remarkable dispersal of negotiating activities into areas previously dominated by hierarchical, top-down decision making.

Negotiating was always prevalent in commerce—buying and selling—long before anybody resorted to training in negotiating skills. During the past 20 years, however, negotiating has extended to all manner of activities and to all kinds of organizational and personal relationships.

People are less deferential than they were only a short time ago and they are less likely to accept what somebody else decides is good for them—they insist much more on having an influence on what affects them. "Like it or lump it" is no longer an acceptable option for those living in free societies.

Withholding consent is a key feature of decision making today. If you need someone's consent you will have to negotiate for it. But negotiating takes time and effort, and does not guarantee success—the other party may still say no. What you are offering may not be enough for them. What they are prepared to consent to may not satisfy your requirements. In this case, one or both of you will have to reconfigure what you are offering if you wish to avoid a failure to agree.

Withholding consent

But what people will consent to is not fixed and certain. For all but regular, routine, minor transactions, such as in a retail store, the outcome of a negotiation is uncertain.

Uncertainty

Uncertainty over what will be acceptable before consent can be obtained is one of the driving forces of negotiation. You can value a property but you cannot force someone to buy it at your valuation, for example. They may have other ideas about its worth and, if you want to sell it to them, you will have to revise your asking price.

In retailing, prices are fixed with a high degree of certainty. Point-of-sale data shows how many people bought which goods at the shop's fixed prices that day (even by the hour!). This gives store managers a great deal of price-fixing power. They can visually scan the shelves when they open and close the shop and compare the two pictures. If the shelves are still full of products, all faced off

Exhibit 3   When to negotiate

● When we need someone's consent

● When the time and effort of negotiating are justified by the potential outcome

● When the outcome is uncertain

Source: *The Negotiate Trainer's Manual*, 1996, p. 6.

in neat lines, then there is something wrong with the prices, packaging, positions or, perhaps, the products themselves. The store managers will take remedial action to vary any, or all, of these causes of slow or no sales.

Thus, your demand to negotiate over the prices of low-value products would carry no weight with store managers because they believe they know, with some degree of confidence, how many other people will buy their products at the store's fixed prices that day. As long as this number clears their shelves of product, they will disdain to negotiate over the price of your groceries.

Most transactions are uncertain

But the terms of the majority of business-to-business transactions are not so certain. Many higher-value products do not have an hourly, sometimes not even an annual, market, hence their market-clearing prices are uncertain. Even experts cannot be certain of the price for which a high-value product will sell, though they are more likely than non-experts to be approximately right more often than they are absolutely wrong. And it is on the ratio of being "approximately right" to being "absolutely wrong" that managers focus their efforts and rest their careers.

Those who believe that they know all the prices at which products will be bought or sold in a complex economy are clearly out-of-work Soviet price planners (which is why they are out of work!).

Observation suggests that no matter how high the price

at which you sell your product, you would still prefer to sell it at an even higher price, and that no matter how cheaply you buy a product, you would still prefer to pay even less for it.

No matter what you get in return for your consent, you will probably prefer to get more, and no matter how little you offer in exchange for someone's consent, you would prefer to offer even less. It is not that humans are irreversibly greedy, so much as they are easily dissatisfied.

Feed a starving man with odious scraps of offal and, once he is full, he will seek better food next time. Raise a generation's living standards to several times those of their grandparents and they will want yet higher living standards for their children.

On such impulses all material progress thrives.

You may abhor these aspects of human nature and you may successfully rearrange your affairs to avoid all material considerations. In consequence, however, you will experience an extremely low standard of living.

I have met many affluent and educated teenagers in a state of aimless discontent who bemoan their (or rather their parents') affluence, but I have never (yet) met anybody actually experiencing abject poverty who did not wish to improve their lot.

Recently, I heard on the radio a pensioner whose ambition to alleviate her "poverty" was to have the state (i.e., the taxpayers) supply her with a heated towel rail for her shower-room! Her grandparents would probably have been overjoyed to have a towel (and would not have looked to the taxpayer to provide it).

NEGOTIATION AS A UNIVERSAL PROCESS

While every negotiation is unique, every negotiation is also the same.

Negotiations are unique because no two pairs of people, or even the same pair on successive occasions, are exactly the same in their attitudes and behaviors. They bring to each negotiation the history of every other negotiation they have undertaken, including those with each other on similar issues.

As Heraclitus said: "You cannot step twice into the same river"—because the river moves on.

Negotiations are the same because all negotiations go through a common process, no matter who they are between, what they are about, which culture(s) the parties are from, or how big or small are the stakes.

The common process of negotiation

The realization that all negotiations are both unique and the same is only some 35 years old. Up to the early 1960s, people regularly negotiated but few, if any, thought about what they were doing in a scientific manner. Of course, once intelligent people started to think about negotiation as an activity worthy of study, it was not long before its common process was uncovered.

The identification of this common process or phases was not the result of a rational, deductive theory of what you ought to do when you negotiate. The phases were identified from observing what people like you *did* when they negotiated. Observation suggested that **everybody who negotiates is a phased negotiator**.

NOT THE BEDFORD TRUCK DRIVERS' INSURANCE POLICY

Years ago, truck drivers were offered what appeared to be a good deal by an insurance company. They could insure their life for a single shilling and their family would receive the equivalent of their annual wage if they were killed while driving a Bedford truck. The small print revealed that their family was only eligible for the award if they were killed by another Bedford truck!

Unlike in this insurance example, you can benefit from awareness of the four phases of negotiation whether or not the other negotiator is aware of them.

This powerful conclusion is good news if you want to improve your performance. You are not required to reform the structure of negotiation, nor must you find another "restructured" negotiator, before you can do better. You just apply your new skills in the same phases that you passed through before you were aware that they existed.

By identifying the common phases, you are in a position to do better than before because now you know what is going on when you negotiate. You know where you are going. And by identifying which behaviors work best in which circumstances, you can practice the most appropriate behaviors. This alone improves your performance, no matter what level of performance you start from.

Know what is going on

Training and, above all else, practice in the behaviors appropriate to each phase displaces the myth that "negotiators are born not made". This is a ludicrous assertion given the need for everybody to negotiate on a regular basis, no matter what "innate" abilities they are born without.

Unless there was a universal process, how could anyone learn to negotiate? Without a common process, there would be as many ways to negotiate as there are people, which would make the entire process random, chaotic and, ultimately, unmanageable.

What is remarkable is that it took so long after the phenomenon of negotiation first appeared, unknown millennia ago, for anybody to consider it worthy of in-depth study. But once negotiation was seriously studied, its basic process was quickly identified.

THE FOUR PHASES

A brief summary of the four phases of negotiation might be helpful at this point.

It could be argued that all your previous experience is a form of **preparation** for negotiation. Should you not have sold an oil tanker before, you are going to be less well prepared to do so than the person across the table who has

Preparation

not bought anything else but oil tankers for the past 20 years. In these circumstances, not adding preparation to your lack of experience in the oil tanker business is likely to prove an expensive way to acquire experience!

Debate

Communication is essential for negotiations to progress. Over 80 percent of the time spent in communication is spent in some form of **debate**.

We can debate constructively (blue) or destructively (red). We can succumb to our attitudes or beliefs, which may not help if they clash with the attitudes and beliefs of the other negotiator. We can rise above clashes of attitudes and beliefs and debate constructively in a search for the basis of a settlement, or we can argue (but not negotiate) about principles, emotions, beliefs, prejudices, the "facts", motivations, ascribed intentions and such like.

Propose

We can only negotiate if we have **proposals**. Proposals are tentative solutions and they have a distinct purple format. They express what one party might want if it is to consider addressing the wants of the other party. Proposals invite questions and clarification, leading the negotiation back to debate.

Ineffective negotiators who indulge in argument and instantly reject proposals with which they disagree are treading water until a more constructive response prevails.

Bargain

A **bargain** is a special type of proposal. It is specific in what the negotiator wants and in what they will offer in return. A purple bargain is always conditional ("If you give me X, then I will offer you Y"), as well as being specific.

There is no room for ambiguity in a bargain because the bargain specifies exactly what is to be exchanged. It is conditional because it would not be an exchange if it offered something without wanting something else in return.

USING THE FOUR PHASES

I am not implying that every negotiation necessarily goes through these four phases in a nice, neat order of, say, 1 through 4, nor that all four phases are of the same duration and sequence in every negotiation. Negotiators can move through the phases in any order and can commence the sequence with any one of the phases.

Some negotiations commence with a *bargain*, when something specific is *proposed* by one party and the other party takes it away for consideration (*prepare*) or by asking questions they start to *debate* it. Alternatively, they could respond with a *counter-bargain* or with a tentative suggestion (*propose*).

A negotiation could also commence with a general exploration of a problem and with a search for what each person wanted (*debate*), followed by adjournments to consider possible options (*prepare*), before returning to a general discussion (*debate*), followed by tentative suggestions (*propose*).

Those negotiators who recognize which phase they are in are more effective than those who remain ignorant of the phased structure through which they are working nevertheless.

As each phase has its own unique behaviors that are more productive than others, the negotiator who knows where what they are doing is likely to lead will be more effective than a negotiator who stumbles along in the hope that something will suggest itself.

It is useful to recognize the purpose of each phase in the overall conduct of a negotiation.

Each phase contributes to the process of reaching agreement. Social processes economize on effort to achieve their goals and it is fair to assume that in today's Age of Negotiation (compared to yesterday's Age of Deference) negotiation has become much less formal or ritualistic to accommodate its usage by anybody. Thus, counting, or naming, the number of phases (and I know of models with 3, 4, 5, 6, 8 and 12 phases!) is much less important than understanding the tasks involved.

Recognizing the strategic task of each of the phases adds to the negotiator's awareness and sharpens their focus. Exhibit 4 restates each phase as a specific task to be accomplished over the time available for a negotiation. It

Exhibit 4   The tasks of the four phases

Phase	Task
Prepare	What do we want?
Debate	What do they want?
Propose	What wants might we trade?
Bargain	What wants will we trade?

Source: *The Negotiate Trainer's Manual*, 1996, p.4.

is a handy guide to negotiators who wish to remain oriented to finding a solution, rather than being over-committed to defending or asserting a position.

NEGOTIATION AND CULTURE

The New Negotiating Edge addresses negotiation as a universal phenomenon and provides a practical toolkit for those who negotiate anywhere in the world. It takes the view that negotiating processes and behavioral styles are not different around the world but are in fact the same.

A great deal of what is asserted about the influence of culture on negotiation boils down to the undoubted differences in manners, courtesies, body language, spoken language, and context, knowledge of which, while essential for successful commercial and social contact, is not evidence of significant cultural differences in the negotiating process.

Negotiators mandated to prepare appropriately in China are no less mandated to prepare similarly in Brazil; and they suffer the same loss of edge if they prepare badly no matter where, or into which culture, they are socialized on the planet.

Debate behaviors take different forms and the

differences can be important. But red, blue or purple
behavior is not unique to this or that culture. And the
notion that all Japanese debate is fundamentally different
in its negotiating purpose from the role of debate for all
Americans—or, surely more contentious, that all Japanese
debate in the same way and do it differently from how all
Americans debate—is woefully contrary to experience.

An individual Japanese negotiator may ask many
questions; an individual American may ask too few. It is
not a cultural weakness on the individual American's part
so much as an individual behavioral weakness. Almost all
members of all cultures do not ask enough questions!

Perceptual differences in time, morals, law, affiliations,
life purposes, ideology and religion and such like abound,
but so they do both within and between people from the
same culture.

The differences are within
cultures

Negotiation as a process is culturally neutral. Different
cultures do not have different processes of negotiation.
The phases of negotiation are universal.

Culture influences the **conduct** of negotiation. It
encompasses the values, beliefs, shared meanings, and
attitudes of a group. It provides a "world view" for its
members and takes in their history, experiences, political
perspectives, myths, folklore, religion, rituals, and social
preferences. Culture drives the group while personality
drives the individual.

Geert Hofstede (1984) defined culture as the "collective
programming of the mind which distinguishes one human
group from another". The other prominent contributor to
views on cultural influences, Fons Trompenaars
(Trompenaars and Hampden-Turner, 1997), defined culture
as "the way in which a group of people solves problems".
Leaping from identifying cultural differences, as defined
by Hofstede and Trompenaars, to assuming differences in
negotiation behavior outside the acknowledged
differences in red and blue styles is almost irresistible, but
unscientific.

Negotiators have to learn to identify and then to cope
with the idiosyncrasies of the business sector in which they

work. They must become familiar with the habits and manners of other societies (travelling on business without knowledge of cultural mores is risky!), but this does not require a search for a different *process* of negotiating in another culture merely because it is another culture. It does require, however, a search for professional competences as a negotiator.

A free gift (i.e., blue-style) concession to an "obstinate" (i.e., red-style) negotiator in China is no different in the predictable outcome of similar behavior (when something is given away without requiring something else in return) from an "obstinate" (red-style) rancher in Texas.

Blue-style behaviors that reward obstinacy, no matter whom they are between or what culture they come from, are poor negotiating practice. In all cases, whether in China or Texas or anywhere else, submissive blue behaviorists run out of patience more quickly than red behaviorists will think it necessary to show a willingness to move. Red-style intimidation, sadly but avoidably, works!

The remedy is to correct the negotiating errors common to all cultures, and not to search for or invent unique, culturally determined negotiating behavior. Red is red and blue is blue in every culture and whenever they interact the outcome is predictable. This is what gives purple negotiating behavior its universal edge.

ARE THERE RED AND BLUE PHASES?

The four phases describe a common process; the behavioral styles, which we consider in the next chapter, identify how negotiators might behave in the phases within that process.

None of the four phases, therefore, inherently leans to red or to blue styles of behavior, though individual people, particularly if they are untrained and unaware, may lean predominantly to one behavioral style or the other. Trained negotiators, however, will choose purple styles of behavior.

No phase is more prone than another to a particular

behavioral style. The phases themselves are style neutral. They simply name the separate phases of the structured process.

How the phases are played depends on the attitudinal and behavioral inclinations of the players, much like speed and acceleration are characteristics of a moving body and not intentional features of whatever is moving. An ambulance with a sick child accelerates towards a hospital under the same laws of physics as a drunk driver accelerating towards a baby in a pram. The physical properties of acceleration are independent of any consequence associated with the acceleration.

The four phases, similarly, are properties of a negotiation process and are independent of the purposes of the negotiators, be it a negotiation between drug pushers or between the Little Sisters of the Poor. Therefore, there is no sensible way to think of preparation as being peculiarly prone to a red style of behavior, or for debate, say, to be conceived of as prone to a uniquely blue style of behavior. Red behaviorists prepare and blue behaviorists debate, but neither behavior style is more common than any other in any of the phases.

Negotiators bring their attitudes and beliefs into their behavior in each phase. Being red or blue, or some combination, is not determined by the intrinsic nature of the phase itself. There are red styles of preparation, as there are red styles of debate and red styles of making proposals and bargains, and there can also be blue-style versions of all four phases.

The role of attitudes and beliefs

Negotiators are driven by their behavioral and attitudinal intentions as they move through the four phases. None of their behaviors is driven by the particular phase they are in.

SUMMARY

Animals decide on food, mates and territory by violence. Humans have the capability (though not always the inclination) to be different. They make decisions by negotiation and have done so for millennia. What was an activity largely confined to traders is now generally practiced by everyone.

Negotiation is defined as the process by which we search for terms to obtain what we want from someone who wants something from us. It encourages decision making by voluntary consent, it is non-coercive and it is an efficient and effective means to distribute what people create. Negotiation is an essential attribute of a sustainable system of wealth creation.

No single decision-making method is superior in all circumstances to any other, as each method is appropriate in some circumstances and is less so in others. Negotiation is appropriate when the time and effort of negotiating are justified by the outcome, when we need the other party's consent and when the outcome is uncertain.

All negotiations are unique but all negotiations also have a common structure. The study of the common structure of negotiation is only 35 years old. In the four-phase version of the negotiating process, the phases are labelled prepare, debate, propose, and bargain. These phases may be sequenced differently, they may be of variable duration and they may be gone through several times in different negotiations.

Negotiation as a process is culturally neutral. Different cultures do not have different processes of negotiation.

For each phase there are both appropriate and inappropriate behaviors, which can be learned. By knowing which phase you are in, and by deploying the more appropriate behaviors, you improve your chances of successfully concluding the negotiation.

None of the phases is inherently red or blue. You can deploy red or blue behaviors in each phase, depending on your intentions. Proposing and bargaining, however, are most effective when they are purple.

RECOMMENDED READING

Ann Douglas (1962) *Industrial Peacemaking*, New York, Columbia University Press.

Geert Hofstede (1984) *Culture's Consequences: International Differences in Work-related Values*, London, Sage.

Colin Rose (1987) *Negotiate and Win: the Proven Methods of the Negotiation Workshop*, Melbourne, Lothian Publishing Company.

Adam Smith (1776) *An Inquiry into the Nature and Causes of the Wealth of Nations*, Book 1, London (John Dent, 2 vols, 1914).

Fons Trompenaars and Charles Hampden-Turner (1997) *Riding the Waves of Culture: Understanding Cultural Diversity in Business*, 2nd edn, London, Nicholas Brealey Publishing.

3 Attitudes, Beliefs, and Behaviors of Negotiators

SELF-ASSESSMENT 1

		Agree	Disagr
1	Negotiators should not reveal their true feelings in case their opponents take advantage.	❐	❐
2	A marginally acceptable deal is better than no deal at all.	❐	❐
3	If an opponent gives me an opportunity to take advantage discreetly, that's their problem.	❐	❐
4	I will renegotiate profitable deals if the other negotiator say they are in difficulties.	❐	❐
5	I look after my own interests and leave opponents to look after theirs.	❐	❐
6	It is generally beneficial to be open about one's true circumstances.	❐	❐
7	I am worried about rejection when negotiating.	❐	❐
8	If opponents are too soft and can't look after themselves, that's their lookout.	❐	❐
9	A good cause is more worthy than power.	❐	❐
10	When opponents buckle under pressure I should push harder.	❐	❐

*B*EFORE reading the rest of the book, please answer some questions to help you identify your attitudes. Don't worry about the "correct" answers, because there are none. Don't pause to reflect in depth on the meaning of each statement.

Simply react by marking whether you agree or disagree with the sentiments expressed. Please complete Self-assessment I now, before you do anything else and before I "contaminate" your ideas with mine.

Every time you negotiate, your attitudes drive your behavior. You are most likely to be driven by one of the two contrasting attitudinal approaches commonly found in people who have not had cause to think about how they negotiate—the red or blue style.

A few people behave almost exclusively according to one approach, but most alternate between the two approaches. Few really think about having a particular set of attitudes and mostly do whatever seems appropriate at that moment.

Identifying the approach you currently prefer, or discovering to which of the approaches you are biased, will help you understand how you and others behave when you negotiate with them. It will also lay the groundwork for what you can do to develop a **new set of behaviors** that will improve your negotiating performance. This improvement will be far beyond anything that is available to you that concentrates merely on refining your present behaviors.

ATTITUDES, BELIEFS, AND BEHAVIORS

A SIMPLE BEHAVIORAL MODEL

In Exhibit 5, there is a relationship between the three overlapping boxes labeled Behaviors, Attitudes and Beliefs. Behavior is at the front because it is the most "visible" of the three elements. You can see, hear and feel other people's behavior, while you cannot be as sure of their private attitudes and beliefs.

Exhibit 5   A simple model

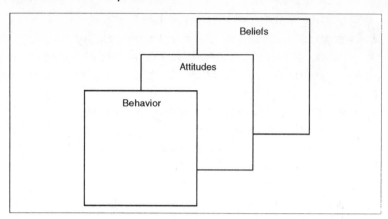

Behavior

People are aware of your behavior when they are affected by what you do. Even if they cannot identify you individually as the perpetrator, because perhaps you are a "faceless bureaucrat", they will know that something has been done to them, particularly if your behavior affects them negatively. For example, when something is stolen from you, you may not know the thief's identity but you know that your possession is missing as a result of their behavior. Negotiators are likely to know when they have been cheated or threatened, or when somebody has taken advantage of them.

Attitudes

With attitudes it is significantly different. Attitudes can be hidden—those that you choose to reveal to others are less reliable as indicators of your true intentions than is your behavior. It may be convenient to express a certain attitude in order to gain a particular effect. It might also be dangerous in some circumstances to express attitudes which are against those who are in a position to hurt you. In such a case, rather than risk harm by expressing your true views, you prudently show only the approved attitudes.

After the collapse of the former Soviet Union it was clear that many hundreds of thousands of people had for years mouthed attitudes mandated by the Soviet Communist Party, without believing a word of what they were saying. Experience under Stalin and his heirs had shown that it was safer to do so. Though Mao Ze Dong called in 1958 for "a hundred schools of thought to contend and a thousand flowers to bloom", his wrath was unleashed later on those who naively believed that it was safe to accept his invitation.

Negotiating experience shows that many practitioners express attitudes that bear no resemblance to their intentions. They speak of trust but they intend only to deceive. While negotiators do not always act with deceitful intent, you have no way of knowing for certain if you can rely solely on what they say. This makes people's professed attitudes an unreliable guide compared to their behavior.

Behind your attitudes stand your relatively firm **beliefs**. Whereas attitudes are short, coded guides to instant behavior—"leave the washing up to my sister", "be polite to neighbors", "he deserves to be mocked" and such like—beliefs are more robust and more complex.

Beliefs

You feel more strongly about your beliefs ("all women should do the washing up", "all neighbors deserve politeness", "all vegetarians must be mocked") because they also explain (to your own satisfaction at least) why you adhere to certain attitudes. This does not mean that you cannot also hold many attitudes that contradict your beliefs.

Belief systems take longer to form than specific attitudes. Your moral code may have a historical foundation in the folk memories of some actual or perceived atrocity against your race, clan, family, or nation. Your beliefs may originate in the religion of your community, or from the teachings of a charismatic figure. Beliefs are handed down from generation to generation, or are forged in the rebellion of one generation against another, which the older regards as a degeneration in society's moral values and the younger regards as a liberating revision of them.

Behavior can be arbitrary, attitudes can be contradictory and beliefs can be hypocritical. Much of our literary heritage is about these very human inconsistencies—what else would be as interesting to read about?

THE RED–BLUE CONTINUUM

Self-assessment 1 is not meant to be a scientific exploration of your attitudes. To the extent that you completed it honestly, it provides a smudgy reflection of some of your attitudes to negotiation, as they were a few moments ago. It is unlikely that all of your responses were untrammeled with doubts; perhaps you misunderstood the statements, you rationalized some of your responses, or you thought of circumstances in which you would both agree and disagree with a particular statement. In SA1 you are not asked for a considered essay on what you might do in varying circumstances. Still, with these and other caveats, your responses are at least indicative.

Checking with the answers to Self-assessment 1 (at the end of this chapter), how many of your answers are **red** and how many are **blue**?

Red ☐   Blue ☐

There are ten possible choices and their distribution places you on an imaginary red–blue continuum running from extreme red to extreme blue (Exhibit 6):

● If you had 10 red responses then you are an extreme red.

● If you had 10 blue responses then you are an extreme blue.

Exhibit 6   The red–blue continuum

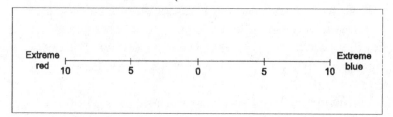

Those who are single-mindedly red or blue are determinedly extreme in their attitudes and in their behavior in all situations. Most negotiators, in contrast, behave according to their interpretations of the individual situation. Your attitudes are more likely to be a combination of red and blue. If your responses revealed, say, six red attitudes and four blue attitudes, then you are more red than blue, but by no means an extreme red.

To translate your combined red and blue scores into places on the continuum, use the table in Exhibit 7.

Exhibit 7   Points on the continuum

No. red	No. blue	Point on continuum
10	0	Red 10
9	1	Red 4
8	2	Red 3
7	3	Red 2
6	4	Red 1
5	5	0
4	6	Blue 1
3	7	Blue 2
2	8	Blue 3
1	9	Blue 4
0	10	Blue 10

When, like most negotiators, you have a combination of red and blue attitudes, you are somewhere between 5 red and 5 blue on the continuum.

Specifically, if more than five of your attitudes are red, then it is likely that you will negotiate in a red manner, particularly under pressure.

Alternatively, if more than five of your choices are blue, then it is likely that you will tend to behave in a blue manner.

The obvious question is: What do red and blue signify?

Broadly, the contrary behaviors of red or blue extremists derive from their beliefs and attitudes to their purpose in negotiating.

WHAT DO RED AND BLUE SIGNIFY?

Red

If, say, you see negotiation as being about dividing up a fixed amount of money, your attitude is moderate red if you intend to get most of it and extreme red if you expect all of it.

If there is only a fixed amount of money available, it follows that striving to get more for yourself means that the other person gets less.

In short, "more for me means less for them". A red player's attitudes produce red behavior.

Blue

Blue negotiators think in terms of "fairness and equity". If they can, blue players press for the creation of more than one pie or, circumstances permitting, they seek to enlarge the available pie.

Their attitude is: "more for me means more for them".

In the extreme, blue players slide from favoring fairness and equity to ensuring that the other players get more, even if this means that the blue players must accept less! Submission from this perspective is regarded as a small price to pay for the purpose of negotiating. A blue player's attitudes produce blue behavior.

RED ATTITUDES

So what are the characteristics of a red negotiator?

Competitive

Red players are **competitive** with the people with whom they negotiate. They see negotiation as a gladiatorial contest, as in competitive sport where the object is to win more of whatever is at stake—be it goals, points, runs, ends, or whatever—than their opponents.

A word such as "opponent" is always indicative of red competitive play. If you see the other player as an opponent—and many negotiators use this word far too liberally—you are bound to develop attitudes that lead to predominantly red behavior.

It is OK to compete with opponents in sport—that, after all, is what competitive games are about and what the laws of these games encourage. Players, within the rules, are supposed to do everything they can to "win" by "defeating" their opponents.

A BASIC (RED) ASSUMPTION OF NEGOTIATION

"In a successful negotiation, both parties gain—but one gains more than the other."

Source: Colin Robinson (1990) *Winning at Business Negotiations: a Guide to Profitable Deal Making*, Kogan Page, p. 33.

Red players are competitive—sometimes hyper-competitive—because they are more concerned with results than they are with having relationships with their opponents.

Red players see no difference between opponents in a sporting contest and the people with whom they negotiate. Opponents are the enemy—they are in the way of you getting what you want—and visualizing them as the enemy legitimizes a whole raft of your red attitudes.

Red players seek **zero-sum outcomes**—what they gain the other loses—and the sum of their gains minus their opponent's losses is always zero.

Red players are **takers** because they always try to take something for nothing or for less than they give. They are

Zero-sum outcomes

Takers

EXTREME RED ATTITUDES

"We recognise that, far from being honest, negotiation is a web of ever more delicate lies. A skilled negotiator will appear friendly if this is the role he considers to be most effective, but will never sacrifice profit for friendship in his business dealings. He will never help unless that is the way to get what he wants and then only if it gives him more than it costs. He will never co-operate if he can avoid it, since this implies giving up something, or worse still, sharing a gain."

Source: Jonathan Sims (1996) *I'm OK – You Think You're OK*, Human Development Centre, p.1.

Exhibit 8   Red attitudes

Be aggressively competitive and non-cooperative

Dominate your opponents

Seek always to win

All deals are "one-offs"

Use ploys and tricks

Bluff and coerce

Exploit the submissive

Source: *The Negotiate Trainer's Manual*, 1996, p. 55.

driven by the results they can obtain.

Books and courses for red players are replete with military language and analogies. In south-east Asia, for example, popular books on business marketing and negotiation draw extensively from Sun Tzu's *Art of War* (c. 240 BC). A whole culture of negotiating has grown up around interpretations of Sun Tzu's maxims that were applicable 2000 years ago to warring kingdoms in ancient China. To the extent that young Asian negotiators are influenced by this popular ancient culture they play red. Indeed, there is a crowded market for books on red behavior in Asia.

Seeking to win

Seeking to win is not regarded other than as a self-evident goal in the competitive game. In US sport, coming second is anathema—"Who loves a loser?"—and while on occasion there are token references to "both winning", Robinson's and Sims's attitudes (in the boxes) more accurately reflect the red negotiator's true intentions.

Bookstalls on "self-improvement" in the US are stacked with guides to ploys, tricks and tactics. Somebody recently mass produced a mouse-mat entitled "10 Dirty

Negotiating Tactics … and their solutions" for sale at $10. Clearly, there is vast scope for "streetwise" negotiating ploys, bluffs and coercion.

BLUE ATTITUDES

In contrast, what are the characteristics of a blue negotiator?

Blue players are **givers**—they seek cooperation and often end up patsies to red partners. For, make no mistake, blue players see negotiators with whom they deal not as "opponents" but as "partners".

Givers

Even a stranger, of whom they know nothing, has the potential to become a **partner**, and they are treated as such (Exhibit 9). Not suprisingly, red players see blue behavior as proof that they have a "live one" on the end of their line and react accordingly with exploitive intent.

Partners

Unless the blue player has the experience and the skills to deal with the red player, they will be exploited.

Blue players seek **non-zero-sum outcomes**—what they gain is not at their partner's expense, and the sum of their gains plus their partner's gains is always positive. Extreme blue players are givers because they are willing to give something for nothing if it means they will reach a deal with someone with whom they seek a relationship.

Non-zero-sum outcomes

Blue negotiators are generally **cooperative**—sometimes hyper-cooperative—because they are more concerned with the relationship they have with their negotiating partners than with the results they could obtain from them.

Cooperative

They do not see their partners as opponents or as obstacles. Partners provide bridges to mutually acceptable solutions to their problems. Negotiated solutions have to be advantageous for both of them.

Their goal is to "**succeed**", not to "win" in a selfish way. They would forgo winning in a scoring sense, if it meant they could both succeed. Indeed, blue negotiators are known to forswear advantageous deals for themselves if it would jeopardize the relationship with their partner.

Succeeding not winning

They regard forgoing winning as a temporary, not a

Exhibit 9   Blue attitudes

Be co-operative—even with aggressive partners

Show respect to all partners

Seek to succeed

All deals lead to others

Eschew manipulation

Be open and play it straight

Source: *The Negotiate Trainer's Manual*, 1996, p. 55.

permanent, gesture, much like an investment in the future, or like some sentimental payback or atonement for their past conduct. Rick's gesture of saving his former lover's husband in *Casablanca* springs to mind, as does Sydney Carton's "far, far better thing that I do" in Dickens's A *Tale of Two Cities*.

Instead of a deal being a one-off only, potentially any deal, because of the relationship it might engender, could lead to others.

Openness

Manipulating a partner for one-sided gain would be impossible for a blue-style negotiator to contemplate. Ploys, tricks and so-called tactics are not part of a blue negotiator's toolkit. They abide by the injunction always to be **open** (within the bounds of sensible discretion) and to play it straight. Their word is truly their bond.

PRISONER'S DILEMMA

Your attitudes, which effectively are hidden and unknowable to outsiders, drive your negotiating behavior, which is mainly visible. This is the basis of the behavioral approach to negotiation.

In Self-assessment 1 you indicated something about

EXTREME BLUE STYLE

"What makes Win-Win Negotiators important, both socially and historically, is that, in modifying their perception of what they need to win, they have redefined what winning means. They consider not just their own goal, but the other person's goal and the common goal. They know that negotiating is not solely a question of how much they will win, but how much the loss will affect the other person. They have no desire to live in an unstable environment of a few winners and a multitude of embittered losers. In short, they don't have to win it all; what's there can be shared."

Source: Tessa A. Warschaw (1981) *Winning by Negotiation*, McGraw-Hill, p. 62.

the red or blue bias of your attitudes. Now you will explore something about the red or blue bias of your behavior and, through this, learn something about the recognition of red or blue behavior in others.

We approach your behavior by what at first seems to be an obscure route. In doing so you will reveal to yourself your behavioral choices as you play or observe some "mind games".

Mind games

One of the most powerful behavioral games in social science is known as **prisoner's dilemma**. It was invented in 1950 and half a century later the deep well of ideas it uncovered is far from plumbed, having already spread from the social sciences to such disciplines as biochemistry, microbiology, genetics, law, and moral philosophy. Early literary versions of the prisoner's dilemma appeared as a story by Edgar Alan Poe (1842) and in a play by Victorien Sardou (1887), which later became the opera *Tosca*, by Giacomo Puccini (1900).

In its modern mathematical format, prisoner's dilemma originated at the RAND Corporation, a "thinktank" in Santa

Monica, California. Despite its relative obscurity (counter-balanced by its superb location!), RAND attracted brilliant scholars from many of the first division of US academic institutions, which produced much exciting work in all kinds of fields. Some of their best work was begun in the unprepossessing circumstances of speculation about how arriving and departing scholars might buy second-hand goods from each other.

There are numerous versions of prisoner's dilemma now circulating, but my version is in Exhibit 10.

Exhibit 10   The prisoner's dilemma

Two prisoners, Slug and Gripper, are under arrest on suspicion of having committed a major crime. They are in separate cells and cannot communicate with each other. The authorities do not have enough evidence to convict them of the crime for which they were arrested. Instead, the prosecutor speaks to each of them separately and offers them the same deal:

"If you confess to the crime and turn state's evidence, you will go free and your former associate will receive a 10-year sentence. If you do not confess but your associate does, then he will go free and you will receive a 10-year sentence. If you both confess, you will receive 5 years each. If neither of you confesses, you will each be charged with a misdemeanour and receive a 1-year sentence."

Aside from concerns about the integrity of the criminal justice system, what is the best course of action for a prisoner who is offered this deal? Not so obvious, is it?

Doing what is best—for whom?

It is a dilemma because the choice of how to behave is motivated by the prisoner doing what is best for himself or doing what is best for the pair of them. This dilemma is a well-trod theme for philosophers and religious mystics over the millennia, with Confucius, Plato, Aristotle, Seneca, Jesus, Hobbes, Kant, and Hume, among many others, having attempted to resolve it.

Unlike the philosophers, the prisoner does not need to contemplate what should motivate the other prisoner, so much as what behavior the other prisoner exhibits when he makes his choice. Moreover, because the choice for one prisoner is complicated by the choice made by the other prisoner, neither of them makes an independent choice. Their choices are inextricably bound together but, of course, are made separately.

Clearly, if they both choose not to confess they would both be better off, compared to their other choices, because they receive only a one-year sentence compared to five years or ten. Thus, this is the optimum choice for both of them (though not for justice). But will Slug and Gripper make this choice? Or will they try to make a choice that is best for themselves alone—confess when the other doesn't confess—and benefit from gaining their freedom?

If Slug decides not to confess, in pursuit of the best joint choice, he risks Gripper choosing to "confess", which gives Slug 10 years and Gripper his freedom.

But why would Gripper not see that the optimum choice for both them is not to confess?

Simple. If Gripper suspects that Slug will defect from their optimum joint choice (don't confess) and that Slug instead will opt for his own personal best choice (confess), then Gripper is vulnerable if he alone makes the optimum joint choice (Slug goes free and Gripper gets 10 years). Thus to protect himself, Gripper would be naive to trust that Slug would opt for the optimum joint choice, and, therefore, Gripper doesn't either.

Wait a minute, you say. Gripper is surely vulnerable to Slug seeing the problem in exactly the same terms, and instead of naively not confessing (which gets Slug 10 years, if Gripper defects and confesses), Slug too might decide to confess, giving them both 5 years. They are now both worse off than if they had stuck to not confessing.

Exactly! This is the dilemma of choice for the two prisoners—and for everybody else facing similar dilemmas in the game of life.

RED–BLUE GAME

Let us examine an extension of the prisoner's dilemma by applying it to what is known as the red–blue game. This game links conveniently to the contrasting attitudes behind red and blue behavior.

Though the original game is played in pairs or teams over ten rounds, we shall play it as a mind game and examine dilemma behavior through introspection. (The rules for playing red–blue in pairs or teams are set out in Appendix 1.)

Red or blue?

In prisoner's dilemma, the choices were to confess or not to confess. In red–blue, the choices are to play red or to play blue. A color is played by revealing a card marked with the chosen colour: red or blue.

In a red–blue game, there are three possible combinations of choice, each with a different pay-off or reward. To play the game two players independently choose and then simultaneously reveal their choice to each other. The combinations of their independent choices and their pay-offs are shown in Exhibit 11.

Exhibit 11   Player's choices and pay-offs

Players' choices	Pay-offs
Both play blue	+ 4 points each
Both play red	− 4 points each
One plays blue, other plays red	Blue player loses 8 points (− 8) Red player gains 8 points (+ 8)

Source: *The Negotiate Trainer's Manual*, 1996, p. 11.6.

Assuming that positive points are preferred to negative points and that you prefer gaining as many positive points as you can, what would be your choice of play for the first round of the game?

My *choice is to play* (*tick one*):
Red   ❏   Blue   ❏

Some people demand that I tell them the purpose of the
game before they choose. You might, for instance, want to
know if you are you to choose according to "what is best
for you alone" or "best for both of us together". Normally, I
would decline to answer that question before you play.
Part of the dilemma you face is that you don't know which
choice other people intend to make and the other part is
that you cannot rely on their claims about their intentions.

Here, however, you are only playing for "points"—it's
not as if you're playing for your life! Suppose, therefore, I
reply that you are to choose what is "best for both of us".

What will you choose to do?

You probably chose to play blue and, if I may interpret
your choice, you chose blue in the expectation that when
you both chose blue, you both get 4 points.

Best for both of us

The problem, however, is that, having chosen on the
basis for "what is best for both of us", you can only assume
what choice the other player will make because you have
no way of knowing. If they choose what is "best for both of
us", they too will play blue. But how do you know the
choice criteria by which they will abide?

Remember, you reveal your choices simultaneously
and, once the marked cards are face up on the table,
neither of you may change your choice of behavior.
Behavior takes place in real time and the past cannot be
changed—you can change your attitudes but you cannot
change your past behavior.

Now, go back a bit, and consider what your choice
would have been if I had said that you should choose on
the basis of what you believe is best for you alone. What
would you choose to do?

Best for you alone

Not so straightforward, is it?

Clearly, your best personal choice is to play red against
the other person's blue, but (and please note this caveat)
this only applies if they play blue when you play red.

As you do not know whether the other person will play

red or blue, you cannot be certain that choosing what is "best for you" will gain you more points than choosing what is "best for both of you". And, worse, if the other person also plays red, choosing what is best for you could net you −4 points and not +8 (see Exhibit 10).

Why should the other person play red? They play red in the expectation that you too will play red. It's back to the prisoner's dilemma!

THE GAME OF LIFE

In the game of life, you must choose between doing what is "best for yourself" or what is "best for both of you". Therefore, it's no good relying on me, nor anyone else, telling you how to behave because you cannot be sure that another person will not mislead you. If you abide by my advice to play blue, the other person can still ambush you with a red.

If the people you negotiate with are among nature's red players, behaving blue is disadvantageous to your interests. If, however, they are among nature's blue players and you always behave blue, you are fortunate, but what restrains anybody else from switching from blue to red ("damn Kennedy's advice!")?

Deciding on the choice criteria of the game of life cannot be delegated to others. When you engage in a certain behavior you have decided on a criteria of choice—your behavior is your choice! Once you have done something, it is forever done. Time does not flow backwards.

As a child, adults told you how to behave and sometimes your experience confirmed their advice; other experiences showed that there were convenient exceptions to any choice rule. If the behavioral exceptions became too frequent to be ignored, your behavior made your previous choice criteria redundant. Later, you formed those attitudes (criteria of choice) that drive your negotiating, and other, behaviors.

COMMON PLAYS OF RED–BLUE

What do you think is the most common choice of players in the first round in the red–blue game?

Here, the world divides into two camps: those (the optimists) who believe that people are, or ought to be, rational (or moral) and, therefore, that they should always seek after what is best for everybody, and those (the realists) who observe that people seldom do other than seek what is best for themselves. What a sad observation of human proclivities!

Yet, the red–blue game consistently shows that the optimists are more often disappointed than right. People predominantly behave in pursuit of their own interests but, in doing so, they usually achieve the opposite outcome to their intentions. Two players attempting to exploit each other usually end up undermining their own interests! The experimental evidence of red–blue games is overwhelming and in this sense justifies the (almost futile?) preaching of the optimists.

Optimists are often disappointed

In thousands of plays of red–blue that I have observed, only 8 percent of players, coming to red–blue for the first time and without pre-game briefing on what choice "should" be made, choose behavior that precludes a blue–blue outcome. Just over half of the players choose to play red in round 1, leaving just under half who choose to play blue. Obviously, blue players have a marginally higher chance that their partner will choose to play red rather blue.

For a blue–blue (or win–win) outcome, both players must play blue in round 1, and must sustain that play throughout all ten rounds.

If your partner plays red in round 1, what should you do in round 2?

Play red, of course!

Some blue players—a very small minority to be sure—play blue again in round 2 (and some, Canute like, play blue again in rounds 3 and 4), in the hope of shaming the red player into blue behavior.

Always playing blue

Shaming in this manner so seldom works that the hope

that it will work is risible. Continuing to play blue when you have received a red is a triumph of hope over experience.

Exhibit 12   Naive blue plays in red–blue

Round	You	Them
1	Blue	Red
2	Blue	Red

The majority of round 1 blue players, finding that they have a red partner, switch to red themselves in round 2. If this continues, both of them end up with low or negative scores over the ten rounds.

Ambush!

Indeed, players who eventually agree to play blue–blue are sometimes ambushed by a red in round 10. Why? Well, a player who remains aggrieved from the round 1 red play of the other player retaliates in the last round for their partner's first defection (because they can get away with it). As commonly, the "guilty" red player of round 1 plays red in round 10 because they expect their round 1 victim to retaliate! The ensuing arguments about "trust" and "betrayal" can become quite heated.

When, in practice, only 8 percent of pairs sustain blue–blue behavior to achieve 48 points each (scores double in rounds 9 and 10), you can see the fallacy in assuming that people will commit to joint maximizing behaviors solely because they "ought" to. If your partners are among the minority 8 percent who behave blue, all well and good. However, as it is much more likely that they aren't, it is risky to behave as if they are.

Win–win

This caution is lost in the noisy consensus among authors in favor of so-called "win–win", or "both win", negotiation. Like motherhood and apple pie, win–win negotiation is a platitude in favor of something that nobody is against, but that, in practice, too few negotiating pairs deliver.

Behaving as if somebody seeks the same win–win outcome that you do is not only reckless, it can provoke the very behavior that you seek to avoid. Your assumption begets the opposite consequence: you proclaim your intentions of playing blue and they craftily exploit you with a red. It is remarkable how annoyed and sulky negotiators can get (like disappointed lovers) when their partner does not live up to their imputed virtues.

TIT-FOR-TAT

Is the answer to assume the worst and behave accordingly?

Not at all. Realism is not about cynically excusing red behavior. But you must understand that blue play is only viable if the other party reciprocates with a blue. In short, a blue–blue exchange has to be worked for before it is a viable choice.

How then do I justify always opening round 1 with a blue in the red–blue game or a blue move in a negotiation? While most blue players are disappointed at the red play of their partners, they gain vital information that would not be available to them if they had played red themselves. They now know, for example, something about the intentions of their partner, because behavior is the safest indicator of a person's intentions.

Gain information

Red players claim they play red either to protect themselves from the red play of others, or to exploit any blue play. Whatever their explanation, you cannot be sure why people behave as they do but, as their behavior is more reliable than their explanations, the safest explanation for their behavior is that their real intention is to exploit you. Accordingly, you protect yourself best by playing red in the next round.

Suppose, however, they did play red to protect themselves? Surely, you could argue, by attributing to them the malign motives of exploitation, we are denying them the benign and legitimate motive of protecting themselves?

Well, first, you are interested only in their behavior and not in their explanations. Secondly, you should always respond in the way that puts your interests at least risk.

Survival

This is a bitter lesson, perhaps, but you should be grateful to your ancestors for learning it (or, at least, for not dying too young through defying it). All of your ancestors lived long enough to breed. Those who didn't— it doesn't matter why—obviously had no descendants! Our ancestors did survive, which is why we are here. Most survived by not taking too many risks; those who ignored risk in favor of trust had fatal "accidents".

A high percentage of people avoid accidents and the most common explanation is that they balance the risks of daily life more effectively than others. The survivors in the 6000 generations that preceded you moved north when the rainforests and grasslands became too scorched; they moved south when the glaciers crept over their habitats. They did not confuse floating logs with crocodiles, or sleeping lions with sleeping dogs, or bright berries with mid-morning snacks, or swamps with dry land, or strangers from over the hill with the friends they grew up with. Above all, they learned not to assume blue intentions from red behaviors.

When assessing somebody's red behavior, your presumption that they have exploitive rather than protective motives is the less risky assumption that makes a difference. Fortunately, the presumption is a working hypothesis and not an irreversible final judgment.

So, if you play blue and your partner plays red, I suggest that you play red in the next round. What will your partner play? Everything now turns on what they do next.

Guide to intentions

Should they play blue, the risk that they are trying to exploit you diminishes. Should they play red, the risk increases. Their behavior is your safest guide to their intentions.

If the risk of exploitation diminishes and, by definition, the likelihood increases that their behavior was motivated

by their need for protection, you may (more) safely play
blue next time, and continue to do so, as long as they
reciprocate with blue behavior.

If the risk of exploitation increases because they play
red again, your red play should continue (should you have
to continue playing) until they abandon their red behavior
by switching to blue.

Exhibit 13   Recommended play in red–blue

Round	You	Them
1	Blue	Red
2	Red	?
3	?	

These simple guidelines for the red–blue game also apply
in the games of life, such as in negotiation, where your
interests are affected by the behaviors of others: you
identify their behavior as red or blue and respond
accordingly.

If they play red, you play red; if they play blue, you
play blue.

Regard your opening blue play as a small investment in
the measured risk of observing from their behavior what
game they are playing.

These guidelines are known generically as "**tit-for-tat**".
They were discovered from a series of competitive
red–blue tournaments in which people were invited to
write computer programs that would be successful when
played against each other. The winner, Anatol Rapoport,
wrote the shortest program (only four lines). In simple
terms it says: "Play blue in round 1 and then always play
whatever the other player played in the previous round".

Consider the alternatives. Always playing blue, no
matter what your partner does, is suicidal—you will last

NEGOTIATION

only so long as you have the resources to make pay-offs to a consistent red player.

Always playing red is also self-defeating, because you will last only so long as you can replace exhausted blue players with, so far, unexploited affluent blue players who still have resources.

Advantages of tit-for-tat

Tit-for-tat behavior has three main things going for it:

- It is "nice" but "ruthless". Nice because it opens with a blue, signalling cooperation to the other player; ruthless because it switches immediately to red only when the other player defects to red behavior. A tit-for-tat strategy never initiates red play.

- It is always "forgiving" of past behavior whenever a red player switches to blue. But it also "forgets" past blue behavior if they switch to red. It does not keep punishing a red player after they have switched to blue, but immediately responds with an instant blue and, as immediately, instantly punishes with a red if they switch to red, no matter how long they have being playing blue. You know for certain where you are with a tit-for-tat player.

- It is an "open" strategy, so simple that young children can identify what a tit-for-tat player is doing after only a few exchanges. Thus, experienced negotiators should spot tit-for-tat behavior easily and can quickly adjust their own behavior. If they play red, they know they will be punished; if they play blue they know they will be rewarded. There is no room for ambiguity.

PURPLE BEHAVIOR

The absence of ambiguity is pretty much a restrictive benefit. In the red–blue game, tit-for-tat is a winning strategy and, to some extent, it is a useful guide to the game of life. But if this was all there was to choose from, I suspect you would feel somewhat disappointed.

Negotiators have long been aware that there are two main orientations in their behavior, though they may not have described their awareness in the terminology of red and blue. Many people speak of "hardness" and "softness" as the two polar extremes of a negotiator's behavior. Others have moved their focus from behavior to motives (a wholly more difficult and ultimately futile phenomenon to try to observe) and have presented the dichotomy as the orientational tension between striving for results versus striving for relationships.

Of the hard–soft choice of behaviors, one approach, that of the "streetwise", is to celebrate it by developing behavioral strategies that seek to enhance one's own "hardness" at the expense of those trapped in versions of "softness".

Streetwise

Chester Karass, for many years the doyen of the "streetwise" presenters (and certainly in his heyday he was the very best of them), argues convincingly in *Give and Take* (1974) that a "hard", or "tough", strategy usually outplays a softer alternative.

For instance, he asserted that "aiming high" would produce better results than aiming modestly, and he supported his assertions both by evidence from his researches into negotiating behavior and from his experience as a senior negotiator in US aircraft manufacturing. His seminars were directed at enhancing results, particularly in the early 1970s, though he swung with the pendulum in the late 1980s towards recognizing the importance of relationships.

The other main source of a reaction to the "hard" versus "soft" dichotomy was that of the Harvard Negotiation Project, led by Roger Fisher and Bill Ury and explained in their book *Getting to Yes* (1981). Unlike Karass, they eschewed turning "soft" negotiators into "hard" negotiators and pointedly declared that the dichotomy itself was a dead end. Instead, they asserted that it was necessary to "change the game" from what they called "positional bargaining" to "negotiation on the merits" and elaborated on four prescriptive principles that together comprise their

Principled negotiation

method of "principled negotiation".

The streetwise approach takes negotiating behavior as it is (it is founded on experience) and creates a practical framework for exploiting other people's negotiating errors by becoming more adept than others at playing the red game.

The principled approach totally rejects negotiation as it is and advocates a rational alternative to the anarchy of normal negotiation by "changing the game". It seeks to turn conflictual stances into joint problem solving, based on non-adversarial attitudes and belief systems, usually and necessarily aided by professional third-party facilitators and using versions of the conciliation methods common in mediation.

A different task

The streetwise approach is unashamedly red in behavioral content and the principled approach is broadly blue, though neither recognizes the language of red and blue. *The New Negotiating Edge* takes a different tack.

It is not necessary to become the reddest negotiator in town nor it is necessary to change the game. The red–blue dichotomy is only resolvable if you do not permit analysis paralysis to pervade your choice of behavior. If you theorize about negotiation too much by looking for rational and tidy explanations of a diverse phenomenon— as diverse as the pairs of individuals negotiating at any one moment—you inevitably try to invent a "new game" to play by using well-known "hard" red or "soft" blue behaviors.

But suppose that both the streetwise and the principled approaches have misread the negotiating game? Maybe it is not a difficult choice between red or blue, nor a choice of which "new" game to play. What if the notion of a rigid dichotomy is only a first cut and not a considered conclusion? Or if the answer lies in the practice of negotiation—what negotiators do when they negotiate a solution—and extreme red or blue behaviors are not an inevitable consequence of negotiating?

Learning to negotiate

Negotiating is not an instinct, fully formed and operational by the time of your first negotiation. You learn to "negotiate" like you learn to speak your native language, through repetitive trial and error and in reaction to the success or otherwise of your attempts at communicating with other people. You are no more a fully competent negotiator—and may never find it necessary to become one—any more than you are a fully competent linguist, perfectly versed in all the nuances of your language before you can speak.

You do not learn to negotiate on your own, any more than you learn to speak on your own. Negotiating is a social activity that you learn in contact with others. This is obvious—too obvious—and its significance is therefore mostly missed.

Negotiation is a means of decision making that fulfills a role in all societies and has done so to one degree or another throughout human existence. It is not surprising that through social evolution—a far speedier process than biological evolution—humankind has developed a commonality of experience of negotiation as a process.

All human groups have some notion of exchange. The rituals and roles vary, but the substance is the same. If exchange is not based on violence then it is based on some form of voluntary consent.

Violence is common to the history (and practice) of all societies. Just as humans recognize violence whenever they see (or feel) it, so they recognize voluntary exchange. Which they choose—violence or exchange—is closely related to their attitudes and beliefs, which derive from the norms of the society in which they are socialized.

Violence or exchange?

If trade is highly developed, people are likely to choose negotiation in some form or another. If they do, the choice of red or blue behaviors echoes the history of humans learning to interact with each other without recourse to violence.

The incomplete social evolution of negotiation is indicated by the fact that the choice between red or blue behavior mainly falls short of what would be more effective in inducing cooperative decision making. But there is no doubt that in the past few decades social evolution has speeded up in most societies and that the prospects for the triumph of negotiation over all forms of coercion, including violence, are better than they were only a short time ago.

DIFFERENCES IN CONTENT AND OUTCOME

The attitudes that drive behavior become "contaminated" by a myriad of almost unrecallable experiences and influences. Hence, it is little wonder that, while negotiating as a behavioral interaction is universal among all humans, the way it is conducted is subject to wide variations in the quality of content and outcome.

The common proclivity for red (hard) and blue (soft) behaviors is not a product of the systemic failings of negotiation as a method. Instead, it is due to the failure of most untrained negotiators to become aware that red versus blue is a dead end as long as the two are separated, but that they can be fused instead into purple behavior. True, some negotiators are neither red nor blue but purple without thinking or theorizing about it, but most of us will require training in purple behavior.

WHAT IS PURPLE BEHAVIOR?

Put at its simplest, purple behavior insists on linking what we want (our **red** side) with what somebody else wants (our **blue** side) to produce a **purple** offer to exchange the one with the other: "You will get nothing from me, unless and until I get something from you."

The next few chapters elaborate and explore the implications of that statement, starting with the red art of haggling.

SUMMARY

What people do—how they behave—is a safer guide to their intentions than are the attitudes they profess. Attitudes can be hidden, as can passionately held beliefs. While significant, neither attitudes nor beliefs are as certain as guides to a person's intentions as is their behavior.

Attitudes are designated as either red or blue. Red

attitudes can be summarized as being about "more for me means less for you". Blue attitudes are about "more for me means more for you".

Red behavior styles are about dividing a fixed pie into unequal portions, with the largest portion going to the red behaviorist. Blue behavior styles are about enlarging a fixed pie or creating new pies, with both parties getting more from the division than they would otherwise enjoy.

In the extreme, a red player claims a larger than fair share and judges their score by their results; a blue player forgoes a fair share and judges their success by the relationship.

Red behaviorists see other negotiators as opponents, as somebody whom it is permissible (even mandatory!) to exploit in pursuit of one's own interests. They also consider it necessary to push harder when their opponents are "too soft". In the extreme, they are arrogant bullies.

Blue behaviorists see other negotiators as partners, and will renegotiate deals if their partner gets into difficulties. They believe that by serving the other negotiator's interests as well as their own, better deals are possible. They believe in the superiority of a good cause, not in the power of enforcement. In the extreme, they are submissive.

Prisoner's dilemma games analyze the conflicts involved in choosing between "joint best" and " only" solutions. Red–blue games allow negotiators to experience the dilemmas of balancing trust and risk in cooperative and competitive contexts.

Nobody can see "inside the heads" of others and therefore their motivations are unknowable. For this reason it is safer to rely on what negotiators do—how they behave—than on their explanations of what they are doing.

Most negotiators who play red do so not because they necessarily want to, but because they must. Protecting oneself from exploitation is legitimate, while exploiting others is not.

In plays of the red–blue game, the overwhelming majority do not manage to maximize either their joint scores or their own scores, because of the retaliation that their red behavior provokes or the exploitation that reckless blue behavior invites.

Tit-for-tat is a simple strategy that has the best chance of optimizing the outcome of iterated plays of a dilemma game, and is also recommended in a negotiation process.

Negotiating behavior is usually mixed between red and blue because it is driven by attitudes associated with both colors, as is the behavior of almost every other person with whom you will ever negotiate. Extremists of either color are rare and not difficult to spot because their behavior is monotonously all red or all blue.

Some authors recommend that negotiators should be adept at behaving red rather than blue because "hard" behavior beats "soft" behavior. Others recommend changing the negotiating game entirely by adopting a "new" set of blue prescriptive attitudes. Neither recommendation is necessary.

The solution is for negotiators to develop purple exchange behavior.

Negotiating behavior can be improved by conscious practice, otherwise known as training—which is good news for you (and for those in the training business!).

RECOMMENDED READING

For the inside story of prisoner's dilemma and red–blue games, see William Poundstone (1992) *Prisoner's Dilemma*, Oxford University Press, Oxford.

For tit-for-tat strategies see Robert Axelrod (1984) *The Evolution of Co-operation*, Basic Books, New York.

For a taste of the "streetwise" approach see Chester Karass (1974) *Give and Take*, Crowell, New York.

For the principled approach see Roger Fisher and William Ury (1981) *Getting to Yes: Negotiating Agreement Without Giving in*, Houghton Mifflin, Boston.

ANSWERS TO SELF-ASSESSMENT I

Agree Disagree

1 Negotiators should not reveal their true
   feelings in case their opponents take
   advantage.   Red   Blue

2 A marginally acceptable deal is better
   than no deal at all.   Blue   Red

3 If an opponent gives me an opportunity
   to take advantage discreetly, that's their
   problem.   Red   Blue

4 I will renegotiate profitable deals if the
   other negotiator say they are in
   difficulties.   Blue   Red

5 I look after my own interests and leave
   opponents to look after theirs.   Red   Blue

6 It is generally beneficial to be open
   about one's true circumstances.   Blue   Red

7 I am worried about rejection when
   negotiating.   Blue   Red

8 If opponents are too soft and cannot look
   after themselves, that is their lookout.   Red   Blue

9 A good cause is more worthy than power. Blue   Red

10 When opponents buckle under pressure
   I should push harder.   Red   Blue

Given the characteristics of extreme red and blue negotiating attitudes, you presumably do not model your own conduct as a negotiator on either of the extremes. Your choices in Self-Assessment 1, however, show the degree to which you have red or blue attitudinal characteristics, so we shall briefly comment on the 10 statements.

1 Negotiators should not reveal their true feelings in case their opponents take advantage

This is clearly a red attitude, partly because it refers to "opponents" but mainly because it expresses fears about others taking "advantage". Red negotiators are suspicious of others, not because they are paranoid (though they may be), but because they do not trust others to behave differently to how they would behave themselves, if given the chance. Thus, revealing your "true feelings" could expose you to red players like yourself.

Indeed, the two main reasons red players give for their resort to red behavior is that they must protect themselves from the suspected red intentions of others. "I behave red to protect myself," they say, "not because I want to, but because I must." The other reason they give, when in a mood to be candid, is that they behave red to exploit the other negotiator.

2 A marginally acceptable deal is better than no deal at all

Only blue players subscribe to this view. How marginal is marginal? And why should a deal—any deal—be better than no deal? For blue negotiators the answer is clear cut: the negotiated deal is the beginning, or the continuation, of a positive business relationship that has merits in its own right.

In the extreme, a desperate blue player would submit to the "sell cheap, get famous" ploy punted by red players to persuade you to take a low price now, in the hope of realizing vague suggestions that you might get a higher price when you have established yourself or your product with your customers. When a buyer has reason to believe that you are in a weak position—your first customer, your first big break, your last hope of staving off creditors—they will push versions of the script that "marginal" deals are better than "no deals".

Red negotiators typically blame their "victims" for what happens in negotiation. Victims are only "opponents" and are unworthy of compassion because sentiment and business do not mix (another red attitude). If their opponents let them take a devious advantage, the red player is not going to feel guilty. Why should they? After all, if the victims don't know how to conduct their business, they deserve to be shown how to do so by those more deserving of survival.

3 If an opponent gives me an opportunity to take advantage discreetly, that's his problem

This is a not uncommon problem as circumstances change. What was profitable may become less so later through causes outside of the influence of the party affected by the changes. Red players, if it is advantageous to them, insist on maintaining the original terms and refuse to budge; blue players consider the changed circumstances and renegotiate in the interests of continuing the relationship.

4 I will renegotiate profitable deals if the other negotiator says they are in difficulties

This is a typical attitude for a red negotiator. Interests are what drive you to negotiate on the issues. When interests are in conflict—a union seeking higher living standards for its members versus a company seeking to restrain its labor costs—the negotiated outcome ideally should address the interests of both parties. This can be made more difficult if one of the parties (or both!) are not interested in the other's interests and only serve their own.

5 I look after my own interests and leave opponents to look after theirs

Blue players aspire to being open about their circumstances and, in the extreme, they can be so open that they risk their partner taking advantage from whatever they reveal. Intentions are closely related to circumstances and disclosures about your circumstances reveal vulnerabilities that can compromise your intentions (and vice versa).

6 It is generally beneficial to be open about one's true circumstances

    If, for example, one of your key suppliers has let you down, you will be anxious to secure alternative supplies quickly. In negotiating with an alternative supplier on price and delivery, you could influence the price against yourself by revealing to them your precarious circumstances.

7 I am worried about rejection when negotiating

If you are worried about rejection you will do less well than perhaps you otherwise could. Blue negotiators are often too worried about rejection. If you fear rejection, you will behave in a manner that avoids being rejected. One obvious way to do this is to mitigate your demands. Instead of offering to settle at $1.4 million, leaving the other party room to negotiate, you may lower the risk of an outright rejection by offering to settle closer to your maximum price of, say, $1.8 million.

Negotiating with oneself in this manner does not guarantee non-rejection. It could encourage the other player to reject the $1.8 million offer, because the unexpected offer of inspires them to be more ambitious. Perhaps they expected a "top" price of only $1.6 million?

8 If opponents are too soft and cannot look after themselves, that is their lookout

The word "opponent" always indicates a red negotiator. Being up against someone whom they perceive to be "too soft" leads a red negotiator to think they have died and gone to heaven. The extreme red player has no inhibitions about taking advantage of a blue player's softness. Because their red intimidatory behavior is aimed at inducing such softness in an opponent, you shouldn't be surprised at the response of red players when you behave softly.

9 A good cause is more worthy than power

Reverence for a "good cause" indicates a blue player. Being on the side of the angels compensates for having to submit to a more powerful partner. The moral superiority of defying naked power with a good cause can be awesome. Unfortunately, a good cause is not enough—the meek have not (yet) inherited the earth.

Power is the ability to get someone to do what they otherwise would not do, while a good cause indicates what you believe they should do. Blue players consistently confuse what *should* be done with what *is* done.

Power does not always succeed in defeating good causes. It depends on the resilience of those who espouse the good causes. But neither does every cause merit its claim to be "good". This is another failing of an extreme blue approach—the presumption that they are in the right and others are in the wrong. Feelings of moral superiority can be sanctimonious and, therefore, irrelevant.

By now, you know that this is a red attitude. You should also be aware of the implications of "pushing harder", particularly when the other party has "buckled" under your pressure. This induces something akin to bloodlust. You are seldom restrained by success—humility is not one of the red virtues—and you push harder because it is in your nature. But, be warned, push too hard too often and the "worm might turn].

10 When opponents buckle under pressure I should push harder

4 *The Haggle*

1   You are in the market for a new mountain bike and see "Phantom Ranger" as just perfect fo
your needs, plus it has the cordless gear changer you have always wanted but could never
afford. The shop's owner tells you she is selling it as a one-off "special" at $350 (about half
price), which is well within your budget and exceptional value at that price. Do you:

   (a)   Think "whoopee" and buy the bike immediately?

   (b)   Visit other bike shops first to see if they have matching offers?

   (c)   Haggle?

2   You are a claims manager for an insurance company. A policy holder has put in a claim fo
$60,000 to replace a boat that was destroyed in an accident that was fully investigated by
a loss adjuster. You are about to write to the policy holder with an offer to settle. Do you

   (a)   Offer $60,000 in final settlement?

   (b)   Offer $45,000 in final settlement?

   (c)   Offer $30,000 in final settlement?

3 How many personal injury claimants do you think accept their insurer's first settlement offer?

(a) 12 percent?

(b) 91 percent?

(c) 66 percent?

THE most obvious place to witness red-style behaviors in the negotiation process is in pure haggling (or dickering, as North Americans call it).

Haggling is disdained by some people, as if it were disreputable. Yet haggling is what a lot of people do when they think they are negotiating. The psychology behind this phenomenon is beyond my remit here. I am more concerned with what haggling can teach you about the process of negotiation. Make no mistake, when you negotiate you are bound on occasion to resort to haggling or to have to handle another negotiator who is trying to haggle with you.

Haggling by its nature is a restrictive method of trading that probably preceded negotiation as we know it today. It persists in many marketplaces (and in tourist traps).

However, haggling and negotiation are not synonymous. They are related but are not substitutes. Haggling is only a subset of negotiation activity and, though some of the elements of haggling are also applicable to general negotiation, you are probably more familiar with them in their haggling forms.

Searching and hiding

Haggling therefore involves two simultaneous strategies, searching and hiding: you search for the other person's "best price" and hide your own. One is coercive, the other deceptive. You try to put the other person in the spotlight and keep yourself in shadow. They do the same to you, so expect a lot of banter and not a little "theater", all accompanied by exhibitions of verbal dexterity, many white lies and a few outrageous ones (which is why tourists

Exhibit 14   Behavioral definition of haggling

> Haggling is about finding out the maximum that the other person would pay, without disclosing the minimum that you would accept.

often love haggling in local markets).

All the motivations for red behaviors are present in the haggle. The focus is on the single issue of price. The parties do not have, nor do they seek, a relationship beyond the time and place of the haggle.

Hagglers are purely results oriented: "How cheap can I get the item?" competes with "How much can I sell it for?"

Pure hagglers are not burdened by future obligations. If you have met for the first time only minutes before you commence haggling, and you do not expect to see each other again, you need not worry about future embarrassments from the deal you have struck. If you regularly haggle together, like dealers in the same market, you keep your relationship at "arm's length"— the personal element is totally removed because "it's only business" and nothing is meant nor taken personally.

The lack of continuity in your relationship makes you both strangers to each other's interests. You have no reputation to build and none to protect. You do not take responsibility for what you say or do or how you behave because there are no comebacks.

Your normal suspicions are exacerbated by the uncertainty of the outcome. You each have a task but, as you are strangers, neither of you knows how far the other will go to accomplish whatever they set out to achieve.

Where experience is lop-sided, because one of you knows far more about the market for the item and the techniques by which haggling for it is conducted, the haggle is lop-sided too. The experienced haggler sets to work on the expectations of the inexperienced and gradually shapes the outcome in their own interests. This is home territory for a red behaviourist and, let's be frank, it's what the inexperienced half expects and, in certain tourist contexts, enjoys.

Listen to any tourist recounting their holiday haggles in the local souk, bazaar or market—in their hearts they know they came off "worse", but at least they were entertained and have something to show for it, even if it is a vulgar fake for which they paid too much. The object ends up forlorn on their sideboard or is given as a present to an unsuspecting relative, and is a memento of their harmless indulgence in a distant culture.

Holiday haggles

As there are at least two of you haggling, there is a gap between the opening, or entry, prices that you both seek. This is called the **haggling range**.

In pure haggling everything comes down to price and, as price is divisible, it is a fertile field for competitive jousting over how much is to be paid or received. The seller tries to secure the highest price and the buyer to pay the lowest. You are in direct competition—the more you get, the more they must give up; the less you give up, the less they get.

It is zero sum all the way. There can only be one winner, not two. You either get it "very cheap" or you pay "too much" for it. And because this is true for both of you, you both know that you are rivals.

FIRST OFFERS

Price is a single dimension. Pure hagglers prefer to see it that way and there is no other way they can look at it. "What's your best price, then?" you ask and whatever answer you get, it's never "best" enough.

The art of haggling does not involve accepting whatever you are offered, especially if it is the first offer. You always act as if the first offer is not the last and that their "best" is not what the Duchess of York would call their "bestest". Behind every offer there is a better one for you—even if what they offer first seems to be marvelous.

The haggler challenges all offers, no matter how good they seem—without, of necessity, causing offence or

---

THE PEACE PROCESS IS NOT A SOUK

Mr Saeb Erekat, Palestinian chief negotiator, accused the Israelis of trying to change the ground rules of the peace process.

"The Israelis no longer stick to the Oslo framework," he claimed. "Instead, they bring up different issues, arguing that because of the nationalistic and far right-wing pressures in the government, they are only prepared to give in on this or that issue—as if they were bargaining in a souk, but Oslo is not a souk. It is a process and we have to stick with it."

Perhaps Earth Summits should be held in a souk?

At the end of the Second Earth Summit at UN headquarters in New York, a spokesperson from the green movement attacked what she described as a "total lack of progress and a very disappointing outcome".

She added: "Instead of adopting anything practical or any measurable targets or any specific obligations to do anything about global warming, all we got were speeches about 'processes', 'strategies' and 'good intentions'."

Perhaps she should speak to Mr Erekat?

risking having the offer withdrawn. This is one habit of a haggler that negotiators would do well to practice.

Consider the problem from the seller's point of view. They don't know what you will pay. True, they might estimate the market-clearing price accurately, but markets are made up of people—perhaps just a single person—at a specific time and place. In an hour, by tomorrow or next month, there will be a different market made up of different people.

If sellers knew for certain the market-clearing prices of everything for sale, they would not need to carry stocks of unsold items. They would become so enormously rich that they would retire from selling, leaving the less successful sellers, who are not yet good enough, to set their prices inaccurately. So, in practice, hagglers deal with sellers who are not sure of their prices.

Along comes a buyer and responds to the seller's opening price. How he does so is instructive.

If he jumps down the throat of the seller screaming "Yes, yes, most definitely yes", the seller concludes that her price might just be a trifle on the low side and, as quickly, she might wonder just how much more she could get for it. Instead of being delighted to have sold the item, she regrets her "best" price.

If, on the other hand, the buyer screams "No, no, a thousand times no" and flees, as if for his life, the seller concludes—particularly if this is repeated by scores of potential buyers—that she is asking too much.

Between these extremes—the over-eager buyer snatching at the deal and the underwhelmed buyer running for his life—we have the haggler, who neither snatches at the deal nor turns it down flat. The game he plays is to appear cool and detached, even uninterested, while he probes the offered price, explains why he is not too impressed with the offer, why, as the deal stands, he cannot pay "that much", and suggests what must be done by the seller to kindle the slightest inclination in him to "take it off the seller's hands".

Meanwhile, the seller appears to be as lukewarm to sell as the buyer is to buy. Sure, it can be treated as a game and both may think they know it is a game, but they can never be too sure it is a game, nor how deceptive a game it is.

When conducted convincingly, the haggle has an important social function. It reassures the seller that her price is not too low and comforts the buyer that his price is not too high. Both seller and buyer avoid the embarrassment of settling too easily.

A social function

Negotiators may also, if they realize that they have settled too easily, resent the deals they strike. It is no good saying they are irrational to think in this way. They just do.

Go in with a demand for a pay rise of $1200 and walk out three minutes later with your boss's agreement to authorise a $1200 raise backdated for three months, and I bet any multiple of the raise you get that you will wish you had asked for more!

Denying that this happens anytime anybody gains anything too easily, or bemoaning their "greed", suggests that you have an awesome capacity for self-delusion (and that you know nothing about young children!).

By haggling over any first offer, good or bad, you do yourself and the other haggler a good turn. They are happier, and you know that they are happier, with the eventual deal. And deals with which people are happier tend to be more robust than the other kind.

Fixed prices and immutable terms are not compatible with a haggle. If the price and all the terms are fixed, there is no role for haggling—it would be "take it or leave it", with nothing to haggle about.

Is it negotiable?

Of course, implied flexibility does not exclude the practice of claiming that some things are "non-negotiable". Spurious protestations are usual in the negotiating "dance", in which a haggler tries to limit the other haggler's room for maneuver. What happens next is a matter of choice and circumstance.

By definition, when an issue is negotiable, there is potential for movement from where the haggler starts to wherever they stick. That potential for movement, no matter how small, is absolutely essential for any haggle to take place, because without movement there can be no haggle. Indeed, generalizing from haggling to negotiation, it can be said that negotiation is about the management of movement.

PRICE HAGGLING

Let's take a simple one-issue haggle: the purchase of a rare book, A *Voyage to the South Seas* by William Bligh (1791), in good but not perfect condition—sadly, it has a torn page, loose prints and part of the original binding has been restitched rather sloppily. Perfect copies of this rare book sell for up to $60,000 and even rarer copies signed by Lt Bligh sell for much more.

Assume that we have two hagglers who are interested in doing some business together. They do not have any previous relationship and they have no intention of having a relationship in the future. These are the classic conditions for a red-style, results-only, one-off haggle.

Barbara wants to buy the book (she trades in rare editions) and Samantha wants to sell the copy she inherited from her uncle. The key issue for their haggle is the price. Barbara has up to $7600 available to purchase this edition of the book and it is worth no more than that to her.

Call the $7600 her **exit price** because she will not offer more than that for this copy. Her first decision is her **entry price**—the amount at which she is going to open for the purposes of starting the haggle.

Exit price

There are no "rules" about choosing entry prices. The best advice I can give Barbara is that whatever she opens at, it is better that she is credible rather than risible.

Entry price

For example, opening at $2000 would be risible if she told Samantha that she is offering that because her daughter is two years old today and she therefore thought it was a good price for the book! Her daughter's birthday has nothing to do with Samantha's price for her book. Barbara's entry price is only credible to the extent to which she can convincingly relate her offer price to the state of Samantha's edition of the rare book and the market prices for similar copies.

Suppose now that Samantha, for whatever reason, must get at least $7000 for her book. This is her exit price. Where will she open?

As with Barbara, there are no "rules" for Samantha to follow when choosing an entry price. She has the same credibility problem. She should know at least one thing: wherever she opens she can expect to settle for less than her entry price, except in the unusual circumstance that Barbara accepts the first offer.

Therefore, with Samantha needing at least $7000, she should set her entry price somewhat higher than this. Let us assume that she sets her entry price at $7800, giving her room for a haggle towards her exit price of $7000.

The current situation is shown in Exhibit 15.

Exhibit 15   The rare book haggle

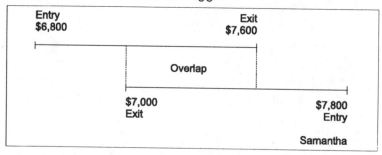

Fortunately, as omniscient outsiders we can read the entry and exit prices for both hagglers. We have access to all four pieces of information: Barbara's and Samantha's entry and exit prices. In practice, however, each haggler only knows three of the four pieces of information in any haggle: they know their own entry and exit prices and they (should) know the entry price of the other haggler, but neither of them knows the other haggler's exit price.

The negotiating range

They have enough information to know the **negotiating range**, which is the gap between the hagglers' entry prices (the $1000 gap between Barbara's $6800 and Samantha's $7800). Now, Barbara knows she could go as high as $7600 (her exit price), but she does not know how low Samantha can go. Samantha knows she can go as low as $7000 (her exit price), but she does not know how high Barbara can go.

Revealing exit prices

Before you suggest that they both reveal their exit prices and save a great deal of time and effort, reflect on your otherwise "reasonable" suggestion.

Take Samantha first. Suppose she reveals that she would accept $7000. What could Barbara do? Accept it perhaps, but almost certainly she would not reveal that she would have gone as high as $7600. Barbara saves herself $600 by keeping quiet about how far she could have gone.

Suppose that Barbara revealed that she would go as high as $7600—what might Samantha do? Accept it perhaps, but almost certainly she would not reveal that she would have accepted $7000. This way she gains $600 by keeping quiet about how far she could have gone.

Whoever reveals their true exit price first risks losing $600.

Perhaps you could amend your "reasonable" suggestion so that each haggler writes down their true exit price and then reveals it simultaneously to the other. This would prevent one of them holding back when the other negotiator revealed hers first. But would your amendment resolve the problem?

Not really. Suppose Barbara wrote down $7600 as her true exit price and Samantha wrote down $7000 as hers. Which would they choose as the agreed price?

Probably neither. They would feel compelled to "split the difference" and to settle at $7300, giving each a gain of $300 over or under their exit price.

This, you might argue, still leaves them better off than having to accept their true exit prices. But how could you ensure that either or both would reveal their true exit price before they split the difference? Perhaps they really are paragons of virtue, veritable saints and, like Caesar's wife, above suspicion—you can't read their minds!

It is safe to assume that if you were haggling you would feel tempted to protect yourself by distorting your own exit price.

In the privacy of their deliberations, Barbara could think through her situation like this:

"Suppose Samantha exaggerates her exit price and writes down $7400 instead of, say, circa $7000, what effect would this have on the final price I pay? Well, instead of splitting the difference between $7000 and $7600 and settling at $7300, we would split the difference between $7400 and $7600 and settle at $7500. This would cost me an extra $200. To avert this, I could protect myself by claiming my exit price as $7200, thus splitting the difference between my $7200 and Samantha's $7400, which ensures that we would settle at $7300."

Meanwhile, Samantha has had second thoughts too. She reasons analogously to Barbara and decides to claim an exit price of $7700, say, forcing a split in the difference between $7200 (or whatever Barbara chooses) and $7700, to give them a settlement price of $7450.

Intending to avert the time and effort of haggling, you have incentivized each haggler to reveal phoney exit points, downwards in the case of buyers and upwards in the case of sellers. Simultaneously revealing their exit points would soon be abandoned as hagglers reverted to traditional haggling.

Overlapping exit prices

In Exhibit 15, the exit prices happen to overlap (Barbara is willing to go up to $7600 and Samantha is willing to go down to $7000). All they really need to know is whether, through haggling, their partner reveals a price that is within their own negotiating range (the gap between their entry and their exit prices). By definition, any price between your own entry and exit prices at the very least is acceptable to you in principle.

If Barbara, for whatever reason, moves from her entry price of $6800 to $7200, say, Samantha knows for certain that Barbara is prepared to pay $7200 for the book. Samantha has a clear choice: accept $7200 (above her exit price of $7000) or press to see if Barbara is prepared, by further movement, to pay more than $7200.

We know, but Samantha doesn't, that Barbara is prepared to pay up to $7600. If Samantha agrees to $7200, the haggle is over. She gets the cash and Barbara gets the book. If Samantha decides to push for more, she may get more or she may not if Barbara, for whatever reason, thinks that Samantha is only testing her resolve.

Consider the situation in which Samantha moves from her entry price of $7800 to $7600, which happens to be (unknown to Samantha) Barbara's exit price. What does Barbara now know that Samantha doesn't?

Barbara knows that a deal on Bligh's book is possible. Barbara could accept the $7600 price immediately and conclude the haggle. She would be advised, however, to continue haggling to see if Samantha will lower her price some more, because every reduction in Samantha's price makes Barbara better off—she gets Bligh's book and saves some cash too.

As we know, Samantha is prepared in principle to go down as far as $7000, but whether she will do so depends on a whole host of circumstances, almost too numerous to elaborate.

For instance, Samantha could get fed up with moving, or could resent that she is moving and Barbara is not. She could decide to make a final offer to Barbara, but one still above $7000, and make a credible excuse for temporarily breaking off the haggle—"I have an appointment at the dentist in ten minutes, so call me this evening." Meanwhile, she will see what price Maggs Brothers, of Berkeley Square, will offer for Bligh's book when she meets their buyer later that afternoon.

Not all exit prices overlap. It is possible that the lowest price Samantha will accept is still higher than the most that Barbara will pay. In this case, after prolonged discussion, neither of them will find the other's offer inside their entry and exit range (Exhibit 16).

Exit prices don't always overlap

Exhibit 16   No overlap in exit points

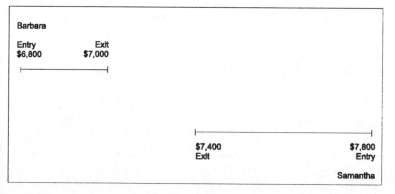

Barbara

Entry   Exit
$6,800 $7,000

$7,400 $7,800
Exit   Entry

Samantha

Unless one or both of them revises their exit prices, the haggle will not conclude with an agreement in this example.

There is another possibility, namely, that the buyer's entire entry–exit range is higher than the seller's (Exhibit 17).

Exhibit 17   No overlap in ranges

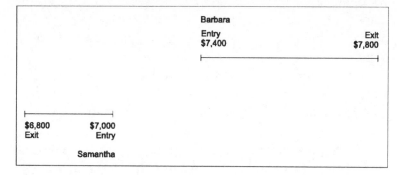

In this exceptional (though by no means unknown) circumstance, Barbara, the buyer, is prepared to open with an offer of $7400 and to go as high as $7800, while Samantha, the seller, is willing to open with a demand for $7000 and to go down as low as $6800! Happy days, you can be sure, for whoever hears the other's entry price first.

If Barbara opens at $7400, what does Samantha do? She would certainly be tempted to say "yes", but, if she does, what effect would this have on Barbara? An instant acceptance by Samantha tells Barbara that she opened too high. She will regret her generosity instantly. So will Samantha, when she remembers that wherever any buyer opens in a haggle or a negotiation, they have a higher exit price too.

Samantha, therefore, should push to see if Barbara will improve on her price.

The same goes for Barbara if Samantha opens with a first demand for $7000, $400 less than her own entry price. Her best course is to search for Samantha's lower exit price.

On hearing an entry price, no matter how attractive it sounds, you should always challenge it, because behind every opening offer there is a better one and your haggling task is to search for it.

Haggling is the means by which Barbara and Samantha are encouraged to explore potential prices for Bligh's book. When one of them (or both) is inside their own entry–exit range, they have a choice to settle at the current price or to continue to search for a better one.

HAGGLER'S SURPLUS

Where there is an overlap in the hagglers' exit prices—and there has to be an overlap if a deal is to be done—some additional terminology helps to appreciate fully what is at stake. Exhibit 18 sets out the factors in a deal, as seen by an omniscient observer.

Think of this example as an insurance claim made by the plaintiff, Patience, against the defendant, David. The fire insurance policy provided a rebuild cover of $550,000 for a large period house.

Unfortunately, the house was totally destroyed by a fire and, fortunately for Patience, the owner, she was up to date with her premiums. As is typical in these red-style disputes, David, the insurance company's claims manager, made a low "final settlement" offer of $200,000. Patience rejected the offer and demanded full restitution of the house under the terms of the $550,000 rebuild policy.

The haggling range is thus between $200,000 and $550,000. As omniscient observers, we know that their exit points overlap: David will authorize as much as $450,000 and Patience will accept as low as $350,000 in final settlement of the claim. However, neither of them knows the other's exit point.

Exhibit 18   The haggler's surplus

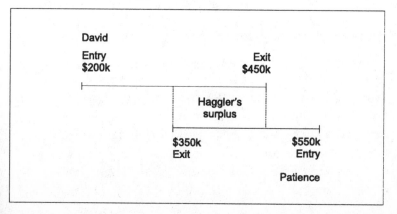

The $100,000 haggling range from $350,000 to $450,000 is also known as the **haggler's surplus**, because if David is forced by Patience's effective haggling to pay out $450,000, Patience is $100,000 better off than if she is forced by David's effective haggling to accept $350,000.

Analogously, if David settles for $350,000, he is better off by $100,000 than if he settles at $450,000. The extent to which they are better off is a measure of the amount they gain over or under what they are prepared to pay if they are forced to their exit points.

David would have a surplus over a possible payout of $450,000 if he could persuade Patience to accept any sum less than $450,000. For example, his haggler's surplus would be $50,000 if she accepted $400,000; $75,000 if she accepted $375,000 and $100,000 if she went down to her exit price of $350,000. Conversely, Patience would have a haggler's surplus of $50,000 if she persuaded David to pay out $400,000 and a surplus of $100,000 if she persuaded David to make his "final offer" of $450,000.

In other words, their haggle divides up the $100,000 range ($350,000 to $450,000) between their overlapping exit points.

As neither Patience nor David knows the other's exit point, they can only calculate their own surplus, which can vary from zero (because they settle at their own exit point) to a maximum given by their own entry point. In practice, their own entry point is unobtainable because the other's exit point is likely to cut off some part of their haggling range. For example, David will not pay out more than $450,000, which is short of Patience's entry point of $550,000, and Patience will not accept less than $350,000, which is more than David's entry price of $200,000.

Don't accept the first offer

Research shows that two-thirds of insurance claimants accept the insurer's first offer, even though in most cases the insurers are prepared to offer more if they are pushed to do so by claimants. Because most claimants accept first offers, insurance companies make low—sometimes very low, almost ludicrous—first offers, in the reliable expectation that there is a relatively high chance that they

---

RED HAGGLES IN INSURANCE

Most people with potential claims for injury do not claim for damages (though, as the UK becomes more litigious, this is changing).

Of the people who do claim, about 17 percent give up without a settlement.

Of the 84 percent who pursue their claims to a settlement, most settle for piffling amounts.

Sixty percent of the claims that are settled are the result of the plaintiffs accepting the first offer they receive.

Only 6 percent of claims that are made get to a court hearing. All the rest are settled (or abandoned) before a trial, often on the proverbial courthouse steps or in a nearby corridor.

Not all claims for damages that are dropped before a hearing are too weak to stand close examination, though some clearly are fraudulent or, at best, frivolous.

Defendants win some of the claims that get to court, and, of course, plaintiffs, win the rest. The outcome of a damages claim depends on the case, the credibility of the witnesses, their behavior, the advocacy skills of the barristers, the credulity of the jury and the interventions of the judge.

---

will be accepted.

Red stances are inevitable in these circumstances. If claimants are daft enough to ignore their own best interests by not challenging first offers, why should insurance companies ignore their shareholders' best interests? Claims managers who are unable to see where the shareholders' interests lie in these matters are soon replaced by others who are not so queasy. Red players dominate in the professional world of insurance claims, whatever PR and marketing spin doctors assert to the contrary.

DISTRIBUTIVE HAGGLING

There is a special case susceptible to haggling in which both negotiators know the amount of the available surplus (though they still do not know the extent of their rival's aspirations). This is where they are haggling over a known fixed amount, such as in the division of the profit from a joint venture, or the amount of an inheritance, or a defined piece of real estate.

Haggling distributes the surplus between them. Both of them know what is in the kitty and, therefore, what is at stake. Save in circumstances where they fight or litigate for it, they must voluntarily agree on the distribution. It is a distributive haggle, with only one dimension on the table. What one gets the other does without in a classic zero-sum haggle.

Zero sum

If one player gets all of the available surplus, the other player gets none; if one player gets 50 percent, the other gets 50 percent (because no part of the surplus can remain undistributed), and if one player gets 30 percent, the other must, perforce, get 70 percent.

Finding an acceptable distribution is not so straightforward as it might seem. If beforehand the players had agreed that they would share the proceeds of their joint venture in set proportions, there should be no problems in distributing them—except, of course, if one of the partners is unsettled by considerations of post-agreement greed (exemplified in John Grisham's *The Partner*, where Benny Aricia tries to change the deal from a $60m : $30m split to a $80m : $10m split).

Partners can also fall out when contributions to the success of the deal are interpreted differently and one of them frets over the alleged injustice of the original shares.

Prenuptial agreements are intended to avert bitter contests over estates, particularly where the partners come to the marriage with very different wealth levels. By fixing an upper limit on alimony prior to the marriage, the partners agree beforehand on the price of the marriage failing. This does not prevent attempts—sometimes successful—to have a court overturn the agreed

APPLYING THE HOOKER'S PRINCIPLE

"Services are valued much more before they are rendered than afterwards—hence get paid first."

Amigo had a tax problem and he wanted to mitigate his firm's liability. Rodriguez, an independent tax specialist, suggested that he be hired to rearrange Amigo's financial affairs by redefining his acquisition of an overseas subsidiary. Rodriguez was hired and saved Amigo nearly $4 million in tax.

A month later, Amigo received an invoice for $100,000. He refused to pay it because it was "far too much to pay for a couple of days' work". He ignored his saving of $3.9 million and the talents of Rodriguez that had led him to the tax plan.

Sanchez did not know he had a further tax-saving opportunity. Rodriguez had spotted one while studying Sanchez's accounts. He asked Sanchez how much it would be worth to him to save $1 million in tax.

Sanchez laughed and asked Rodriguez if he could save him that much.

Rodriguez said: "Probably not."

"Well," Sanchez asked, "how much can you save me?"

"That depends on how much it is worth to me to find out," replied Rodriguez.

"If you can guarantee me savings of $1 million," Sanchez said, "I'll write you a cheque for $100,000 right now."

This time, Rodriguez smiled and got to work as soon as the cheque cleared.

distribution in a divorce. And, of course, the mere fact of suggesting a prenuptial assessment of the consequences of a failed marriage (hardly a romantic touch!) could itself produce a prenuptial failure.

To avert (niggling) haggles, potential partners are advised not just to state the proportion of the future distribution but also its basis, so that a specified variation in circumstances triggers a specified variation in a previously agreed distribution. Where the proposed revision of a distribution is vexatious only, it can be excluded on the grounds that none of the agreed circumstances for a new distribution has occurred.

SUMMARY

Pure haggling exemplifies pure red-style behavior. Hagglers are results oriented and do not have, nor do they seek, long-term relationships. Haggling is about dividing a single amount—usually the price—between two parties. Each wants as much of the available amount as they can get.

Haggling is about determining the most that someone will pay without disclosing the least that you will accept (and vice versa).

Hagglers do not accept first offers. They challenge first and all subsequent offers. They engage in verbal bluffs to secure whatever they are after. They manage movement from their entry points (where they open) towards their exit points (from which they do not intend to move further) and try to stay inside their haggling range (the gap between their entry and exit points).

Hagglers open credibly and try to persuade the other haggler to move towards them. They know their own entry and exit points and the entry point of the other haggler, but not the latter's exit point.

Where exit points overlap a deal is possible (but not certain); where they do not overlap a deal is unlikely unless one or both move from their exit point. The gap between overlapping exit points is known as the haggler's surplus because it represents the amount to be divided.

The closer haggler A settles to haggler B's entry point, the greater the haggler's surplus B secures; the closer to B's exit point, the smaller the haggler's surplus B acquires.

Where the haggling ranges do not overlap, a deal is impossible. Where entry points overlap, the first one to open is at a disadvantage because this invites the other haggler to take advantage of this information by revising their own entry point.

Where the amount to be divided is known (a legacy, an amount of profit) the haggler's surplus is also known. Where the division is not set down beforehand (the terms of the will; the profit-sharing formula; the prenuptial agreement) haggles can be fraught.

RECOMMENDED READING

James C. Freund (1992) *Smart Negotiating: How to Make Good Deals in the Real World*, Simon & Shuster, London.

Howard Raiffa (1982) *The Art and Science of Negotiation*, Belknap Press, Harvard University, Boston, pp 45–65.

Richard Walton & Robert McKersie (1962) A *Behavioral Theory of Negotiation: an Analysis of a Social Interaction System*, McGraw-Hill, New York, pp 11–45.

1

(a) A major mistake if you do. If her first offer is about half the price you would expect to pay, what price is her second—or her last—offer? Always challenge first offers. If you buy first offers you teach sellers to open with higher prices!

(b) Seems sensible, but is it? By the time you get round the other bike shops and find none of them can match her offer, she might have sold the bike to somebody else.

(c) Yes. By challenging the first offer "bargain", you might discover a better bargain—her last, not her first price—and, if you don't, by putting up some resistance to her price, you avoid giving her "seller's regret" from the realization that she could have got more for her bargain.

2

(a) Not if you want to remain in business. Only special circumstances would provoke you into such generosity.

(b) Much better. Depends on how much pressure they are under to settle quickly. Perhaps they have seen another boat and $45,000 would go a long way towards acquiring it; or perhaps they feel uneasy about their claim because of so far unidentified contributory neglect on their part.

(c) Ecstatically better! There is a good chance they will accept this—or any—first offer for reasons similar to (b). If not, they have a long way to go to get anywhere near $60,000 and, as this will take a long time, even with threats of litigation, at what point below $60,000 will they prefer the certainty of a settlement to the prolonged disappointment of waiting for their money?

3

(a) Way off target! If the proportion was anywhere near 12 percent, the average settlement offer would be way above what it is in practice. Insurance companies take full advantage of their clients' willingness to sell themselves short. This is why red players do well as claims managers for insurance companies (blue players go into softer professions).

(b) You're an incorrigible red player having a dream after a heavy night out spending your annual bonus in the "Claims Adjuster of the Year Award"—you won the Order of Merit in the "Impervious to Sobbing Widows" section (for the third year running). Pity you have to wake up, but meanwhile smile and dream on.

(c) Yes, incredible as it may seem. Sixty-six percent of those in dire need of their insurance claims settle first time—whatever they are offered. This behavior only encourages red players to exploit their soft blue customers and have no qualms about taking their bonuses for doing so.

5 Red, Blue, and Purple Ways to Prepare

1 You are in dispute with a supplier over some poor-quality printing. In preparing to meet with their production manager to discuss the problem, do you:

 (a) Collect evidence of the details of the poor-quality brochures?

 (b) Examine the printing contract to see what recourse you have?

 (c) Instruct your accounts department to suspend all payments to the printer until this problem is solved?

2 Your monitoring service has let you down. The remote sensors reported a system failure in the refrigeration units in one of your stores, but due to its operators' misunderstanding the alert procedures they failed to ensure the timely arrival of repair engineers. This cost you about $25,000 in stock losses because the temperature of the units rose 4° above zero. On what should you concentrate your negotiating efforts:

 (a) Why their operators misunderstood the agreed alert procedures?

 (b) How much compensation they will pay to cover your losses?

 (c) How to prevent this happening again?

> 3   When you have no time at all to prepare for a negotiation, do you:
>
>   (a)   Rely on your experience of similar situations?
>
>   (b)   React to what the other person has said?
>
>   (c)   Listen to them and adjourn at the first opportunity?

*A*LL management gurus advise on the necessity for preparation. Widely advised, this is less frequently practiced. And where and when it is practiced, it is frequently done badly.

It is no different with preparation for negotiation. Honored more in the breach, preparation time is seldom allowed for, though preparation is required of juniors by their bosses.

Preparation takes time and time is often the first scarce resource to be sacrificed. Preparation is nevertheless assumed to have been done and, for the most part, negotiators get away with not doing it because errors arising from the lack of preparation are subsumed in the often messy confusion of events.

Negotiations are a disorderly affair. Players with different agendas are easily diverted into less important issues. They carry a lot of irrelevant baggage, react and provoke each other in equal measure, have selective recall and do not listen too closely. It is easy to hide poor preparation—even ignorance—in the ensuing and meandering bluster.

While both negotiators are equally unprepared, it is not always evident to those to whom they selectively report.

Hence, though everybody knows they should prepare, there is not a high chance of being found out if you skip it, either willfully from arrogant lethargy, or with genuine regret due to other pressures on your time.

Unwilling to sail against the tide of human behavior, I am not going to crusade against what you feel compelled to do by habit or circumstance. Instead, I think it more

PREPARATION IS A NECESSITY

Using the time you have

useful to consider what happens when you prepare in the time you do have.

Negotiators, unfortunately, usually rely for behavioral guidance on their attitudes far more than their interests. Before your meeting, predispositions in your intentions dominate your thinking. In short, your preparation behavior is red or blue biased.

THE RED PREPARER

If a picture is worth a thousand words, a real-life scenario must be worth twice that. So, in place of two thousand words, read the following example carefully:

Iceberg

You are a deputy manager in a store which is part of the large branded Iceberg group, which specializes in frozen foods and has branches across the country. On entering the premises at 8 am on Friday morning, to prepare for an 8.45 am opening, you found the refrigeration controls for the entire shop flashing "Alert".

On checking, you discovered to your horror that all of the display and warehouse storage units were above the maximum permitted temperature for goods for sale to the public. This meant that none of the food products in these units could be offered for sale, nor could they be refrozen. Instead, they would have to be destroyed and replaced. As this would take time to organize, if you could not restock quickly you would lose at least a day's trading—usually a good one at that, because it was a Friday, and probably Saturday's as well. You estimated this to mean losses of $15,000 of stock, equating to $30,000 in gross sales revenue.

Staff were already arriving for work and you had to act quickly if you were to stop a disaster from becoming a nightmare. You set your people to work to clear out the defrosted units and sped to your phone to call Frigo, the refrigerator company, to report the failure of their systems and to call out their repair team. It was imperative to get the refrigerated units functioning as soon as possible.

To your surprise, Frigo knew of the situation and had

already arranged to have a maintenance engineer at the store by mid-morning. When you told him that you needed engineers immediately, the service manager informed you that your "store manager" (he could not remember her name) had agreed yesterday afternoon to a mid-morning callout, which was unavoidable as all their engineers were off-site on other jobs. As it took 40 minutes to travel from Frigo's depot to the store, and the entire engineering team was in a meeting until 10.30 am, he could not get anybody to the store before 11.15 am.

At this news, you "exploded" and demanded that he got his engineers out of the meeting and send them on their way immediately. Your store was in chaos and you wanted engineers who knew what they were doing on the premises by 9.30 am, if not sooner. You slammed the phone down, and ten minutes later you rang back demanding to speak to Frigo's general manager. He too was in the meeting! You got his assistant and brusquely complained of your dissatisfaction and she promised to convey your urgent message to her boss.

Next, you called your own store group manager at Iceberg's head office, informing her of your fruitless calls to Frigo and of what you had immediately organized at the store. You also told her that in your opinion the costs of the failure would have to be met by Frigo, as they had failed to act quickly and were still not due at the store until after 11.15 am. She agreed to ring Frigo immediately to demand their assistance and promised to send down extra staff to help you with the unloading of the units. An emergency supply of foods to restock for the weekend and beyond was also promised, though she could not send it until she knew how long it would take for the refrigeration service to be restored. Meanwhile, all normal deliveries would be suspended.

Have you got the picture?

As a manager, your first task is to get remedial action under way, before you decide on your response to the consequences of the emergency. Head office will want a full report on what happened, what caused it and what you did about it. The lost stock and sales will have to be accounted for and, as you believe the refrigeration company to be culpable, you expect Iceberg to seek compensation from them.

POSSIBLE REACTIONS

Now, I'll hold it there for a moment, while we explore possible reactions to the problem and how your choices influence the outcomes available to you. In doing so, I shall also introduce some ideas about preparation for negotiation and how they are influenced by your style of negotiating behavior. I readily accept that this is an unusual treatment of preparation techniques, but I want to get away from standard treatments of negotiation preparation that only purvey approved practices, as if the way people prepare has nothing to do with their proclivity for red or blue behaviors. I shall also word the presentation as if you are behaving in the manner I describe.

TACTICAL PRESSURES ON ATTITUDES

The dominant thought in your mind is that you have been let down by Frigo. Doing something about this is all you have time for just now.

You think tactically. Your attitude is: "Doers do, they don't dally."

You are angry with Frigo's reaction to your phone call and with their lack of urgency—as if a staff meeting took precedence over a collapse in the refrigeration system at one of their major clients! You are aware that the Frigo system is brand new (your store only opened six weeks ago). If your anger grows, it is because you feel pretty incensed and determined at this moment. The picture for you is clear—there are no clouds on the horizon. That Frigo will be forced to pay compensation for the situation is beyond doubt.

Now, add in the tactical pressures of dealing with the emergency:

- Supervising staff who want to know where to pile the defrosted food—with two out of three rubbish containers full already, where should they dump the growing piles of spoiled stock?

- Making sure that no food gets into the public's hands on health grounds—who is to stand guard while you find a secure way to do this?

- Deciding whether to take stock of what they are disposing of—if so, who is to do it?

- Giving instructions to the staff sent to apologize to customers entering the car park in expectation of doing their shopping

- Estimating when the shop will be back to normal and open for business—customers will seek reassurance

- Taking phone calls from head office, Frigo, various food suppliers, querulous customers and curious colleagues in other locations

- Turning away lorries that arrive with normal deliveries for the store

- Plus a myriad of other tactical decisions that usual accompany breaks like these in daily routines.

You are told that the general manager of Frigo is on his way along with his engineers. Your own stores group manager is also coming down to see for herself what happened. ElectroAlert, the service company that monitors the refrigeration system through remote sensors, is expected soon and its managers want to have a meeting, presumably to shed blame. Two of your supervisors have also asked to see you.

You do not have much time to prepare yourself for the aftermath of the incident. Yet you are going to have to deal with it soon, including perhaps having to commence negotiations with some of the key players involved in the problem. Yes, it is an everyday story of preparing under duress.

How you react to the situation is not ordained by what you should do in theory. "Sunday-best" behavior is for Goody Two Shoes, and she ain't here. What you would tell your boss you would do in a theoretical scenario is different from what you actually do when confronted by real emergency circumstances like this.

RED AND BLUE RESPONSES TO PREPARATION

Consider a typical red response to the deputy store manager's problems.

Finding someone to blame

To protect yourself, you must find somebody else or something else to blame. Your attention is concentrated on commenting forcefully on the events, to all who will listen, and on providing yourself with explanations to feed repetitive cycles of possible questions from your bosses.

Frigo is clearly in the wrong because, for their own ends, they "bamboozled" the employee who rang them into accepting a less than proper response—how could Frigo let the freezers wait for inspection and repair until Friday when they were told about the alarm alert on Thursday afternoon?

It doesn't make sense to you and, if someone's behavior doesn't make sense, you are forced to speculate—usually malignly—about their motives. This conditions and justifies your own reactions to their behavior, reinforcing your red behavioral proclivities as in a vicious cycle.

"You didn't respond" becomes "You didn't want to respond", which becomes "You deliberately didn't respond because you thought you could get away with it". Accusations spread like a pebble's ripples in a still pond.

Before long, urged on by supportive staff, for whom the disaster is a welcome spark of excitement in the dull routine of their jobs, you refine your red blaming assertions in readiness for confronting Frigo's staff with the mess they have created.

Frigo did not ask to speak to the store manager, you speculate, because they thought they could get away with "soft-soaping a junior employee into taking second-rate service". Well, now they have got their come-uppance! Their willful neglect caused the problem so, you conclude, they must pay compensation to solve it.

A tough line is necessary in your view, with no concessions, no giving in, and no surrender. It's no time to "take prisoners". And if Frigo argue, your bosses must threaten them with "no more work from Iceberg".

This should be the last of the six new stores to be built in which Frigo gets the contract to install refrigerators. The publicity alone will kill Frigo's business, you hope.

Your approach combines your deeply felt grievance with your red attitudes, working to absolve yourself from blame. Frigo has got you into trouble. Their neglect has put you in jeopardy with your own employers and if anybody is going to get blamed for this, it certainly is not going to be you.

Preparing for a fight is not difficult for a red player. It is a semi-automatic, knee-jerk reaction that clouds your judgment. You only consider your own view of the matter and you ignore, or downplay, any nagging doubts that might occur to you. The "facts" are to be squeezed into your blaming framework by playing up Frigo's culpability and downplaying any suggestion of your own contributions to the disaster.

Preparing for a fight

There are some things you must attend to immediately, just so you get everybody at the store singing from the hymnsheet you are scripting. First, you must get hold of Gladys, the senior supervisor, who was left in charge yesterday and who telephoned Frigo yesterday afternoon with news about the alarm.

The store manager is presently on annual leave and, as her deputy, you are covering for her during her absence. You rehearse your reasons for taking a half-day's holiday, because the first question the store group manager is going to ask is why you were not present yesterday afternoon. You may have to "adjust" some of your reasons to make them more convincing:

- You had already worked 14 days without a break—normally you would have had two days off

- Thursday is the quietest afternoon of the shopping week

- Gladys is an experienced supervisor

- She had your home phone number—it's there on the wall (better remove the memo that is half hiding it)

- Gladys hadn't called you out, so you had no idea there was a problem until you came in early this morning and by then there was nothing you could do to avert the disaster.

Blue attitudes

Quickly taking Gladys aside, you listen to her (blue) narrative. She reports that the alarm light on the delicatessen counter began flashing at 2.30 pm and she rang Frigo to report it. It was a "level-one" warning only and, she reminded you, this had happened twice before since the new store opened. On both occasions it was a minor fault that was quickly fixed and did not pose any real threat. Yesterday the temperature had risen from −3°C to near zero, which was still over 2° within the safety range.

The man at Frigo (she didn't get his name) explained that all of his engineers were busy elsewhere that afternoon and, unless he heard from her by closing time (7 pm) that the temperature rise had continued towards +2°C, he would schedule a maintenance callout for 8 am. If the temperature rose any further she was to call him immediately, and he would have somebody come out as soon as his engineers got back from their assignments, around 6.30 pm. He did not mention anything about them having a meeting the next morning.

Gladys had accepted, almost submissively, this arrangement and she reported what she had done to night security at head office. As the temperature did not change before 7 pm, she assumed it would be all right to accept Frigo's response and did not realize the serious danger she was running that everything would go down. She allowed Frigo to put the store at risk and did not want to make a fuss.

She did not call your house because everything seemed in order and, as the temperature had not changed, she thought it was like the previous two incidents, a minor defect. She also thought it best to let you "enjoy your well-earned afternoon off".

You went over it all again with Gladys, emphasizing how sensible she had been and that no blame whatsoever was attached to her. It was all Frigo's fault, you assured her. That Gladys said the timing of this morning's callout was at Frigo's insistence, because it suited them not to come then, was good news from your defensive stance. Also, they had clearly misled her about an 8 am arrival by not mentioning their staff meeting.

Gladys had clearly behaved in a submissive blue manner but, as this leaves her open to future criticism and not you, the devious red in your attitude set allows you to feel quite relaxed about her role in the crisis. Red behaviorists prefer to have soft blue types working for them because they are easily "dumped" on during a crisis.

Next, the man from ElectroAlert arrived to report that their monitors had picked up a "level two" alarm in the delicatessen unit at 7.15 pm (by which time the store would have been empty), going up to level three at 7.55 pm in a couple of the units. This meant that the system in the delicatessen unit had completely crashed by 7.55 pm but, when ElectroAlert reported this to the night security people at Iceberg at 8 pm, they were told that the security staff "knew about the alarm situation and that it was under control". They were given the same message when they contacted head office at 8.30 pm, to report that their monitors were signalling system failures in all of the display and storage units in the store.

For some reason, night security had interpreted the logged report from Gladys at 2.50 pm to mean that the Frigo engineers were "on the premises dealing with the problem". Her report, it was discovered later, had said that an engineer from Frigo "was coming to the premises at 8", which was transcribed as 8 pm on Thursday and not as 8 am on Friday. She had put her best gloss on Frigo's response (a typical reaction from a submissive blue!). For this reason night security had assumed that the Frigo engineer was at the premises when ElecroAlert called them at 8 pm and they also assumed that the later alarms were caused by Frigo's engineers initiating controlled shutdowns!

This is even better news for you because it puts the entire incident in its most serious "system-crashing" mode after store opening hours and therefore outside of your responsibility. It was now fully in the laps of Frigo and ElectroAlert. You are almost home free!

If Frigo had responded by sending an engineer shortly after 6.30 pm and before 8 pm, as you convinced yourself you would have insisted on if Gladys had telephoned you, the problem might have been averted. You can now build up your availability and willingness to come back in ("a captain is never off the bridge"). You could also, if necessary, acknowledge Glady's "misguided" gesture and hint at her inexperience and, if pushed, her "neglect" (also a typical red behaviorist's reaction when sacrificing the submissive blues they have around them).

You feel that now you have a plausible case and you are ready for the meeting with Frigo's general manager. But are you?

In the time available you have sorted out the best line of attack, should Frigo try to evade responsibility for their culpability, and, given sufficient time to settle the issue with Frigo, you could have the whole business of who is to blame cleared up before your general manager arrives.

But will you? What about the interests involved?

Red-style negotiators are more concerned with who is right than what needs to be done. If they think at all about the latter, they confuse it with the former. Hence, if they are convinced that they are in the right, that is sufficient justification for them because they believe that whoever is in the right dictates the solution.

But what if their preferred solution is also wrong? A mistake in focus diverts attention.

As the store is in the right in your view—it is all Frigo's fault, with minor parts played by ElectroAlert and night security at head office—the question of compensation is settled: Frigo pays. QED?

Hold on a minute! This is only true if compensation for the breakdown is the main negotiating issue, which it isn't. What the deputy manager has done is jump to a false conclusion. Who says that compensation is the main issue for the store?

It may become an issue, but the deputy manager did not arrive at that conclusion by a method that sought to identify the store's interests.

The **search for interests** should be the first step in preparation. It can take seconds, when that is all you have got, but it must be done, however little time you have. It is a rock-bottom element of preparation.

To search for interests ask: What does the store want? We know what the deputy manager wants—no blame—but that need not be in the store's interests.

Ask why the deputy manager wants no blame. Does the answer serve the store's interests?

In general, probably not. If the deputy manager is incompetent, it is surely in the store's overall interests (though not those of the deputy manager) to become aware of it. So the interests of the store and those of the deputy manager can conflict.

What might the store want that serves its interests? Well, what it doesn't want is for the incident to happen again. The store's interests include preventing accidental defrosting of its food stock caused by the avoidable incompetence of employees or a supplier's failure to respond to alarms caused by machine malfunctions. The costs in public reputation, customer confidence, hygiene, and public health are incalculable. For a store dependent on its brand name in the frozen food sector, these must be its prime motivations. That is what an interest is—a motivation for your wanting something.

In this context, is compensation for the system failure a prime interest? Not really.

It might assume greater importance later, but for now the immediate interest is to get the refrigeration system working again, and to ensure that it keeps working correctly from now on.

No store's interest is served by you, the deputy manager, having a furious row with Frigo's general manager. Such a row, or behavior that leads to one, is incompatible with committing Frigo to whole-hearted cooperation in finding a permanent solution to the failure of its refrigeration system. As it stands, a red-style row is on the cards that will not address any of the store's interests.

You want to marshall a critical case against Frigo. By putting a critical case across forcibly you will aim to coerce Frigo into accepting the blame and paying compensation. At the very least, your personal tactical task is to divert blame from yourself.

How it will play out is another story. At present, all of your scarce preparation time is concentrated on this end, and almost all of it has been wasted and is counter to the store's interests.

STRATEGIC PRESSURES

This time, imagine that you are Iceberg's stores group manager and you have received an early report from the deputy store manager of what happened some time on Thursday night. As the first task of a manager is to take remedial action, you are pleased that this is what the deputy store manager appears to have done. You know that the next thing he must do is find out what went wrong technically with the refrigeration system (not with the reporting arrangements) and get assurances from Frigo that a total system failure of this nature will not happen again. These are number one priorities.

You must **think strategically**. Senior managers prepare and implement; they don't "shoot from the hip".

Thinking strategically

You are aware that Frigo's system is almost brand new (you were present when the local MP opened the store only six weeks ago) and you know that similar Frigo systems are planned for six other new Iceberg stores across the country. If there is something wrong with the design, this is a good time to find out, before additional tenders from Frigo are accepted and contracts are issued.

This thought prompts other questions.

- Where are you in the tender approval process with Frigo? Check with your business development manager in charge of contract approvals about the status of the Frigo tenders.

- How do your technical people rate the Frigo system against its competition? Better get somebody from the technical evaluation team down to the store to help assess what went wrong.

- Frigo's system is still under warranty, so it must be covered by Frigo's insurance. Better get a claims officer from your insurers to confirm this.

- An early meeting with Frigo's general manager would be a prudent precautionary step. Check where their GM will be this morning and suggest a meeting as soon as possible at the store.

- What immediate steps need to be taken to ensure that the incident is not repeated? What must the store's staff do that they weren't doing? What must Frigo's staff do that they weren't doing? What happened to your monitoring service?

- Tactically, you should take the heat out of the current situation and concentrate on putting it right. Solve the problem first and hold an inquest afterwards. Concentrate on your strategic interests and do not get diverted into a squabble or a game of "pass the parcel".

PURPLE RESPONSES

As Iceberg's stores group manager, consider **purple preparation** to deal with your problem.

Your intention is to concentrate on solving the problem for the longer term. This means attacking the *problem* and not the *people* through whom the solution must work—make people part of the solution.

Something is clearly wrong technically because the entire system went down. You do not know why the incident was triggered off, so at this stage nothing is to be gained by jumping to conclusions.

Cooperation

To get at the truth you need open and full cooperation from everybody involved and you don't want key people, through fear of being blamed, to clam up defensively. Finding out why the system crashed is more important than seeking out the "guilty". Punishing a hapless victim is a trivial matter compared to training people not to be victims. In any case, if somebody did cause the problem by their unintentional actions, there is still something wrong because standard operating procedures failed to kick in to override an individual's neglect. That is why leaving people like Gladys, with submissive blue tendencies, without remedial training in becoming more assertive is an unwise economy for an organization.

Search for the truth

A truth-seeking approach is necessary. No witch-hunts. No personalizing the problem. No blame seeking. Approach the problem with an open mind and listen to what people have to say—that is what you should teach your staff. The technical data will show what happened and what needs to be done.

Preparing to search for the truth is not difficult for a

purple player. It is a semi-automatic, almost knee-jerk reaction. You are not judgmental until you have the full facts. Other people's interpretations of the "facts" are treated as contributions to the quest for the truth, and will be weighed in the balance when you have gathered as much information as you can. You expect people, at first, not to trust that you mean what you say about not looking for scapegoats.

There are some things you must attend to immediately, so that you get everybody at the store singing from their own hymnsheets, preferably uncontaminated by pressure from other people with individual agendas.

You certainly must see ElectroAlert and get copies of their monitoring sheets and their responses, for comparison with the logs held at night security.

You feel that now you have something like an effective agenda and you are ready for a meeting with Frigo.

Purple negotiators are more concerned with what needs to be done than with who is right. A mistake in focus diverts scarce resources, including time, to wrong solutions and usually exacerbates the problem.

What are your concerns?

A purple behaviorist will not ignore an individual's concerns, nor demand that they are set aside, and certainly would not use mere hierarchical authority ("I'm the boss and I decide what is important") to enforce a corporate viewpoint on an individual. Purple behaviorists are empathic to individuals and seek to understand why they take the stances they do.

The deputy store manager wants no blame on himself. And why? Because if somebody else is blamed then personal disasters, like demotion (loss of face, loss of income) or, worse, unemployment ("How will I provide for my family?"), will be averted. The deputy store manager's red reaction to the problem is to personalize it; understandably, because that is what serves his personal interests. But that does not serve Iceberg's interests. Managers should have a different agenda.

The distinction between a purple-style and a red-style approach in the Iceberg meltdown case is more than a

Differences in approach

difference in emphasis. When the players go from preparation to face-to-face meetings, the differences in their approach will be shown in how they conduct the debate phases and in the form that proposed solutions will be presented—and in whether a negotiated solution is possible.

Of course, your purple approach is conditional on Frigo putting their full effort into identifying the technical problem with their equipment. You will also not want them to try to hide their culpability or design weaknesses in a manner that might affect your company's pending decisions on new contracts. You will be looking for evidence of Frigo working closely with your technical people to make sure that nothing like this can happen again.

If evidence emerges that there is a major design fault in Frigo's equipment, you will not seek, including by submissive collusion with Frigo, to protect your earlier decision to award them the contract for the store. The interests of the store are your sole concern and you will be assertive, not submissive, in all your dealings with Frigo.

In the purple approach to preparation you will require—either explicitly or implicitly, depending on the circumstances—that Frigo's managers address your interests with alacrity and that they guarantee that there will no repetition of the fault in the system.

In return, you will address Frigo's interests—new contracts—in a positive manner. If events show that this is not happening, then you will deal with this new situation with assertive determination: Frigo will get nothing from you unless and until you get what you require from Frigo.

Purple behavior comes from having **positive attitudes**, including those of partnership with suppliers whom you rely on to contribute to your business's added value. Your aim is high results and strong relationships, not some weak compromise between them.

Purple preparation is outlined in detail in the next chapter.

SUMMARY

Preparation takes time, but it is time well spent. Unfortunately, "busy" managers, with many demands on their time, don't take sufficient time to prepare. They rely too much on their red or blue biases to guide their preparation.

Red behaviorists react too quickly and think too tactically, usually based on what is good for them personally and not what is good for the enterprise. They concentrate, for example, on avoiding blame by passing it to others. They rehearse accusations, justifications and grievances, and any remedies they come up with usually address their own personal interests only. Extreme red behaviorists go too far in blaming people rather than addressing the solution to the problem.

Soft blue behaviorists also think tactically—how to resolve the tactical problem with the least fuss and embarrassment, so as to ensure that they do not strain their relationships with their suppliers. They are more likely to accept whatever they are offered, even at risk to their interests, and to downplay the behavior of others that negatively affects the organization because they don't like getting other people into trouble.

Purple behaviorists think strategically. In dealing with some kind of failure they are more interested in ensuring that the system does not fail again, rather than in arguing about who was at fault and how much compensation they can get.

They begin with the organization's interests and, if the system has failings or weaknesses, they prefer to search with the other parties for solutions to the problems. They are people oriented, without going too far in softly protecting people from the consequences of their behaviors, or, in this case, their lack of appropriate behavior.

1

(a) Well, you certainly will need accurate evidence if you are to pursue credibly a complaint about poor quality, including to what extent, if any, your instructions to the printer and the materials you supplied were contributory factors to the poor quality. Those factors outside your control, and wholly within the printer's, would be considered carefully. A "powerful" case can collapse from information that you have overlooked or of which you are ignorant. Revealing such information puts red demeanor at risk.

(b) Maybe, but after you have considered the steps to be taken as in (a). If you have been negligent in aspects that are wholly under your control, your rights under the contract terms are compromised.

(c) A precautionary red step, almost as if you anticipated a fight. This move increases your leverage, in case it is needed, but could be provocative. The accounts department did not cause the substandard work. This opens up two "fronts" for you to fight on.

2

(a) This is of interest, and could form background to the design of a remedy to prevent future repetition of the problem, but it is not the most important issue for the negotiators.

(b) Definitely not. Compensating for past events is a job for red-style lawyers, not managers.

(c) Yes. This is the first task for the negotiators and coincides with the best interests of the parties. Management is about preventing damaging things happening that otherwise would. To ensure it never happens again the cooperation of all concerned is required.

3

(a) For routine negotiations that you conduct regularly, this might be tempting on the grounds that it is all you have time for in the circumstances. The habit of responding this way, however, is difficult to curb even when you do have more time to prepare properly.

(b) Just a step along from (a) and all too often the limit of preparation for many people. Even quite complex negotiations are handled this way by quite senior people. It is a sign of a reactive management style.

(c) By far the best response, if you are truly thrown in at the deep end and the option of finding time to prepare is completely denied you. Try working weekends or staying on after 5 pm.

6 Basic Purple Preparation

1 You are negotiating a commercial lease with a tenant and he insists on including the phrase "time is of the essence" in the document. This concession is of no consequence to you at all. Do you:

   (a) Willingly agree to its inclusion?

   b) Grudgingly agree to its inclusion?

   (c) Wait and see how important it is for the tenant?

2 After studying the negotiable issues in detail, you conclude that on most of them you regard their importance as crucial to your interests. Does this suggest that:

   (a) You can take a tougher red stance with the other negotiator?

   (b) He will take a tougher red stance with you?

   (c) You are relatively weaker as a result?

3 You are depending on winning future business with a client and, at present, you are the preferred bidder. A problem has come up that could jeopardize your preferred bidder status and, therefore, your winning of future business. In these circumstances, do you:

(a) Ensure that the client's interests take precedence over yours?

(b) Put your interests before those of the client?

(c) Judge the importance of each party's interests on their merits?

*B*ECAUSE preparation is pivotal to the success of a negotiation, finding time to prepare is not an alternative, it is mandatory. But laxness in preparation is not confined to those of a red disposition. Soft blue players can be just as lax and ill prepared as red players.

You must not confuse red with being "bad" and blue with being "good", any more than being prepared is a moral virtue. You can prepare well for evil purposes, as any witness to the work of Adolf Eichmann could testify.

Preparation done well improves your effectiveness as a negotiator, whatever your intentions. And to do it well, you have to rise above your behavioral biases, as we saw in the previous chapter. There is a rock-bottom minimum of things you must do if you are to prepare well.

I have already mentioned some of the elements, for example that some of your scarce time is well spent on identifying your **interests**. This means searching for those higher-order objectives, such as raising your living standards or maintaining your profit levels. Wanting to raise your income is an **issue** and the amount by which you want to raise it is your **position** on the issue.

Minimum preparation

Time spent identifying the negotiable issues and deciding on your positions is seldom wasted, provided that your ruminations are plausible, not fanciful.

To be specific, in identifying your positions on the issues you must think about your negotiation **range** on each issue, which leads you to consider your entry and exit points.

So if time is absolutely at a premium, identifying your interests, issues, positions and ranges constitute the rock-bottom elements of preparation.

INTERESTS

Most negotiators adopt red or blue stances on the negotiable issues and articulate what they want relatively easily. Often they never get beyond the issues to consider their interests, mainly because they conduct negotiations blindly.

What are your interests?

Interests are found by asking why you want what you want. Why do I want it in this form rather than that? Wants are **what** you want, interests are **why** you want them (see Exhibit 19).

If you are thirsty, you want water. If your need for water is pressing because you are severely dehydrated, your interest in acquiring water overrides your concerns about its cleanliness or its cost. When Chris Ryan, a member of the SAS patrol Bravo Two Zero, avoided capture by the Iraqis in the Gulf War, he was so thirsty at one point that he drank chemically contaminated water. His interest in survival overcame his reservations at drinking what he suspected was contaminated water.

Likewise, we grade or prioritize our interests. This forces us to prioritize the negotiable issues because the issues deliver our interests.

In the Iceberg store's case, preventing a repeat failure of the refrigeration system is a prime interest and, therefore, negotiating conditionally on those issues that will prevent another failure is also a high priority. Because this is a conditional approach, it is purple behavior.

Hardly anything that the deputy manager did in preparation addressed the interests of Iceberg or the priority issues that would deliver them; quite the reverse. He used scarce preparation time in constructing a sanitized version of the events so as to help him escape blame.

Exhibit 19   Interests, wants and positions

Interests	Wants	Positions
Higher living standards	More income	$5000 more per year
More security	People-proof fencing	15 feet high on all sides
Better education	Go to university	Get in with 3 Bs
Higher profits	Raise prices	By 10 percent
Conservation	Less fishing	Reduce by 35 percent
Free ride	Restrict copyrights	Reduce to 5 years
Protect own talents	Extend copyrights	Increase to life + 100 years
Acquire power	Independence from Britain	Self-government by 1962
Continuity of supply	Fail-safe systems	Specific guarantees and penalties

Interests can be delivered in more than one way. The way you initially think of is not the only way to deliver your interests. This is important if the wants of the two negotiators are incompatible, as presently formulated.

By considering your interests, other forms of addressing them can be explored and, if these other forms are found to be acceptable, that could be enough to break a deadlock.

A LESSON IN INTERESTS FROM HISTORY

From the mid-eighteenth century, Britain's foreign policy towards continental Europe was driven by the admonition: "never allow any European state to be so powerful as to permit it to dominate Flanders Plain". On that basis, Britain chose allies and fought wars for over 200 years.

Wars against Spain, the Netherlands, France and Germany, and, latterly, Britain's resistance to Soviet ambitions during the Cold War, are explained by the application of the Flanders Plain admonition against whichever power came closest to qualifying as a threat. Considerable blood and treasure were expended (not always wisely or well) to deliver Britain's interest in preserving its independence.

At the turn of the twenty-first century, Britain continues to pursue this core interest, but now the "battlegrounds" have shifted from Flanders fields to the corridors of power Brussels (itself sited on Flanders plain!).

The same interest in preserving British sovereignty is served by different means, though now the negotiable issues are different. *Plus ça change, plus c'est la même chose.*

ISSUES

Interests are served by the negotiable issues.

An issue is negotiable when a decision on it requires the voluntary consent of both parties—it is a joint, not a unilateral, decision. For a decision to be implemented, except by force or stealth, each of you must consent to it.

You must spend time identifying negotiable issues because these form the agenda of negotiations. Sometimes the negotiable issues are obvious—the clauses of a contract—but sometimes they do not emerge until views are exchanged.

An exploratory meeting to exchange views on matters of common interest between two companies may lead them to discuss merely "keeping in touch", then agreeing issues to do with "spheres of influence" and "joint marketing", and so on through to "joint ventures" and all the way to negotiating a full-blown "takeover".

Until something emerges from the initial discussions as worthy of a second look, drawing up an agenda of negotiable issues would not be feasible, except in the loosest possible general language.

Issues are about what we want and, because they are jointly decided, what we want is constrained by what the other negotiator wants. We cannot write our own paycheck in a wages dispute (would that we could!), nor do we unilaterally write our own price list without consideration of the market.

What we want

In a free society, individuals, in a domestic dispute over what is reasonable behavior, do not have a unilateral right to impose their views on their partner (though they might try to do so). If they are to continue to live together voluntarily, they will have to come to a joint decision about what is acceptable behavior.

PRIORITIES

Having identified the issues, the next most important task is to prioritize them. This is an important dynamic of exchange. It is the means by which a negotiated solution becomes possible.

People do not normally prioritize what they want in the same rank order—they do not value everything in the same way. If they did, trade, though not totally impossible, would be severely restricted and negotiation would not be such a common way to make decisions.

Your priorities are your valuation of the issues. If you value something very highly, then acquiring it or holding on to it will have a higher priority for you than if you value it hardly at all.

Valuing the issues

PERPLEXING PRIORITIES

Just after the Second World War, a rumor quickly spread where I lived that some chocolate was on sale at the local shop. For many kids this was our first chance to taste real chocolate. Running round to the sweet shop, clutching my precious ration coupons and tuppence, I joined the throng of kids at the counter and eagerly awaited my turn.

Eventually, I was given a small bar of the "Five Boys" brand of chocolate in exchange for the coupons and tuppence. Almost before I had left the shop, I had eaten the chocolate and I was in a state of wonderment.

Then it struck me! Why was Mr Higginsbottom, the shop owner, selling chocolate? Why wasn't he eating it? Surely, he knew how wonderful it tasted? I concluded he was mad.

Fifteen years later, I realized that Mr Higginsbottom was perfectly sane (I was studying economics). He clearly preferred collecting coupons and pennies from little urchins like me because he had lots of chocolate and an empty till. We kids manifestly preferred a bar of chocolate to keeping coupons and pennies because we had no chocolate and had no other use for our coupons and pennies.

Mr Higginsbottom's priorities were different from ours.

If you are dehydrated, a can of cola is worth much more to you than some salted French fries. If I am ravenously hungry, and salted fries look appetizing, I might value them much higher than a can of cola.

Now, if you own the fries but prefer the cola, and I own the cola but prefer the fries, it does not require much of a leap in imagination for us to fathom out a deal, in which you get my cola and I get your fries.

Generalizing to more complex negotiations, ascertaining your relative valuation of the issues

Ranking

Exhibit 20   Prioritizing the issues

Ranking	Comment
Crucial (High)	What you must get if you are to do business—a deal breaker, as things stand, if not settled within your range.
Important (Medium)	What is important for you to get but it need not be a deal breaker—it depends on "how the deal stacks".
Desirable (Low)	What you would like and will try to get, but not a deal breaker if you don't.

constitutes a basic step in rock-bottom preparation. To prioritize the issues you have to rank them, and the simpler your method of ranking them the better (remember, you are squeezed for time).

You could rank them "1, 2, 3", with 1 being the most important priority for you through to 3, the least important, or you could name them "high", "medium" and "low", or "crucial", "important" and "desirable". As long as you rank them into no more than three categories, it doesn't matter what you call them.

Your intention is to get as much as you can, but you know before you start that you will not get everything (if you could, are you asking for enough?). You rank the issues to look for trades, with the intention of trading things that you value less for things that you value more.

TRADING RANGES, NOT POSITIONAL POSTURING

You have most room for maneuver among your lower-priority issues—that is why they are only desirable and are of lower priority. You have least room among the higher-priority issues—that is why they are crucial. But you do have room for maneuver on all issues, otherwise they are non-negotiable and in the "take-it-or-leave-it'" category.

Getting stuck

Getting stuck into a positional posture is not helpful. Sure, it happens—often too easily—but positional posturing is the antithesis of negotiation and not an inevitable characteristic of it. Those people who fall into this error usually have no sense of what is meant by prioritizing. They confuse the rhetoric of presenting their case with holding to an inflexible position.

Purple negotiators do not think in terms of a single position on an issue because they are always looking for potential trades across the positions on each of the negotiable issues.

They think in terms of a range of positions on each issue, from their entry position, where they intend to open, to their exit position, from which they intend to move no further.

You have already met the negotiation range in the dynamics of the haggle. A pure haggle occurs along a single dimension, such as price. When there are numerous dimensions, or ranges, as is common in all but the most pure of haggles, you can explore numerous combinations of positions along the ranges at your disposal on the issues.

Positional posturing, however, is like a sad case of amnesia, where a so-called negotiator has forgotten, or thinks it smart to act as if they do not know, that negotiation is the management of movement.

Expecting the other person to give in

Insisting on a single immovable position is not negotiation. It is a strategy based on expecting the other person to give in. Where both parties adopt this strategy, perhaps because they have been provoked into it, a negotiated solution is unlikely until they change their postures.

Assessing negotiation ranges

Preparation involves assessing the negotiation ranges open to you. Unlike in a single-issue haggle, you have several dimensions along which to move in exchange for movement by the other negotiator. You need not suffer psychic pain from losing what you give up when you move, because you move only in exchange for movement across some other issue. Which combination of movement across the issues satisfies your interests is for you to decide, constrained only by your negotiating partner's legitimate desire to service their own interests.

Thus purple preparation is a strategic activity to identify your interests, to prioritize the negotiable issues that serve your interests, and to assess the range of positions between which you can move to gain the consent of the other party to the overall deal. Searching for a negotiated solution that meets as many of yours and the other negotiator's interests is feasible as a strategy.

FRIGO'S PURPLE PREPARATION

The clearest way to see these elements at work is to return to the Iceberg case. This time you will be in the role of the general manager of Frigo, the refrigeration company.

Your assistant cut into the staff meeting and told you what Iceberg's deputy store manager said had happened to his store's refrigeration system last night. You immediately closed the meeting and assigned engineers to an MRT (maintenance and repair team) to drive to Iceberg immediately. You recognized that this was a serious emergency in one of the new stores of a major customer and only a swift response was appropriate. Your interests in new contracts coincided with Iceberg's interests in getting its store back to normal working.

While you were preparing to leave for the Iceberg store, a call came in from Iceberg's stores group manager and she confirmed that her store's entire system was down. You quickly confirmed that an MRT would be on site in under 30 minutes and that you would arrive about ten minutes after them to supervise operations personally. You assured her that everything would be done to restore the system as soon as possible and you acknowledged that it was Frigo's responsibility to find out what went wrong, to put it right and to ensure that it did not happen again. This was the first time that there had been a total failure in any of your systems.

Frigo

En route to Iceberg, you called your service manager on your car phone and asked what he knew of the events leading up to the emergency. He informed you that he had taken a call yesterday afternoon at 2.35 pm, from somebody describing herself as Iceberg's "store manager" (he didn't catch her name), to the effect that the alarm on the delicatessen counter had flashed a "level one" precautionary warning that the temperature was zero degrees. He reminded you that this had happened twice since the store opened six weeks ago, and that on both occasions your MRT had found a minor fault in the settings of the units, which they sorted out in a few minutes. At no time, in your engineers' view, were the faults of sufficient seriousness to suggest that a "second-level" warning was imminent or likely.

When Iceberg rang, all your engineers were off site, both on PMs (preventive maintenance) and on callouts (repairs), and would not be back until 6 pm. Your service manager had suggested to the store manager that he schedule a callout to her store for 8 am, but that, in the unlikely event that the alarm went to a level-two warning, if she rang him before 7 pm he would divert somebody to her, as soon as they arrived back at Frigo. He also told her that if she called, Frigo would need after-hours access to the store. She said she was not authorized to give that but "something could be worked out". She seemed relaxed about waiting until the morning for the callout. He was sorry, but he had not known that the staff meeting had been moved to the morning.

This did not sound too good to you from a customer service point of view, but you did not have time just now to enquire further. You reviewed the overall situation as you drove:

● Frigo had tendered for the sale and installation of four complete systems as part of Iceberg's expansion program. Iceberg was evaluating your bids at this moment and if Frigo qualified as bidders—which until 20 minutes ago seemed a formality—you would be negotiating with Iceberg by the middle of next month.

- The contract value exceeds $200,000 per store and a large slice of Frigo's business was at stake. It was of great importance to you to win the contracts.

- You called your design chief for a quick report on what she knew about the state of Iceberg's technical evaluation. She reminded you that reliability was one of the cardinal points in Iceberg's RFPs (request for proposals). All Iceberg stores were to be linked by remote sensor systems into a centralized 24-hour monitoring service.

- You recognize that the most important priority was to guarantee non-repetition of the system failure. That was what Iceberg would go for and it was imperative that you satisfied them on this if they were to say "yes". Everything reasonable must be done to provide a credible service, which Iceberg would probably want to be supported by guarantees, perhaps also by penalty clauses. You will have to live with penalties if you are going to turn round this disaster into a triumph.

- What must Frigo do that they weren't doing? What must Iceberg do that they weren't doing? What had happened at the remote monitoring service when the level-three alarms went active? Whatever else is done, you must get your MRTs directly plugged into Iceberg's monitoring service and arrange for 24-hour access to Iceberg stores in emergencies. How can you make the system foolproof? You feel confident that you are technically very competitive with other refrigeration companies, but a system failure is a poor advertisement for reliability.

- You must take the heat out of the current situation and concentrate solely on putting it right. To do that you must solve the problem first and hold an inquest afterwards. There is more than just the Iceberg contracts at stake here, because if there is a defect in your designs you had better know about it before your customers (and your competitors). You need answers, you need them fast and they had better be the right ones.

● As a precautionary step to contain the fallout from the problem, you want an early meeting with Iceberg's stores group manager. She mentioned that she was going to be at the store this morning, so you called your design chief back and suggested that she come to the store too. Iceberg's technical people would probably arrive as well and you needed to provide technical back-up to the MRT and credible technical assurance to Iceberg's assessors.

Using your time well

In this way, you have used your journey time well and you have laid the foundation for more detailed work as your understanding of the problem deepens.

Commercially, winning new business from Iceberg is highly significant. However, to ensure that result it is essential that you keep your existing contracts, because it is unlikely that you will win new business if you lose your technical reputation through a failure at the new store.

If you had been preparing at your desk you would have sketched an "issues map" (Exhibit 21) to help clarify the issues and the priorities.

To maintain the existing contracts, you must address what are bound to be Iceberg's major concerns: namely,

Exhibit 21   Frigo's issues map

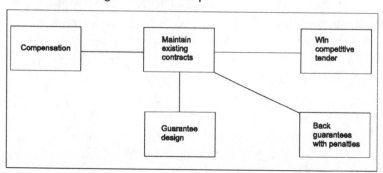

are your designs robust and can the top managers risk recommending your refrigerators? If you lose technical credibility, they will not risk awarding new contracts to you.

Hence, your own high priority must be to find out what went wrong, not so that you can pass the blame, but so you can be seen to put it right.

Even how you handle the emergency—and face it, Frigo has not done too well since 2.30 pm on Thursday—could influence Iceberg's purchase decision.

You anticipate that Iceberg will want any guarantees that you offer to be backed by a schedule of penalties for non-performance, both retrospectively for the existing contracts and prospectively for new ones, on the grounds that a guarantee is only worth what you will suffer if your system fails.

Note also that the issue of compensation for the store's losses from this incident is not linked to the retention of the existing contracts. Effectively, it should stand alone, reflecting what you have already decided—that compensation is not a high priority, either for Frigo or for Iceberg, and to make it a priority would be a negotiating mistake for you both. How compensation is handled, when it eventually surfaces as an issue, depends on how the other four issues are handled by the people involved.

In Exhibit 22, the preparation planner sets out the issues in the rock-bottom format for illustration. The details of the ranges for each issue are vague at present—in case the minutiae takes us too far from our learning objectives. In the real world you would continue to refine your details as you responded to what Iceberg and you deliberate about.

No excuse

Given your knowledge of your own job function, making a first cut at the preparation tasks would not take you much longer than it took to read the case and, by using this rock-bottom method, no negotiator has an excuse for being completely unprepared because of time constraints.

Exhibit 22   Frigo's rock-bottom preparation

Negotiable Issues	Priorities	Ranges	
		Entry	Exit
Competitive tenders for new business	Crucial	At tender price (profit @ 27%)	Profit @12%
Retain current contracts	Crucial	As is	Lower % profit
Performance guarantees	Important	Loose	Tight
Penalties	Desirable	Nominal	Penal (wide *force majeure*)
Compensation	Desirable	Insurance	Insurance plus *ex gratia*

MORE THAN ONE ISSUE

Negotiation is different from a haggle when you have more than one negotiable issue. In pure haggling, you are restricted to verbal dexterity and the chat lines and banter of a street market. You have nothing to trade, except a greater or lesser amount of whatever is up for haggle.

In negotiation, while verbal dexterity is no disqualification, it is not sufficient. You secure movement by trading across the issues, some of which are more important to you than others.

Familiarity with the dynamics of simple haggling is useful for negotiators. The negotiator's surplus, for example, has the same significance for the negotiator as the haggler's surplus does for the haggler, with the difference that instead of dividing up just one surplus on the one and only issue of price, in negotiation there are as many surpluses as there are issues. This gives much greater scope for finding a deal out of the multiple trade-offs you can create.

A negotiation, however, can become a haggle by default. The negotiators can agree on all of the disputed issues until there is only one left (usually the money!), over which they will be forced to haggle. When this happens, it comes down to which party must settle earliest, which has more power or, even, which has the most patience.

Haggling by default

A far better negotiating strategy is to keep all of the issues on the table and to settle none of them finally until you settle them as a package. You can make provisional agreements, under the formula that "nothing is agreed until everything is agreed", and avoid ending up in a haggle on the last issue.

Another way is to negotiate on as many issues as you can find. This is known as a tradables approach. A tradable is anything over which at least one of the parties has discretion. A tradable can be used, in conjunction with other tradables, to promote a settlement, provided that at least one of the parties values some of the tradables more than the other party. Many tradables are found by experience.

TRADABLES

Sellers, for example, know that sometimes the affordability of regular installments is more important to the purchaser than the total amount they will eventually pay (that is why hire purchase was commonly known as the "never never"). The sheer convenience of a credit card mitigates the higher rate of interest debtors pay compared to other debt instruments obtainable from their bank— including the bank that issued the credit card! Likewise, how much is to be paid in a deal may be less important to the debtor than when it is paid. By finding other tradables to those on the table, it is possible to break a deadlock.

SOME TRADABLES?

Borrowing a large sum of money and paying it back by equal installments from the day it is borrowed—how about paying it all back in a single balloon payment at the end of the loan period to coincide with the fruition of the project (such as the sale of the property development)?

Unable to provide tangible security for a loan—how about assigning an insurance policy to the lender for the duration of the loan?

Reluctant to add to direct labor costs plus employment taxes—why not make non-contributory pension payments that are tax efficient (they can be credited against corporation tax)?

Anxious to reduce political damage by buying abroad—why not agree a local offset purchase?

Negotiators search for tradables, some that are intrinsic to the deal, some by creative application to the issues, and some suggested by the other negotiator's concerns.

SUMMARY

There is a rock-bottom preparation method that is applicable in varying circumstances and under different time constraints. It consists of determining your interests and searching for those of the other party.

Your interests motivate you to prefer one solution to another. Interests encompass your fears, hopes and concerns about various solutions. They are why you want something in one form as opposed to another, including accepting the status quo.

Issues are what you want and they form the agenda of the negotiation. They deliver your interests, though interests may be delivered by various sets of issues, not necessarily those that comprise the current agenda.

Negotiable issues are prioritized by their degree of importance or their value to you. Those issues of high importance, or those that are crucial, are what you must get if you are to do business (deal breakers). Other issues may be important and whether they make or break the deal depends on what you gain or give up to get them. Those issues that you would like to get, because they are desirable but not overwhelmingly necessary, are unlikely to be deal breakers.

Negotiators think in terms of ranges and not fixed positions.

Positional posturing is the antithesis of negotiation. To develop a negotiation range, you identify your entry and exit positions.

You should negotiate on more than one issue and trade across several issues, rather than becoming trapped into haggling on a single issue (such as the money). Nothing is agreed until everything is agreed.

To facilitate multi-issue negotiation you should search for tradables—anything over which you or the other negotiator has discretion—as this assists movement. Movement on one issue, in principle, can be compensated for by movement on another issue or issues.

ANSWERS TO SELF-ASSESSMENT 4

1

(a) No. Just because something is of relative unimportance to you, it does not follow that it is unimportant to the tenant. If he wants it, he values it and how much he values it, compared to you, is of singular importance to you in the negotiation.

(b) No. You will not agree to its inclusion without trading it for something that is more important to you.

(c) Wait and see how important it is for the tenant? Yes. It is not what it is worth to you that is decisive. It is what it is worth to him and what he is willing to trade to get it.

2

(a) If the outcome is crucial to you, then you are more dependent on the other negotiator. Taking a tougher red line is less advisable when you are desperate on the outcome than when you have many options.

(b) His proclivity to red behavior is unlikely to be influenced by how crucial the issues are to you, unless, of course, you permit him to know how desperate you are.

(c) You are relatively weaker as a result? Yes. The more issues you decide are crucial to you—an elementary beginner's error—the weaker you make your negotiating stance. You have fewer options with crucial issues.

3

(a) Most likely to be necessary. If you do not deliver the client's interests, you are unlikely to remain the preferred bidder.

(b) Hardly a sensible stance. If you are seen to put your interests first and this does not deliver her interests, she is likely to address her interests only, which may not include you being the preferred bidder.

(c) Your own interests naturally are of great importance to you, but if the situation requires you to address her interests first, you would be well advised to do so. You cannot compare the merits of each party's interests.

7 *Fights, Arguments, and Discor*

1 You are negotiating with a colleague over parking spaces for your respective teams, and
   he makes a factually incorrect statement about your entitlement to parking places. Do
   you:

   (a) Stop him just there to correct his factual errors?

   (b) Shake your head vigorously, indicating your disagreement with his statement, but
        say nothing until he is finished or gives way?

   (c) Say and do nothing until he is finished?

2 The other negotiator is obviously quite angry and winds up her tirade with a clear
   threat of what she will do if she does not get her way. Do you:

   (a) Ignore her threats and concentrate on rebutting her claims?

   (b) Demand that she withdraw her threat if you are to continue negotiating?

   (c) Counter her threat with one of your own?

3 The other negotiator makes a statement with which you profoundly disagree. Do you:

(a) Tell him that he is grossly mistaken and then explain why?

(b) Ask him why he believes that his statement is true?

*T*HERE is a huge gulf between being treated as an opponent and being treated as a partner. Good manners can hide the distinction. However, when your patience is tested and irritation strains your inclination to be polite, happy banter can slide into verbal jousting with people whom you regard as opponents and with whom you feel you are in competition.

People who see those with whom they negotiate as opponents are inclined to stay behind their mental ramparts, scanning with radar-like suspicion for signs of malign motives. They are edgy, like a tennis player on the baseline, waiting for their opponent to serve.

Partners are more relaxed when they negotiate. Their manners, tone and genuine banter express the state of their relationship. They are relaxed because they are not suspicious. Partnerships develop out of behavior, not rhetoric. The road to partnership, however, is strewn with obstacles—including the wreckage of failed attempts at partnerships—and it is not well trodden.

Partners

The majority of negotiators are not partners. Most negotiators regard themselves, if not explicitly as opponents, implicitly as at odds with each other. Sometimes it is a one-sided affair, as between a "hard" red style buyer and a resilient seller who is trained, and determined, to be far more blue than red. Sometimes the status of being a conscious opponent is reciprocated—two solicitors, for example, vigorously representing their clients in an apparently intractable dispute.

At other times, openly tense exchanges can break out into bouts of positional posturing. Such is the intensity of these verbal clashes that people new to negotiation can be forgiven for concluding that no progress is likely to be made on the disputed issues. Of course, their pessimistic conclusions are sometimes true, but fierce rhetoric is usually an unreliable guide to the likely outcome of a dispute.

How negotiators regard their relationships influences their conduct and the outcome of the negotiation. Things said in the heat of a disagreement can rupture personal relationships to such an extent that they may never recover, just as a calmer handling of disputes could reinforce them.

RED FIGHTS

Fights are at the extreme red end of the red–blue continuum. There is no friendly relationship between fighters to speak of, only a wholly hostile one. A past good relationship is no protection against the intensity of a fight, as marital breakdowns can testify. "Hell hath no fury" when lovers fall out.

Stereotypes

Similarly, a pervasive belief in an "enemy" stereotype—racial, religious, ethnic, sexual, and so on—can work through to the most atrocious of behaviors. As the stereotypes are usually accompanied by selective histories of previous atrocities—"proving" the authenticity of the stereotypes—many layers of mutual hatred and mistrust must be peeled back before tentative steps are possible towards normality in the relationship.

Time cures many things, but bitter disputes can remain in the collective memory of a group generations after the events that caused the disputes. Listen to an Armenian on the conduct of Turkey towards their people, or a Jew on Hitler's Holocaust, or a Kazakh on Stalin's terror. The enmity between Hutus and Tutsis exploded into genocidal atrocities in Central Africa a few years ago, following closely on the depredations of Serbs, Croats and Muslims on each other in Bosnia. Sectarian hatred in Northern Ireland goes back 800 years and, for many of those involved, what happened a long time ago is as real as if it happened only last week.

Fights in a negotiation context are seldom physically bloody though they can be psychologically bruising. They can creep up on you in the steady accumulation of minor irritations, resentments, anxieties and slights before they erupt into a fierce exchange of angry abuse. Or they can suddenly explode in your face from nowhere, unannounced and without warning.

Fights break out because at least one person is absolutely determined to end the status quo and at least one other person is as determined to maintain it. Peace is the acceptance by all of the status quo. But in many situations the continuation of the status quo is impossible and, therefore, resistance to change and consequential disputes are inevitable. Where the contest is between two determined and unrelenting parties, disputes turn into fights.

When fights are physical, the scope for negotiation, or even mediation, is severely limited. Two countries at war are driven to negotiation by the military victory of one over the other, or by their mutual exhaustion and ruin. Ending fights by negotiation between victors and vanquished is still no bed of roses, even when the military power is one-sided. The victor sets the terms and finds an authoritative body among the vanquished to agree the surrender. When Nazi Germany unconditionally surrendered on 7 May 1945, it was in no position to resist Allied terms for peace.

Where both sides are exhausted and willing to contemplate the alternative of peace, negotiations are not so one-sided, but a country's resolve to negotiate in good faith blows hot and cold. An unexpected breakthrough on the battlefield can cool a government's ardor for peace. It stalls while it pursues its military advantage. The other combatant pressurizes for speedier progress at the peace talks, or slows them down if it believes it can reverse its military disadvantages. Fighting can break out again while the parties are in sight of peace. The most difficult peace to negotiate is where either or both of the belligerents are not totally convinced that they are militarily exhausted and

Status quo

ONE MORE PUSH, LADS

The solidarity and determination of seamen during a ferry strike began to weaken after three weeks, as it was clear that while lorries were delayed for a few hours by the strike, the lorry companies were finding alternative sailings with rival ferry companies. Defections of strikers back to work slowly grew from a few dispirited individuals to a steady trickle of threes and fives. The union leaders decided to hold a meeting of the 2000 remaining strikers to take soundings of their commitment to continuing the strike.

On the morning of the meeting, news broke that lorry drivers, kept waiting for up to eight hours or more, had blocked the ferry terminal with their lorries "in protest at the delays in getting a place on a ship". This news electrified the meeting and reversed the slump in strikers' morale, because if no lorries could get in or out of the port, this put severe pressure on the ferry company, which had so far resisted the union's demands. With all ferry companies now losing business, the determination of the company's management was severely tested.

The strikers voted overwhelmingly to continue their stoppage and many of the seamen who had returned to work rejoined the strike. Three days later the lorry blockade ended (they were threatened with being engaged in an illegal "secondary strike"). With this, the strikers' morale sagged again and the union sued for peace, followed by an orderly return to work.

---

that they should sue for peace.

Strikes

Bitterly contested strikes terminate in a manner similar to wars. If the balance of advantage comes to favor one of the parties, peace talks stall while the advantage is exploited or reversed. The impetus to peace talks is the diminishing prospect of victory and the consequent threat of demoralization for union members or managers and shareholders.

THREATS

People fighting verbally state their stance forcefully and back it with aggressive body language. "No surrender", "no way", "over my dead body (but preferably yours!)", and other intransigent expressions and displays of determination are common. Threats are exchanged, loudly. The other side's threats are belittled—"We'll bear any burden, pay any price"—and one's own are emphasized and embroidered—"I'll sue you for every penny you've got and then some".

This is called commitment. You are so committed in public to a course of action that your listener would be well advised to take heed. You do not have room for maneuver, there is no flexibility and, to underline these assertions, you demonstrate your commitment by numerous devices. One common one is to make public pledges of your intentions to fight to the bitter end.

Commitment

Depending on the credibility with which your pledges are received, your message can have its desired effect. If your listeners believe that you are serious, they will conclude that any flexibility over the issues will have to emanate from their side, not yours. Commitments that are not credible—you will kill anybody who smokes at work—are treated with disbelief and derision (watch professional wrestlers mouthing off before a match).

Another device is to make threats. These can be of two kinds, deterrence or compliance threats. In deterrence, you draw a "line in the sand" and tell the other party that they must never cross it, but that if they do, you will execute whatever you have threatened. In a compliance threat, you initiate a course of action (sanctions, say) and threaten to continue it until the other party desists from whatever you announce they must not do.

Threats

Your intention—and, as important, your capability—to carry out your threat determines your listeners' reaction.

The degree to which implementing your threat is likely to damage your listener also determines how they react. Hitler was not deterred by Britain's warning of war if Germany invaded Poland in 1939 because he misjudged Britain's intentions and capabilities; Ian Smith did not comply with British demands for a "majority rule" constitution in Rhodesia in 1967 because he correctly judged the value of Britain's intentions and capabilities.

More often than not fights are preceded by threat behaviors. Threats do not always achieve their intended objective. People threaten in order to force you to comply without them having to use force. Instead, you could react, contrary to their intentions, by stiffening your defiance or by initiating the action from which they have attempted to deter you.

In the 1950s game of "chicken", affluent American teenagers drove cars towards each other and the first to swerve was "chicken" (but alive). Those who preferred to die than swerve were safe when playing against a "chicken", but not so safe when they weren't!

Put up or shut up

If one party's deterrence fails they must "put up or shut up". This could provoke them to "put up", and both must take the consequences. In the Cold War decades, a failure in nuclear deterrence would have rapidly escalated to end human life on the planet. If the Soviet Union had, for example, invaded Germany and NATO had carried out its commitment to regard "an attack on one member as an attack on all members" (Article 5), escalation would have led to a massive thermonuclear exchange. If, however, NATO had "shut up" when its bluff was called, its loss of credibility would have been so total as to remove it as a serious deterrent to Soviet invasion.

In a compliance threat, implementing punishment may prove to be effective if its impact really hurts its target. If it doesn't hurt as much as expected, it is not a punishment after all.

The imposition of a ban on international air travel into and out of Libya has not, at the time of writing, had the desired effect of bringing to trial the two Libyans accused of the bombing of PanAm flight 103 over Lockerbie in 1988. Strikes, intended to punish an employer sometimes wither because the employer does without the striking employees for longer than the strikers are willing to do without their wages. Also, economic sanctions have been shown to be relatively weak and not likely to produce early results, suggesting that punishment strategies need to be carefully thought through before they are implemented.

Once a verbal fight escalates to physical action—once the dogs of war are let loose—it is difficult to escape damage to both sides. It is far easier to destroy that it is to create. Negotiation, though an alternative to fighting, can all too easily slip from a verbal altercation into a physical one.

Damage to both sides

People who want to fight will do so. Unfortunately, if they want to kill each other too, they will. This leaves fights that degenerate into bloody stand-offs very difficult to control. Mediation methods are helpful, though not always practical. For mediation to work, the parties have to *want* it to work. It is not easy to get to the stage of considering mediation as a potential solution, once bloodlust is rampant among people willing and able to fight.

"NO MORE MR NICE GUY"

Asset Management plc (AMP) owns, among other properties, a row of high street shops built in the 1950s. The property is run down and suitable for demolition. AMP received outline planning consent for a new shopping mall on the site six months ago, but last month before detailed architect's drawings were commissioned, the Iceberg Group offered to purchase the entire site for $1.4 million. Iceberg intends to clear the site, submit its own detailed plans to the local planning authority, and then build a superstore to the same design as its other successful projects across the country.

Back to Iceberg

AMP accepted the Iceberg offer because the present value of the net profit from the sale is greater than the net profit from financing its own development and leasing the mall. Iceberg required vacant possession of the site. This condition was not that onerous because the tenants of the shops had only 18 months of their 15-year leases left to run and they were already under notice to quit.

Before Iceberg's offer was received, AMP's leasehold property division had successfully negotiated terms with five of the six tenants for them to quit early (one had already gone and four others had converted to new short-term leases, giving AMP the right to issue a month's notice to quit). In exchange for their cooperation, AMP agreed to pay these tenants compensation—varying from $40,000 to the largest tenant (Honest Sam's Used Cars Emporium, with 600 square meters) to $16,000 (Dorothy's Lingerie, with 60 square meters).

One tenant (Mrs Luigi's Pizzeria) had refused to cooperate and had indicated that she intended to continue her business in her shop until her lease ended in 18 months' time. Hers is the smallest shop at only 50 square meters. Eighteen months ago, Mrs Luigi's last three-yearly rent review for her tenancy resulted in her pizzeria being assessed at a rent of $12,000 a year for the final three years of her lease.

She protested at the new rent on the grounds that her business had been hit by the opening of Mr Lo's modernized fast-food pizza outlet, almost directly opposite her own shop. She claimed severely straitened financial circumstances as a result of the competition. AMP took this into account and, as a "goodwill gesture", agreed informally to abate her rent to $6500 per year. AMP calculated that it would take a year or more to relet the shop to a new tenant—the building looked, and was, rundown—and for a lease of less than three years' duration it might not attract much more rent than $6000 anyway. They also did not press her to undertake repairs to her shop, assessed by their surveyors as likely to cost around $2500, for which she was responsible under her lease.

When AMP's new plans for the properties were finalized and Mrs Luigi was left as the only tenant not cooperating, they faced the problem of what to do with her. As all attempts at negotiating had proven fruitless, they considered their options. She sought more than their offer of $14,000 for quitting early and, clearly, she was relying on AMP's keenness to progress to their new building project.

AMP was reasonably certain that Mrs Luigi knew nothing about their selling the site to Iceberg. The project would not become public, unless Iceberg announced it, until detailed consents were sought from the planning authority. AMP preferred to hold off from making the Iceberg plan public until Mrs Luigi agreed to an early termination of her lease. If Mrs Luigi learned of AMP's plans before she signed, she would almost certainly expect extra compensation over what she had already demanded.

Iceberg were ready to go ahead with the deal provided they were assured of the date when they would acquire vacant possession of the entire site. AMP could not guarantee vacant possession for 18 months, unless Mrs Luigi agreed to go early. Mrs Luigi, by holding up the deal, would soon cost AMP about $8000 a month in lost interest on the $1.4 million. Moreover, there was always the risk that Iceberg would not wait 18 months and would seek another site in the town.

In considering their options, AMP managers came up with a red fighting plan to drive Mrs Luigi out legally (though it would not be good PR if the local media picked up on her story: "Widow Hounded by Grasping Landlord", etc.,). Because they expected her to continue to decline their original offer, AMP had a contingency plan, basically along the lines of "no more Mr nice guy"!

The earlier informal goodwill gesture of abating her rent from $12,000 to $6500 would be withdrawn and they would demand the unpaid portion of back rent. Similarly, the concession of not requiring her to make good the repairs (mainly plaster work) at a cost of $2500 would be withdrawn and a legal notice would be issued to her to carry out the repairs, on pain of AMP's arranging for the work to be completed, with the bill sent to Mrs Luigi for payment. Because they intended to demolish the building anyway, the "repairs" issue was a pressure threat.

To "persuade" her to quit earlier than in 18 months, AMP would also initiate robust actions around her business. The vacant shop next to hers would be boarded up for "safety" reasons, as would the others whenever they became vacant. The dilapidated state of the site would create, from a food hygiene point of view, an unpleasant environment which could be talked up into a health risk.

Depositing scraps of food in the empty shops would attract rodents, stray cats, dogs, and even foxes, and the sight of staff from pest-control firms working in the building (from prominently parked, well-signed vehicles) would damage her business, perhaps even cause it to be closed, if the local council were "persuaded" to consider the presence of the rodents to be a food hazard.

By selective destruction of parts of the old building— holes punched through the roof, broken glass, unhinged doors, unstable stairs, flooded basements, etc.—the weather could be relied on to make the area an unpleasant place in which to run a food business. "Emergency" scaffolding, boarding, and wire fencing would "need" to be erected.

If vagrants were attracted to the area—hopefully accompanied by drugs raids—the resultant disamenity would drive Mrs Luigi's remaining customers to cross the road to the rival pizzeria and, hopefully, she would fail financially.

Of course, these antics would tread close to the boundaries of legality and good corporate governance. They are illustrations of—and not my suggestions for—the way fights are conducted. If you have doubts that they happen, attend any local court to hear of the antics of neighbors against each other when the objects of their disputes are merely trivial, like the height of boundary fences, the overhang of trees, the behavior of cats, and the parking of cars on common ground. When a large amount of money is at stake, red-style fighting can get serious.

RED ARGUMENT

The difference between a fight and a red argument is one
of degree. They are both associated with red styles, with
fights at the far red extreme of the continuum and red
arguments the next stop. Arguments can easily turn into
fights—and fights, less easily, can "soften" into arguments.

In negotiation, and not just in collective bargaining, red
argument is the norm.

Red argument is the norm

Contractual disputes are far from a tea party and
international negotiations can be fraught places for timid
people. Domestic disputes, interpersonal disputes and
disputes between neighbors are often conducted as
relatively intense red arguments.

Some people love a "good" argument and, when the
other person is of like mind, no lasting harm is done. In my
experience, though, the same people who like good
arguments do not like to lose an argument, which makes
good losers of arguments a rare species.

Most people resent arguments that contradict their
prejudices and undermine their stances. Giving in
gracefully is not an option when you feel humiliated by
sarcasm, found wanting of "facts" and devoid of the
comfort of a conscionable case. The step over from arguing
a contrary case to personalizing a disputed point is a small
one to make and, once personalities enter the fray, all
manner of difficulties loom and can become entrenched.

Courtroom arguments, when the issues are seriously
contested by the defense and the prosecution, are
conducted under a set of strict rules and, to keep the
disputants in line, they are benignly presided over by a
judge (whose stewardship and decisions are subject to
appeal). Yet they too can get heated, no matter how
detached from emotions the professionals profess
themselves to be. In a negotiation, there are no rules, no
judges, no appeals, and no lack of personal bias. Little
wonder, then, that red behaviors in negotiation are so
common.

Rationally, you might consider it sensible for
negotiators to adapt those behaviors that have the best

FALLACIOUS RED ARGUMENTS

1 **Prominence**. Because something is prominent it does not mean it is important—one recent error does not invalidate a year's good conduct.

2 **Popularity**. Because "everybody knows, or agrees", it does not mean that the argument is valid. The truth is not established by majority vote.

3 **Expertise**. Experts from one field are not necessarily experts in other fields, or experts for all time in their own field, especially once they've left it.

4 **Changing the subject**. Red players ask "Whose side are you on?" if you challenge their silly proposal.

5 **Defective personality**. Discredit the proposer by opprobrium.

6 **Provenance**. A red ploy that attacks the origins of an idea.

7 **Straw man**. Distorts the case in order to attack it unfairly.

8 **Slippery slope**. Extreme consequences of modest proposals block change.

9 **Selective evidence**. Quotes only evidence for, not against, a proposal.

10 **Phoney dilemmas**. Excludes all but two unattractive options to force a choice of one the red player favors.

chance of securing for them their objectives. As your objective is to get your way in the dispute, behaviors best designed to achieve that end should be most favored.

Observation suggests, however, that most negotiators do not think in a rational manner. Negotiating behaviors are often reactive because they are driven by the emotions people feel towards the issues. If anything, people act as if they believe that their emotions, given a free rein, will produce for them their desired outcomes. Showing how strongly you feel about an issue is part of the theater of convincing the listener that you intend, because you deserve to do so, to get your own way.

Not thinking rationally

Red-style negotiators, in this climate, stoop to any device, any stratagem, any trick or ploy to impress their will on the person whose consent is required for them to get what they want. There is no point in being timid when expressing your determination, the courtesies of a courtroom notwithstanding, and such good manners and restraint as are normal in friendly discourse are swept aside in hot pursuit of the objective of winning the position on which you have decided to make a stand.

It surely has not escaped your notice, however, that such red behaviors are not one-way tickets to success. Ironically, when you gain success from behaving as a red player, your being successfully argumentative teaches the "loser" to mimic your red behaviors. Those negotiators who lose to argumentative bullies mostly learn to respond in kind and, before long, a culture of argumentative negotiating behavior spreads like a fungus.

A culture of argument

The lively argumentative behaviors that were common in labor negotiations shocked those observers more used to less fraught styles of debate, as many red behaviors were taken for granted by those practicing them. Lively red argument and pressure tactics are not confined to labor negotiations—they have been studied more closely by labor specialists, that is all—because red argumentative behaviors are found in abundance in most negotiations between parties that have felt grievances.

Roger Fisher and Bill Ury wrote *Getting to Yes: Negotiating*

Agreement Without Giving In (1981) in reaction to adversarial negotiating cultures. Their book has had a significant impact on problem-solving and mediation techniques. A similar reaction also propelled Neil Rackham and his associates at Huthwaite Research to demonstrate a decade earlier the poverty of negative red-style negotiating behaviors. By holding up a mirror to the pronounced argumentative behaviors of many negotiators, they showed that constructive debate could replace what was as unpleasant as it was unnecessary for its exponents to endure.

Arguments degenerate quickly, from being mildly irritating to being outright annoying and deeply provocative. Fights leading to deadlocks are an obvious risk.

Where representatives of hostile interests confront each other, long periods of posturing may have to be endured, while the parties imperceptibly edge towards negotiating the terms under which they coexist.

Having a clear understanding of—and patience with—this adversarial version of the negotiating process is a challenge to anybody who would be a sponsor, or honest broker, and who tries to push those involved towards searching for a negotiated outcome, rather than killing each other (or their economic enterprise). Observers of disputes in Israel, Palestine, Kashmir and Northern Ireland learn to be patient, with good reason, though it is far easier to be patient as an observer than it is as a participant.

IRRITATION

It is by no means only headline negotiations that monopolize red argumentative behaviors. They occur in all levels of negotiation. Irritation can flare up from the way one negotiator speaks to another.

True, you may believe that the other person is being overly sensitive in finding your jokes or sarcasm less funny than you do and that it is their problem, not yours, if they react negatively. But their sensitivity becomes your problem if, by irritating them, they become less than committed to considering your proposals. If you seek their consent, it seems prudent not to make it less likely that their consent will be forthcoming.

Irritating an "opponent" is predictable behavior from a red player. Irritating them provokes their unease and underlines how unimportant their feelings are to you. Gratuitous insults, slights and sexist or racist putdowns can have a devastating effect on a person's sensibilities, which is why a red player resorts to them and some red players are so ignorant of the feelings of others than they irritate without realizing what they are doing.

WHERE AM I?

National sensitivity is a factor in socializing across cultures. At what to you is the most trivial of levels, you can commit a *faux pas*. One unintentional *faux pas* you might get away with as a stranger's slip, but continually commit the same *faux pas* and your listeners might conclude that they do not want to socialize with you.

A filmstar from California, promoting her latest film, began her news conference at the Edinburgh Festival by exclaiming: "How pleased I am to be in England once again". She was surprised at the immediate, not so *sotte voce*, groans among the assembled press, and on enquiring what was the problem, she was told by an aide that she was in "Scotland not England". She buried herself deeper when she shrugged her famous shoulders and commented: "Scotland, England—what's the difference?"

INTERRUPTIONS

Interrupting someone is acceptable in certain situations. Negotiation is not one of them. Friends discoursing socially accept reasonable levels of mutual interruption— listen to two friends and notice how many sentences are unfinished and how they often cut into each other's pauses, with comments, allusions to past events and gestures of rapport.

People who do not know each other well interrupt much less—and often apologize if they interrupt when they had mistakenly thought the other person had finished. They give way by gesture, if they both try to speak at once.

Negotiators do not like being interrupted (though they often interrupt in practice) and if the interruption level rises too high, it becomes a weapon of argument ("I listened to your point of view, will you please listen to mine!").

You must be familiar with politicians negatively responding to interruptions on television, though some interviewers are adept at cutting in on implausible answers. Such interviewers also have a reputation for being "aggressive" and not fooled by celebrity flimflam. Some politicians choose their interviewers and insist on agreeing the questions to be asked before going on air.

Negotiators who interrupt too frequently indicate that they are not interested in what is said by somebody else. Their own views are what counts and other speakers had better not speak while they are being interrupted. They aim to put the other negotiator off balance by interrupting them and they try to divert them into rebuttals of whatever the interrupter has said (often with the sole intention of provoking them).

ATTACKING AND BLAMING

Attacking and blaming are among the most frequently used red argumentative behaviors. They seldom miss their targets and almost always provoke a response.

If you are attacked, you defend yourself. Your carefully worded statement can be attacked as "nonsense", "rubbish", "lies", and such like. You can be attacked with a verbal onslaught covering many points and assertions. Because all attacks have weak points, many tempting targets present themselves for rebuttal and not all of them are relevant to the substantive issues in the dispute.

How do you react to an attack?

Do you counter it to demonstrate that you are not to be pushed around? If you do, don't be surprised if, after a few exchanges, you are both into a full-fledged attack spiral, with imminent prospects of a loss of control and no certainty as to where—or when—it will end.

Attack spirals often lead to a fight, as much for what is said during them as for what is now at stake. To the disputed issues are added loss of face, emotional hurt, and a sense of injustice and anger.

Blame cycles are not much different in their evolution. If you blame somebody, they justify themselves, sometimes by counter-blaming you ("We could not deliver on time because your instructions were so unclear that we could not read the address!"). People point the thick end of a telescope when looking for somebody else's contribution to a problem, and the thin end when looking at their own.

Accidents are the unintentional outcomes of somebody's behavior and that person is blamed for the accident. But the culprit is not obvious when blame is passed like an unwanted parcel. Courts of inquiry sit long (and expensively) searching for someone to blame. They get it "right" (to the satisfaction of the inquiry) as often as they get it "wrong" (to the dissatisfaction of those blamed) and, when they get it "right", it often remains controversial.

Negotiations are seldom a judicious enquiry into whom to blame, and they do not approach, even remotely, the necessary conditions for an objective examination of the "facts". People in dispute decide on blame on flimsy, sometimes fictional, evidence, selectively "nursing their wrath" until it boils over into indignation. Once let loose, a blame cycle rolls over into an attack spiral and the protagonists are carried away by their hostility towards the accusations and their accusers. Even the act of blaming creates cycles of recriminations—"You started it", "No, I didn't, you did".

People who want to argue will do so. People who, instead, want to debate have a difficult time of it because, as neither person can control the other, neither can be sure

Reacting to an attack

DEBATE

that the debate is other than a fragile truce about to drift into an argument. It takes two to tango, so to speak, and constructive debate imposes conversational restraints on speakers and listeners alike.

If the restraints collapse under the effort to abide by them, you will revert to argument, or worse.

If, however, negotiators find adhering to the restraints productive of their interests, they mutually reinforce their joint commitment to a constructive negotiation.

SUMMARY

How you perceive the people with whom you negotiate—as opponents or partners—determines how you behave towards them. If they are opponents they are likely to be treated in a red style.

Fights are at the extreme red end of the color spectrum. They involve conduct just short of physical harm, though they can include psychological abuse. Fighting is a pressure tactic, where anything legal (and sometimes illegal too) is used to achieve the desired objective.

Negotiations to end a war or a strike have similar dynamics, with the negotiators blowing hot and cold as events alter the incentives to pursue a peaceful solution.

Threats encompass behavior that precedes a fight. There are two kinds of threats—deterrence and compliance. A deterrence threat persuades you not do what you otherwise would do; a compliance threat persuades you to stop doing what you otherwise would continue doing. To be credible, threats must be backed by a capability to carry out the threat and a willingness to do so.

Arguments are also red style, just short of a fight. In their various guises, arguments are the norm in negotiations. With effort (and training) argumentative behaviors can be avoided. They involve behaviors such as irritating remarks or gestures, interruptions, and attack or blame cycles.

Subsidiary red behaviors such as sarcasm, point scoring, name calling, imputing motives, being patronizing, and insulting are also common in an argument.

RECOMMENDED READING

Roger Fisher & William Ury (1981) *Getting to Yes: Negotiating Agreement Without Giving In*, Boston, Mass, Houghton Mifflin.

Paul R. Pillar (1983) *Negotiating Peace: War Termination as a Bargaining Process*, Princeton, NJ, Princeton University Press.

Neil Rackham (1972), "Controlled pace negotiation: as a new technique for developing negotiating skills", *Industrial & Commercial Training*, vol 4, no 6, pp 266–75.

Thomas Schelling (1960) *The Strategy of Conflict*, Cambridge, Mass, Harvard University Press.

Thomas Schelling (1966) *Arms and Influence*, New Haven, Yale University Press.

1

(a) To "stop him just there" is a euphemism for interrupting him. Nobody likes being interrupted and it seldom, if ever, helps if a negotiator does so.

(b) Body language that is visually interruptive is still an interruption and earns the same disapprobation as a verbal interruption. Sometimes a speaker acknowledges a visual interruption but continues speaking, with a parenthetical sideswipe at the would-be interrupter ("I see you don't like me raising these facts but that's your problem not mine").

(c) Correct. If his case is built around the factual error it will collapse more quickly if you wait to reveal the truth. Nothing is gained by interrupting.

2

(a) Yes. Threats may be made in the heat of a rhetorical flourish. They are better ignored, particularly early on in the negotiations.

(b) Pointless. It is unlikely that she will, and then what do you do. She can use weasel words to excuse the threat, claiming she was only drawing attention to some unhappy consequences of your failing to agree. A threat "withdrawn" is still on the table.

(c) This could spark off a threat cycle, which will take you both away from negotiating a solution. If it comes to a fight, so be it, but it is more likely to become a fight if you exchange threats—and if you show you are fazed by them.

3

(a) Telling someone they are wrong and then telling them why is a sure way to stop them listening while they compose their reply to your announcement.

(b) Correct. The best way to handle disagreement is to question the person with whom you disagree. Their case is either substantiated by their answers—in which case you are not embarrassed by announcing your disagreement—or it is undermined, in which case you have not embarrassed them for holding an incorrect viewpoint.

8 *Debates, Signals, and Concord*

SELF-ASSESSMENT 6

1   Denying press reports that a secret deal had been negotiated to release two French
    secret agents from prison, the New Zealand Prime Minister said: "There is no question
    of the prisoners being released to freedom". Did this mean that:

    (a)   They would be released from their jail?

    (b)   They would not be released from their jail?

2   Two negotiators had been disputing the issue of compensation for a supplier's failure
    to supply a brand of fabric conditioner the previous month. The retail customer was
    demanding compensation of $7000 for profit from lost sales. The supplier pleaded
    force majeure (a factory that supplied them with the brand's plastic bottles had been
    on strike) and said that he "could not accept a direct connection between
    compensation and the failure to supply as it would set a serious precedent". Should
    the retailer:

    (a)   Continue to demand justifiable compensation for the accurately calculated lost
          profit?

    (b)   Take the supplier to court?

(c) Demand an *ex gratia* payment of $2000 for a local promotion of the brand of fabric conditioner?

3 A software designer is pushing for an amendment to a clause in the contract that requires her to relinquish copyright control of her product to one of the world's largest software producers. She desperately wants to place her designs with the producer but does not want to lose her copyright. The other negotiator says his company must have control because it needs to protect the product when it issues licenses to subcontractors, and its size alone inhibits piracy because of its reputation of suing for heavy damages from anybody who pirates its copyrights. Would you advise the software designer to:

(a) Licence her copyright to the software producer for 20 years?

(b) Trade her copyright for a higher royalty?

(c) Refuse to assign her copyright?

*D*EBATE is about purple behaviors that contribute to negotiators serving their own interests without trespassing on the interests of others. Nothing is agreed without their consent and neither party needs to fight or argue in an attempt to dislodge a person from pursuing their own interests, provided that they respect the other negotiator's right to do likewise. Each person's interests are recognized to have the same degree of legitimacy to them as one's own interests have for oneself.

Purple negotiators follow Adam Smith's advice that the best way to satisfy your own interests is to address the interests of those who have what you want.

Soft blue behaviorists, who willingly sacrifice their own interests for the interests of others, display the opposite behavior to that of the red behaviorist who consciously forces the other negotiator to sacrifice their interests.

Self-denial by the extreme blue behaviorist serves the self-centered acquisitiveness of the extreme red behaviorist. Neither red nor blue behavior, therefore, is healthy from a negotiating point of view.

The purple behaviorist's recognition of the mutual legitimacy of interests is not normally formalized by a prior and explicit understanding. During the debate phases it will flower, or at least become implicit, through the behaviors of the purple-style negotiator. In a longer-lasting relationship between two negotiators, recognition of the mutual legitimacy of their interests will be made explicit by their behaviors.

Of course, a purple negotiator's efforts may be rebuffed, cast in their face, and mocked by red counter-behaviors. It is not implied here that everything is "sweetness and light", nor that purple behavior is necessarily naive. Of difficult negotiators, and red-style "saboteurs", we have much to say later. For the moment, familiarity with what constitutes normal purple debate is required.

STATEMENTS

From observation, negotiatiors' most common debate behavior is to exchange information through **statements**, partly by each negotiator taking turns, as is normal in civilized human discourse, and partly by their statements facilitating the necessary explanation and exploration of the differences that prompt their search for a negotiated solution.

Without the mutual exchange of statements, progress would be impossible. Not that the mere exchange of statements guarantees progress, as the continuing North Korean–United States "negotiations" at Panmunjom formally to end the Korean war (1950–53), would amply testify. The Panmunjom conferences can justifiably be called the original example of the "dialog of the deaf".

Tone

Statements delivered in a hostile tone generate a predictable effect. They can be delivered in a neutral, even a friendly, tone with more positive results. Neutrality of tone is more conducive to progress—and clarity of intent—than is hostility, which is more closely associated with arguments and fights.

Choice of tone is an early decision for negotiators. It sends a message or, more correctly, the listeners receive a message, about what they think you intend. How the message is received fashions the tone of the responses it provokes, which is why neutrality of tone—neither aggressive nor deferential—is advised, unless you prefer to "negotiate" by argument or to "win" by fighting.

Purple negotiators reinforce the tone of their statements by their assurance behaviors. With strangers, with whom you have no relationship, you may not know beforehand how are you going to be treated, how you are going to fare, whether your interests will be served by the outcome, whether there will be a satisfactory outcome at all.

ASSURANCE

As the negotiation exchange gets under way, vague answers to your concerns may emerge. In due course, they are more or less answered when you are in a position to accept or reject the negotiated deal. Until then, varying degrees of anxiety are inevitable.

Assurance behavior addresses anxieties about the way decisions are to be made (the process) and the decisions that will be made (the outcome). You can provide assurance by asserting that you are in the "solution business" and that current difficulties, while openly acknowledged, are only obstacles to be jointly overcome.

By disclaiming any intention to act at the expense of others' interests, without, of course, committing to act against your own interests, you can calm fears that you will behave negatively towards the other party. This may inhibit them from succumbing to the temptation to resort to negative behaviors themselves out of fear of your intentions. The purpose of your purple assurance behavior is to create a positive atmosphere for each of you to explore whether a negotiated solution that addresses each party's interests is feasible.

QUESTIONING

Questioning is the clearest example of behavior that distinguishes purple debate from red argument. Red arguers use questions as a weapon; purple debaters use questions to elicit information that will help in the search for a solution.

Indeed, in some red arguments I have observed, over 45 minutes have passed with nobody asking a question of any kind at all—even a sarcastic and presumably rhetorical one like "Do you think I'm stupid?". If questions are asked at all by red negotiators, they tend to be intimidatory, put in a badgering manner, with no room for doubt as to what answers they expect. Or they may be loaded questions that are part of an attack sequence along the lines of "answer 'yes' or 'no'" ("Do you still take bribes?").

Purple negotiators ask more questions than red arguers or blue submissives and also listen more carefully to the answers.

ACTIVE LISTENING

Active listening does not feature in most people's repertoire of social skills. Evidence shows that most people have defective listening skills. They switch off their attention and can barely repeat what has been said, particularly in a prolonged negotiation exchange.

When you think you know what someone is going to say, you don't listen closely; if you disagree with what you think they are going to say, you only nominally listen; and if you disagree violently with what you believe they believe, you don't listen at all.

Of course, you are practiced in pretending to listen. You know how and when to grunt as if you are listening and you even try to do other things, like read a newspaper, watch TV, or beat time to a favorite tune, when people talk to you. You may not do this too much as you begin negotiating, but in a prolonged negotiating sequence you probably slip into unconscious habits (doodling, sorting papers, quarrying in your ears) when your attention wanders.

SUMMARIZING

Questioning is an important negotiating skill. Its incidence in debate is a measure of your commitment to understanding the other negotiator's interests and positions on the negotiable issues. The extent to which you can **summarize** to their satisfaction their views and their versions of what has happened, or is at stake, complements your questioning and listening skills.

Summaries hit several targets simultaneously.

You can unambiguously demonstrate that you are listening to the other person if you can accurately summarize their views on a disputed issue in words with which they agree. This overcomes the first and most basic requirement of people who have a grievance—that you listen to them. In summarizing at difficult moments in the exchange, you can defuse tensions and emotional outbursts, in a manner that keeps the discussions on an even keel.

Acknowledging that you understand how strongly someone else feels on an issue averts the necessity for them to demonstrate to you dramatically or disruptively their strength of feeling.

Lastly, summarizing a position, including your own, is a neat way of clarifying for yourself and for others what is at stake. This keeps you focused on the problem and prevents you from being overawed by its apparent complexities or misled into less significant byways.

Summaries, like questions, have a higher incidence among purple than among red negotiators. When negotiating in a team, one of your number should ideally be included because of their facility for paying close attention to what transpires and for translating their observations into summaries that are neutral, truthful and, above all else, brief. Any other kind of summary will be discredited and become part of a red argument or, at best, just waste time.

MANAGING MOVEMENT

Negotiation is the management of movement; not that everybody sees it this way.

Red behaviorists see movement as something only the other side does, not themselves. Among red-style negotiators, succumbing to pressure to move is seen as a sign of personal weakness. But move you must, because an extreme red strategy of never moving places on the other negotiator the full burden of adjusting their aspirations to yours. This might be successful if you are dealing with a blue submissive, but it will cut no ice with a purple trader.

Two negotiators, each subscribing to the practice of not moving before the other moves, may wait a long time. Some "tough" (red) negotiators see this as their role. "Who blinks loses" is their motto. They play a macho game of staring down the other person and their demands.

Negotiators who feel they have the power also feel able to stand up to the other person and defy them not to move. Large companies, dealing with smaller ones, are often characterized by their immovable stances on issues that are of some importance to the smaller company.

Two solutions

All negotiations begin with at least two solutions to the same problem: yours and the other person's.

You want a bigger price, he prefers a smaller price; she wants it delivered in penny packets, you want it delivered in bulk; he wants payment in 30 days, you prefer to pay in 60 days; you want to plea bargain to "mild harassment", she demands nothing less than "rape one", and so on.

The problem is to find a third solution, different from the initial solutions, that will be acceptable to both of you. This cannot be achieved if you both stick to your entry solutions, nor can it be achieved if you insist that the only solution is your own and that if the other person wants a deal, they will have to abandon their solution in favor of yours.

What is to be done if both of you insist on "no surrender"? If negotiators see movement as a sign of weakness—and many do—how come they manage to reach an agreement, eventually?

THE LANGUAGE OF THE SIGNAL

Negotiators do not learn to move by participating in a training course. Long before the first negotiating skills

---

TIMES CHANGE

In the early days of large-scale computing, giants like IBM, and smaller companies like Digital, ICL, Hewlett-Packard, Prime and Amdahl, negotiated sales but not their contracts. You signed them, small print and all, and that was that. Vendor's contracts ruled.

Computing was in its infancy and technical expertise was relatively rare. Data processing managers were scarce and tended to be "locked in" by the major suppliers because of their technological dependency on—and familiarity with—a single system.

With the technological leap in the powers of microprocessing, the rapid increase in power of PCs and minicomputers, and the cheap availability of independent software, "Big Blue" and the others found market power swinging against them.

Big users of computing power, like government departments, public utilities, and multinational companies, had enormous budgets for computing services and also had access to vast technical and user expertise. Power swung to the buyers from the increasingly competitive sellers (some went out of business, others lost tens of millions of dollars until they reorganized).

Vendor's contracts were rejected in favor of procurer's contracts pushing the buyer's interests, not the seller's. All aspects of the vendors' contracts became negotiable.

---

training courses (in the early 1970s), negotiators coped with the problem of moving without giving in. Some were adept at it, others not so good, but almost everybody who negotiated managed either to do it, or to react when somebody else was doing it, without too much strife or stress.

Problems of movement are exacerbated by the contexts of a more formal negotiation. They occur in other social contexts too, such as when one person wants to suggest something to another, which might be displeasing, embarrassing or controversial. If you hold back from bluntly revealing your suggestion, for any reason, you face the same predicament as the negotiator.

Someone wishing to lay court to another is unlikely to come right out and announce their intentions without some preparatory soundings first (unless they are inebriated, naturally bold or just plain ignorant).

Perhaps it is fear of rejection that inhibits most people from trying to jump from a non-relationship to intimacy in one go. If they do so jump, this itself suggests—and may safely be taken as such—that their commitment is less than serious. In turn, this might inhibit their intended partner's willingness to commence a long-term relationship with them. (The conventions for a casual dalliance are somewhat different!)

The strategic problem remains: how to make your potential intentions clear without frightening your intended away? Too bold and your brashness repels, too timid and your wimpishness is scorned. So, how do people cope if they are torn between holding back and pushing on and between the fear of failure and the joy of success? By **signaling**, of course. Romantic fiction abounds with hopeless purveyors of courting signals, as well as those so skilled that their reputations precede them.

The messages negotiators send are not always the ones received. You may not realize that the other negotiator is signaling or realize that you are. You may not appreciate how to respond to somebody else's signals, or what to do when they do not respond to yours. Just because you are relatively familiar with signaling behavior from various social situations, it does not mean that you are fully competent at managing it. Though signaling is a messy business—providing much material for dramatists and gossip-mongers—fortunately for human relationships, in the main it works itself out.

Take two negotiators who are firmly stuck behind their ramparts, asserting their inflexibility and their total lack of room for movement. How do they convey their stances? By the language they use, which is sturdily stated and unqualified in its absolutes (Exhibit 23).

Exhibit 23   Absolute language

"Nothing less than an immediate lifting of the beef ban is acceptable to my government."

"It is absolutely impossible for us even to consider a dilution of our shareholding."

"Nobody could ever meet that delivery target."

"I wouldn't even bother putting that proposal to my board."

"We demand the immediate cessation of troop movements."

Their language is meant to convey their steely determination. To the uninitiated, language like this depresses the faint-hearted and provokes the more resolute. They respond with attempts to convey just how certain they are that the exact opposite of what is being rejected will have to be accepted by those who are so certain that it must be rejected.

If it remained like this, negotiation would become a minority activity that could only succeed in very narrow circumstances. Because negotiation succeeds in a wide range of circumstances, something else besides the face value of people's assertions, must intervene to move the parties from their stubborn stances.

Something does intervene and it operates through subtle changes in the language used to convey the original absolute rejection. Compare the restatements of Exhibit 23 with those that contain a signal that subtly modifies the rejection (Exhibit 24).

Exhibit 24   Signal language

> "Nothing less than an early lifting of the beef ban is acceptable to my government."
>
> "A dilution of our shareholding would be very difficult to accept."
>
> "Nobody could ever meet that delivery target without extraordinary costs."
>
> "I would be loath to put that proposal in its current form to my board."
>
> "We demand the immediate cessation of troop movements close to our borders."

Can you see the signals? Can you see how the wording has changed and how it modifies the previous statements?

An "early" lifting of the beef ban is less red than an "immediate" lifting; what is "very difficult" is not "absolutely impossible"; to meet the target it only costs more; change its "present form" and the proposal goes to the board; and you can continue moving your troops anywhere but "near our borders".

Subtle changes   Signals are subtle changes in language that shift the message from absolute to qualified relative statements. They loosen the strictures of a positional dispute. What was impossible to consider becomes potentially possible.

And the message lies in its potential. The person signaling is not committing to movement but only to a *potential* for movement. There is much else to do before what is potential becomes an actuality.

She has agreed to go out to dinner with you; she has not committed herself to being the mother of your children—that isn't even remotely on her agenda.

Rush at a signal too fast and you will find the signaler will pull back; ignore it and they may tire of waiting for signs of potential movement.

PERFIDIOUS GAUL?

Two diplomats were disputing the intentions of the New Zealand government towards the release of two French agents, jailed for their role in the bombing of the Greenpeace ship, *Rainbow Warrior*, and the death of a crew member.

The New Zealand diplomat insisted that his prime minister had assured the diplomatic service, only the previous week, that the two French agents would serve their sentences in full. The British diplomat disagreed, and quoted from that morning's *Times* what the New Zealand prime minister had said the day before: "The French prisoners would not be released to freedom."

"There you are", said the New Zealander, "they will not be released."

"I don't think so", replied the British diplomat, who clearly understood a signal when he saw one. "Your prime minister says 'not released to freedom' and I would guess he means that they will be released soon into the custody of the French, perhaps to serve their sentences on a French island in the Pacific."

This is what happened—though the French then released them back to France and freedom, long before their sentences were served in full.

THE PURPLE MESSAGE OF THE SIGNAL

A signal addresses the common problem negotiators face when they are inhibited from moving through fear of giving in and of sliding down a slippery slope to surrender. This makes them hold back rather than plunge forward. Blue negotiators who move too soon and too far, often without testing the water via signaling, take great risks and are too easily exploited by red negotiators who hold back. Submissive blue movers, once they start softening their stance, can't help moving until they give in. Overly timid negotiators, like overly timid pilots, don't last as long as the assertive kind.

The signal does not announce a unilateral decision to move. That would indeed invite, never mind risk, a slippery slope. A signal is a tentative indication of a willingness to consider a move if, and only if, the other party is prepared to consider reciprocating in some way and does not treat the signal as a move in itself.

The simple signal is a behavioral convention adapted from social contexts other than negotiation. People learn to signal in a variety of contexts and find it very easy—and natural—to use signals in the specific circumstances of a negotiation (Exhibit 25).

Exhibit 25 Some hidden messages in signals

"I'd have immense difficulty in getting that past my board"—It would not be altogether impossible

"The answer is 'No', as things stand"—Amend it in some way and it may be "Yes".

"Our normal terms of business preclude discounts"—Our non-normal terms include discounts

"We cannot accept liability"—Please accept an *ex gratia* payment

"Sack all contract labor"—Give us more overtime

"We won't increase income tax rates"—We intend to reduce income tax allowances

"There is no way we can afford a 7 percent pay raise for all employees"—How about 7 percent for the very low paid and 4 percent for the rest?

Signals are tentative—they can be withdrawn if their reception threatens to compromise an adopted position. Rejection of a courtship signal is often enough for the parties to continue as normal and as if nothing had happened (though not always, as in the American phrase of "hitting on" someone, which suggests it was too demonstrative or too threatening to be ignored). Rejection of a negotiating signal by ignoring it terminates the episode, at least temporarily.

Willful rejection by exploiting a signal is least likely to lead to a productive exchange between the participants: "Ah, I see, so now it is no longer 'impossible', it's only 'difficult'. How long will it take you to agree that it is 'possible' and no longer merely 'difficult'?"

This carping and negative response drives a signaler back behind their ramparts and will prolong the argument or even start a fight.

The signaler's intent is to gain recognition that mutual movement is possible. That is why the signal is tentatively expressed and casually dropped into the phraseology of the dialog, unannounced and unadorned. If it is responded to by the listener, the possibility of considering the prospects of movement from the current stance is almost assured. It is only a possibility and not yet a commitment.

The signaler's intent

The purple signaler seeks assurance that it is "safe" for them to discuss the conditions for mutual movement. They judge how safe it is to continue along this line depending on their interpretation of your response. They are saying in effect: "If hostilities are temporarily suspended [and note that signals can be sent in the midst of a fierce exchange] and I will not be punished for my willingness to consider movement, then I might be ready to do so."

THE PURPLE RESPONSE TO A SIGNAL

To respond to signals, you have to listen for them.

Normal active listening standards are not good, therefore many signals are missed. As signalers cannot be sure whether their signal was ignored by you out of intent or accident, it may be necessary to repeat the signal in different forms. Ultimately, the signal may have to be presented explicitly:

> "Look, we can argue all day, and almost have, about why you cannot accept clause 7.2, as it stands. So let me be frank. What form of amended wording, or compensation, would be appropriate for you to accept the substance of a clause like 7.2?"

If the response is wholly negative—"Nothing will ever induce me to accept 7.2"—you know where you stand with this person: on the brink of a failed negotiation, assuming that clause 7.2 is, and remains, crucial to your deal. Should 7.2 be negotiable, you can explore what other issues you could trade to compensate you for moving on 7.2.

You have to be careful to discriminate between a negotiator's defense of a sacred interest and their playing a red game, in which they defend everything in sight in order to compel you, unilaterally, to do all of the moving. By playing a resolute red, they may be attempting to structure (i.e., lower) your expectations.

Mostly, signals are responded to positively. If they weren't, precious little progress would be made when negotiating. It is not always clear cut, however, and some red players cannot resist point scoring when given an opportunity:

> "I'm glad to see that you are dropping your intransigent opposition to my reasonable proposals, so, in the interests of making some progress, let me hear what your latest new position is."

Add in a sarcastic tone, and we commence our own mini-dialog of the deaf.

Responding constructively

How should a purple negotiator respond who wants to be more constructive?

Simple: follow the signal and don't attack the signaler. When someone changes a statement from something being "impossible" to "it would be difficult", your best response is to follow the change in language: "When you say it would be 'difficult', could you elaborate on the nature of the difficulties?"; and later, perhaps: "In what way can we assist you in overcoming these difficulties?"

If the other person changed their stance, they are in the best position to explain what the change means, so you do not have to guess or interpret what they mean. Just ask them.

Once you follow a signal, by asking non-sarcastic and non-point-scoring questions and, of course, listening carefully to the answers, a whole new episode in the negotiation opens up. It pays to be purple!

From two opposed original solutions, expressed as the entry points of each position on the issues, you can move on towards exploring tentative possibilities for movement away from these entry positions. You become aware of the other party's interests, as they see them, and of their priorities and how, and perhaps why, they differ from yours.

Purple negotiators recognize that no negotiated solution is possible if it behaviorally excludes the other party from serving their own interests in some way, and to their satisfaction. Consciously identifying their interests makes for a more likely package than allowing only one of the solutions you both first thought of to become the sole basis of the joint solution.

To avoid a "hit-or-miss" first solution being the only solution you consider, you both have to explore facets of your initial positions that are currently unacceptable. Only purple signaling can safely deliver that exploration process to you, which is why it has become more common.

WALLOWING TECHNIQUES

People are not always willing to state clearly their problems, concerns, or even what they want, just because you think they should. For various reasons they may resent your questioning—they see you gathering evidence with which to criticize or mock them, or they suspect that you are about to try to sell them something.

When lack of progress sparks off disappointment and frustration leads to threats, you will have to do something else if you want a settlement.

STRUCTURED QUESTIONING

One behavioral technique that you can use is a structured sequence for your questioning, developed for sales people by Neil Rackham. He called it SPIN® in 1987, though its antecedents in sales behavior were around for many years earlier. Today it is presented in various (dis)guises by numerous presenters in the sales training business.

Situation questions

Most people ask questions about the **situation** that the other person thinks they are in. "How's business, Mrs Luigi?", is one common introductory question you are bound to use in many social contexts. Assuming she bothers to answer other than vaguely—and without a bold riposte—you press on with other situation questions: "How is Lo's affecting your trade?" (to which she might reply "Mind your own business!"); "Where are you going for your holiday?"; "What do you think of fish prices?", and so on.

Some situation questions are essential but, according to Rackham, asking too many of them bores (and irritates) the person who is asked them.

Problem questions

Sales people usually ask their questions as the "hook" on which to sell you something. These "hooks" are called **problem** questions. You ask questions about any problems the person might have in the situations they describe and which your product allegedly solves.

In processing problem questions, you acquire the information you need to formulate a proposal, but Rackham's research in 30,000 sales interviews showed that sellers do best if they do not formulate or present their proposals as soon as they identify that a prospect has a problem that can be resolved if only they buy the product.

Below-average sales people (and influencers) move too

fast to reveal their products, or their solutions, to problems or needs that they may only have casually identified in the briefest of ways from their initial situation and problem questions. Just because somebody under general questioning hints at a problem or need they have, it does not mean that they are in any sense as passionate as you are about solving it at that moment, or through your solution.

Anybody aware that they have a problem—they are thirsty, for instance—may consider it to be only one of many problems they have at that precise moment. They identified their "thirst" as a problem only because you asked them a question that brought thirst to the surface of their attention.

They may also have other problems that warrant their immediate attention (they are late for a meeting and have no time to get a drink—or talk to you) which you don't know about. Trying to sell them something at this moment is a mistake. They are not fully receptive until their awareness of their need to solve their problem rises to the top of their personal agenda.

By asking **implication** questions that explore the consequences to them of not solving the problem, your questions bring their needs right to the fore. If the implication of being thirsty on a hot day, while late for an appointment, is that they will suffer severe distress from dehydration, they could have a driving accident and miss the appointment altogether. And drawing out the implications of having an accident (say) leads them to focus on the seriousness of doing nothing about their thirst.

Implication questions

Here, I will introduce a short elaboration on the technique that Rackham did not identify and for which he is not responsible—so don't criticize him for it! I just find that it helps negotiators to remember what to do because it involves such a vivid image.

Briefly, you get people to wallow in their problems and, as most people like to talk about themselves (i.e., to wallow in their own concerns) to sympathetic listeners, it is

Wallowing

not difficult to encourage others to wallow in the implications of their problems.

Many people who don't encourage listeners to wallow are simply not interested in what others have to say (they only want to sell or tell them something). Those negotiators who do practice wallowing techniques on others certainly are memorably different—and achieve better results—than those who don't.

Exhibit 26   A wallowing sequence

"How much profit will you forgo if you terminated your business in these premises before your lease runs out?" (Implication)

"What kind of problems would this create for you?" (Implication)

"How would you manage without a regular income?" (Implication)

"What would be the effect of having to live on your capital?" (Implication)

"If you had to cancel your holiday in Florence, when would you see your grandchildren?" (Implication—invitation to wallow)

"How do you feel about that?" (Wallow, wallow, wallow)

Some say that by letting people think about their problems, and by asking them implication or wallowing questions, they will tend to postpone a decision on what to do. But they ignore what the questioning sequence achieves.

You want Mrs Luigi, for instance, to reveal her version of her problems—you don't want to impose on her your version of them—so that when you make proposals to

resolve her problems you address her needs as fully as
you can (which may not be to the full extent that she
expects). At present you are searching for the key items in
her refusal to cooperate with AMP, while you gauge her
expectations and priorities.

Value questions

At some stage—negotiation is an art not a science—you
will move on from the implications of Mrs Luigi's problems
with AMP's short lease to the **value** to her of resolving the
problems.

Rackham, understandably from a marketing
perspective, slightly fudged the name of the last step in
the SPIN® sequence (Situation, Problem, Implication and
Need-payoff) to call it "need-payoff", not "value", which
would produce the less acceptable pneumonic SPIV! On
the grounds that a "rose by any other name smells as
sweet", I prefer to leave it at "value", provided you accept
that it is Mrs Luigi's valuation in her own words that is the
important consequence of SPIN®-type questioning and
not what it is called.

Value questions seek to highlight for Mrs Luigi what it is
worth to her to solve her leasing problems and, by
implication, what it will cost her if she doesn't solve them.

Asset Management plc

If, in her own words, she places a value on solving these
problems, you can make an accurate judgment as to what
it is worth to her to resolve them and she too can judge
what it is worth to her for you do so.

LISTEN TO MRS LUIGI

You are familiar with the quandary that Asset Management
plc is in, following Mrs Luigi's rejection of its offer of
$14,000 for quitting her lease early. Red behaviorists in
your team mock the "goodwill gestures" you made 18
months ago and react to her current stance entirely
negatively. She is, in their firm view, typically ungrateful for
AMP's abatement of her rent and for waiving the repairs to
her shop.

You, on the other hand, appalled by the red fighting
behaviors they advocate in their "contingency plan", recoil

from the risks to AMP's reputation if their red behavior became public. These risks are too serious to contemplate (always remember that disaffected employees, who can blow the whistle on you, hold your future in their memories).

Experience shows that fights get out of hand.

Suppose somebody did suffer food poisoning as a result of AMP's "pressure" and Mrs Luigi was closed down. How would that be a victory if the authorities traced the contamination to vermin which was brought on to the site by AMP employees? Heavy fines, if not jail sentences, could follow, causing permanent damage to AMP's business reputation. What would Iceberg do then? Criminal-like acts by AMP could void Iceberg's contract to buy the site.

Purple debate

So what could AMP do instead? How would purple-style debate help you to find a solution out of which there are only winners?

A meeting with Mrs Luigi is advised at which you listen and do not threaten. You would use a structured questioning sequence, such as SPIN® or its derivatives, and seek some level of rapport from simple wallowing techniques.

What does she want? Why won't she move? How does she see her future?

Mrs Luigi has hinted that one of her problems would be the loss of profit for the 18 months in which she will not trade if she quits early. The amount of profit can be estimated from her books. It is an empirical question, not a subjective wish. She says that she is suffering straitened financial circumstances because of Mr Lo's competition across the street, which you acknowledged when you abated her rent, so any monetary value she places on the future lost profits is capped by realistic numbers and cannot be inflated by her.

Contrast this to your jumping in with an offer to compensate her as soon as she signals that she is concerned about the profit forgone if she accedes to a four-month rolling lease. You would be too hasty and, more than likely, you would be ineffective because assertively inclined Mrs Luigi would not regard your offer of compensation as other than a "first offer". She would push for more than whatever you offer and also, as she has not raised all of her problems and objections to quitting her lease, you would be in for a longer shopping list (believe me, Mrs Luigi is as sharp about her business affairs as is the vinegar on one of her chips!).

By proceeding using your own version of a questioning sequence, you will amass critical information about Mrs Luigi's positions, interests and anxieties. You would also glean something of her aspirations about what she wants. As important, you also send messages about your purple-motivated empathic intentions, perhaps establishing some rapport with her by creating a helpful atmosphere for the presentation and debate on your proposals as the next stage of the negotiation. This is the role of purple debate as opposed to red arguing or fighting.

Mrs Luigi's demands may not be exorbitant when they are assessed but, even if they are, you still need to know about them. Suppose, however, she outlines her concerns in her own words and these boil down to the following:

- Closing her shop takes away her means of earning a living and her independence—she's made pizzas here for over 20 years.

- She forgoes 18 months' profit if she shuts now—it's not much but still positive (say, $18,000) and just enough for her to get by on.

- She wants time to find another shop in the area to serve her customers until she is 65 (six years on) and then wants to sell her pizzeria as a "going concern" to fund her retirement. For this she needs capital to fit out a new shop like Mr Lo's.

- She also resented being mocked by the first man who came down to see her from AMP, who told her she was a "silly old bag who stood in the way of progress".

Listing Mrs Luigi's concerns is not an absolute commitment to resolve them as they stand, but it is an offer to consider them or some alternative, provided that it does not weaken your ability to address your own interests. It is also a firmer basis for a purple negotiating stance if you know how she sees the problems she has with your proposals—particularly if she expresses them in her own words. False views of other people's perceptions are a weak basis for designing an enduring settlement.

Don't ignore people's concerns

Now, I am certainly not suggesting that soft blue sentiment should rule your business decisions, and it's not to tug at your heart strings that I state Mrs Luigi's four concerns. Even holding to cold business decisions does not mean that you ignore the concerns of people with whom you do business.

In Mrs Luigi's case, you must do business with her in order to do your business with Iceberg. She and her concerns stand between you and $1.4 million. Therefore, for as long as this remains the case, her concerns are your concerns.

In contrast to a red fight, you could, for instance, distance yourself from the wilder outbursts of whomever spoke to her first, disclaiming his professionalism (an apology won't do you any harm either). You are here to resolve the problem to your mutual satisfaction (assurances) and you intend to try to meet as many of her concerns as you can consistent with AMP's interests.

Your questioning sequence is constructive and it is known to work. You listen in order to summarize her points to her satisfaction—and for your own edification. You note her signals and respond positively, and prepare both of you for the exchange and discussion of tentative purple proposals.

SUMMARY

Debate behaviors in the purple style do not threaten the other party's interests because purple players acknowledge the importance to both parties of their interests.

Purple debate behaviors include neutral statements, regular assurances of constructive intent, positive questions, neutral, truthful and brief summaries and signals. Above all, they recognize the importance of active listening skills.

Negotiation is about the management of movement and this is accomplished by signaling. A signal is a change in the language used in stating one's current positions. Definitive rejections or defense of a stance are qualified—"impossible" becomes "difficult", etc.—and conditions are hinted at by which a solution could be considered.

An appropriate questioning sequence is one that goes beyond instantly solving somebody's problems (or trying to sell them something) to one that explores the implications with them of not solving their problems or concerns (using sympathetic wallowing techniques), leading them to value the costs and benefits of resolving some or all of their problem.

Debate is about finding out what they want and letting them know what you want. It is usually more effective than an argument or a fight.

RECOMMENDED READING

Neil Rackham (1987) *Making Major Sales*, Chapter 8, Aldershot, Gower.

Neil Rackham (1988) *Account Strategy for Major Sales*, Chapter 3, Aldershot, Gower.

ANSWERS TO SELF-ASSESSMENT 6

1

(a) Yes. By adding in the words "to freedom" he was signaling that they would be released to a French jail instead of remaining in a New Zealand jail.

(b) No. You have not recognized the signal.

2

(a) This is an option, of course, but how far you will get with it relies on the supplier's determination to prevent a precedent. You have missed the significance of the signal: "direct connection between compensation and the failure to supply". What does he mean by that? Why not ask him?

(b) Another option but your case will turn on the words *"force majeure"* and whether they cover this case. It could cost you $7000 for your solicitor to get a legal opinion from counsel, before you get near a court.

(c) Yes. Follow the signal. An *ex gratia* payment does not directly, nor even overtly, connect money to you with the failure to supply. Joint promotion of the fabric conditioner brand also advertises your store in your locality.

3

(a) Yes. This way she keeps her copyright because it is returned in 20 years, and she benefits from the software producer's protection of it from pirate exploitation. She also gets a royalty for every copy sold.

(b) An option, but one that forgoes her ownership of her copyright. Depends on the monetary value of the trade, perhaps.

(c) Another option. Keep pushing on the software
    producer. Depends on the balance of power and how
    feasible it is for a parallel product to appear. Is she in
    business for the money or the personal glory?

9 *Difficult Red Negotiators*

1 The man you are negotiating with has a bombastic and rude manner. He interrupts constantly and loudly and at a pace that does not allow interruptions of his flow. He is emphatic and threatening and shows no interest in your point of view. It is almost a one-way transaction. Do you:

   (a) Retaliate in kind with matching behavior?

   (b) Wait for an opening to say your piece?

   (c) Agree to what he wants?

2 The financial director of a large customer is an abusive and domineering person, who has a fine repertoire of swear words, and will not accept "No" for an answer. She expects you to sit there and take it and theatrically waves her arms about and throws papers around when she wants to make a point. Do you:

   (a) Behave in a contrasting manner and keep your cool?

   (b) Agree to what she wants?

   (c) Wait to say your piece?

3   Your boss is a bully and seldom has a word of praise for what you do, but flies into a paroxysm of rage if you make the slightest mistake, including over the most trivial of incidents. Do you:

  (a)   Let him know of your dissatisfaction with how he treats you?

  (b)   Ignore his behavior and otherwise do not let it affect what you do or how you do it?

  (c)   Try your best to humor him and keep out of trouble?

*W*HO is difficult? Usually somebody else. Few people look in a mirror and see a difficult person. Many who are told that they are "difficult to work for" are genuinely shocked to discover how others see them. With shock come disbelief, denial and disappointment—they feel "betrayed" by disloyal subordinates. So beware, it's risky career-wise to be the messenger.

   Why is it always the other person who is "difficult"? Why is it that every negotiator I have questioned about "difficult" people has always been able to identify—at least in their mind's eye—one or two other people who qualify for the accolade?

   When asked to discuss the ways in which these people are difficult, they come up with a number of common characteristics. One, of course, is that they do not like dealing with certain individuals because they do not like them. Instant dislikes are common enough, as are slowly growing dislikes, and disliking someone makes them "difficult".

   Think back to a recent upsetting incident concerning the way you were treated by a stranger, be it while pursuing a telephone enquiry, or asking for help in a store, or the way a complaint of yours was handled. It did not take much for you to be angered by some perceived slight or slipshod treatment, did it?

   I am willing to bet that you have had cause to bemoan somebody's attitude to your interests in the past 48 hours!

People who are in a position to make life harder for you are prone to be irritating. Petty bureaucrats, "jobsworths" (as in, "it's more than my job's worth to let you do that") who are sticklers for their own interpretations of their precious routines and rigid procedures, people with aimless discontent or grudges who take them out on anybody unfortunate enough to come within their ambit of discretion, and people who are merely irascible and bloody-minded, all make life miserable for the rest of us. Trying to negotiate with them can be a pain. But that's life!

I am not thinking about these types of people, however, when asking who is difficult to cope with in a negotiating sense. Difficult negotiators in the sense discussed here are those people who systematically deploy red behaviors to produce the outcome that they want, whatever your intentions.

Intimidation

There is a difference between having to deal with people who on occasion are irritating and annoying (we all have "off" days) and having to suffer the intimidatory behaviors of a red-style negotiator. For them, intimidation is a calculated act. By domineering and bullying they get what they want from (most) other people.

Probably, in practice, you do not distinguish between the one-off tantrums of someone who is thoroughly "pissed off" by something you have done to them and the repetitive tantrum style of the difficult negotiator. You should distinguish these cases because the former are very different from the latter.

Depending on context, humoring certain bad-tempered people is an appropriate strategy, if a little demeaning, to get what you want. Once, however, their tempers are excited as a result of your sledgehammer response, everything gets out of control. What is just an inconvenience becomes a major personality clash.

If you are in a hurry and they are not, and they are in the driving seat, you can really be made to suffer—"little Napoleons" thirst for excuses to show others just how important they are to those provoked enough to challenge them. Give them an audience and they are ecstatic. (Clue: avoid challenging little Napoleons in public.)

The difficult people I consider here are serious obstacles in a negotiation. Their behavior prevents the resolution of differences by a joint decision, except when you acquiesce in whatever they decide. To that end they use aggressive red styles of debate, backed by threats and sanctions, to compel you into deals that meet their interests, not yours. They are, in short, operating at the extreme red end of the red–blue continuum.

MATCH OR CONTRAST?

How should you react to a person who is being "difficult" in this sense?

Should you react by matching their difficult behavior with similar behavior on your part, or by contrasting their behavior with your intentionally non-difficult behavior?

That is how people usually and starkly summarize their choices. As choices, however, they are inadequate, as you will soon realize when you try either of them.

Neither matching nor contrasting behaviors work for very long because it is extremely difficult to keep them going for more than a few exchanges. And you are left with the classic problem of what to do when whatever you choose to do is shown not to work.

Advocates of matching or contrasting strategies seldom take into account the reaction of the difficult person to their blatant counter-manipulation.

Exhibit 27   Matching or contrasting behaviors?

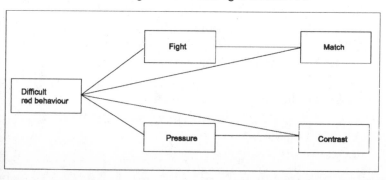

In Exhibit 27, the two strategies usually suggested for dealing with difficult red behavior are counterpoised, as are the usual reactions of the difficult person. To see what happens when you apply either strategy, look at it from the red behaviorist's perspective and not from your own.

MATCHING

Take matching behavior. How does the red behaviorist perceive your reaction?

Your intention is to match his behavior by playing red yourself so that you make him change his behavior into something less difficult. But why should your red behavior change his red behavior if his red behavior is not changing yours? Does this mean that you are immune to his red behavior but he is not to yours?

He does not roll over and play dead. And why should he?

His red behavior aims to intimidate you into submission, but your evident resistance suggests to him that that he is not pushing you hard enough, yet. So it is more likely that he will continue intimidating rather than give up, which is precisely what you are inclined to do if your matching red outburst doesn't work on him.

Think it through. Either you back off when he pushes or you resist. If you back off, then your submissive reactions confirm the efficacy of his red behavior. If you don't back off, this suggests that you have not yet got his message, so he escalates his red pressure.

What is true for him is true for you. If your resistance causes him to back off—it might with some people, but observation suggests otherwise for the vast majority—will you drop your matching behavior or will you continue matching? Observation suggests that you will continue.

Why? Because once you engage in a red matching strategy to make him back off, you must keep your red pressure on in case he recommences his initial intimidatory stance! Only in theory is it possible (though unlikely) that your red counter-stance will cool him down from red to reasonable.

And this leads directly to the fallacy behind your

intentions in using intimidatory red counter-behavior. Even
if it had been shown to work, your red matching strategy
traps you into continuing to behave in the red manner that
you were meant to be resisting when it came from him.
What didn't work on you—because you resisted—is
supposed to work on him! Believing that he won't resist
your red behavior, though you can successfully resist his, is
pure arrogance.

Or are you dead brilliant and everybody else is just
plain stupid?

Of course, there are rare occasions when matching
might work (in negotiation everything works at some time
or another!) and a small minority of people probably exist
somewhere with whom it is certain to work should you find
them. But workable behavioral strategies must be valid on
the majority of occasions when circumstance dictate that
they should be used, not just on those few exceptional
occasions when they might work.

Experience suggests that if you match intimidatory
behavior, irrespective of your motives (and you can hardly
reveal your motives convincingly, can you?), most difficult
people will fight back. They do not give in—after all, you
didn't, did you?

The exchange becomes an intimidatory challenge,
escalating as each of you strives to convince the other that
you are the most determined to win. As to who started the
contest of wills, it no longer matters. After a few exchanges,
who is to blame for the red-style row is no longer
distinguishable.

Matching behavior as a strategy is doomed on most
occasions. Your matching manipulation—despite all the
good intentions you claim for yourself—becomes just
another case of two red-style negotiators fighting each
other in their normal aggressive manner.

What then of contrasting behavior? Does it fare any better?   **CONTRASTING**
Unfortunately, it doesn't.

As a strategy it has similar flaws to matching behavior,
not least because it assumes behavior on the part of

others that is not demonstrated by you.

Again, be less egotistical and consider the interaction from perspective of the red behaviorist.

Her intentions are to intimidate you and, lo and behold, in the first exchange, you behave as if you appear to have been intimidated!

Now, from her point of view, how different is your behavior from what she would observe if you had been genuinely intimidated?

Remember, she cannot see inside your head and she has no way of knowing that what she is witnessing is but a "clever" sham on your part. You behave as if you are intimidated, which means, as far as she is concerned, that you are intimidated.

How will she react? Will she desist from her intimidatory behavior now that she appears to be achieving her intentions? Unlikely!

If her intimidatory behavior produces the submissive results that she seeks, then she has all the more reason to keep you in line by keeping her pressure on you.

Of course, it may be that the more you contrast your behavior with hers, the lower she might drop her red pressure, if only relatively speaking, but there is only a very slim hope that she will feel the need to drop it completely. She is still inclined to demonstrate that she is more determined than you are.

She reads your behavior as weaker than hers as she has considerable experience of dealing with soft-blue style negotiators. The more your blue behavior contrasts with her red behavior, the more extreme she reads your blueness to be.

Bullies make the submissive suffer—they don't give them a cuddle!

What do you intend to happen when you contrast your behavior with hers? Presumably, you hope in some way to "shame" her into curtailing her sharply contrasting red behavior and, in an act of contrition, you want her to stop trying to intimidate you.

What are your chances of success? Not high, for much

the same reasons as efforts at matching intimidatory behavior are futile.

Why should contrasting behavior triumph over intimidation? The intimidator intends you to submit and, as far she is concerned, the surest sign of your submission is exactly what you are displaying.

Where she intimidates—loud voice, extreme gestures, speaking quickly, interrupting, threatening, arguing, blaming and belittling—you deploy their opposites—speaking quietly, offering meek gestures, giving way to her interruptions, recoiling from her accusations and forswearing threats to her.

Privately, you know that you are not really giving in—but try to convince her of that! She sees only how you behave, not what you are thinking, and she believes what she sees. She concludes that her intimidation has worked, so she keeps intimidating.

What a quandary! Neither matching nor contrasting is a sure-fire way to react, yet both are advocated sincerely by many experts in interpersonal skills as behavioral counters to intimidatory red-style behavior.

NEITHER STRATEGY WORKS

Admittedly, I have heard eloquent, even passionate, advocacy of both behavioral responses, complete with anecdotal support of their alleged success. When examined closely, however, the supporting evidence is highly selective, more like "one-offs" than generally applicable behavioral responses that you can rely on.

In all possible human interactions there are many possibilities and successful cases of matching or contrasting strategies are among them, but they are also extremely rare.

You could hear of someone walking along Sauchiehall Street in Glasgow and meeting a millionaire who gave them £500 for no other reason than they were in the right place at the right time. One isolated incident like this would not justify you spending your spare time wandering along Sauchiehall—or any other—Street, in the hope of meeting a millionaire similarly disposed to give away £500.

You are more likely to meet a mugger who relieves you of what money you have already got.

In most attempts to match or contrast a red negotiator's behavior, sooner or later you will feel compelled to adopt full-scale red behavior yourself or to give in. In matching their behavior, your inability to force the red player to back off forces you to escalate from an argument to a fight, or to submit. In contrasting their behavior, the same inability to shame the red player into switching to blue behavior forces you to switch from blue to red argument, or to submit.

Neither behavioral strategy is advised for purple players.

BEHAVIORS AND OUTCOMES

How do you resolve the dilemma when the choice between matching or contrasting behavior is not really a choice at all because they both invariably lead to the same result? Not obviously, nor easily, but resolve it you can.

Their behavior or your interests?

The place to start is by asking what causes you to accept that your response to somebody else's behavior is best determined by *their* behavior and not by *your* interests?

When you pose the behavioral dilemma in the normal manner—match or contrast?—you allow somebody else, in effect, to determine how you behave. You are reacting to their behavior.

Reactive behavior, while perfectly necessary for competitive games like tennis—if your partner plays to your backhand, you do not use your forehand—is woefully inadequate for negotiation.

Behaving reactively in negotiation makes you a prisoner of the other player's intentions and leads directly to the false dilemma of matching or contrasting. To escape from the false dilemma you must escape from reactive behavior.

First, ask yourself why a red-style negotiator uses

intimidatory behaviors: to influence or, better still, to determine the outcome, if they can.

Linking their red behavior to their intended outcome is their paramount motivation. They behave in a red way because they have found that it gets them what they want. Experience of the outcomes achieved by their past red behavior guides their current behavior.

Now, if you react the way they expect, they will achieve the outcome that they want because their intimidatory red behavior overrides either your matching or contrasting responses.

But suppose you neither match nor contrast? Suppose you do not allow her behavior to determine yours?

DISCONNECTING

Suppose, in short, you break the connection between their red behavior and their intended outcome? How would this affect the negotiation sequence?

No one should assume that the strategy of **disconnecting** red-style behavior from the outcome is easy, nor that it is certain to succeed. It isn't on either count. If it were easy and certain to succeed, it would be far more common than are the futile strategies of matching or contrasting.

To disconnect red-style behavior from the outcome is to deny the other person the prize they seek. And this is why disconnecting as a behavioral strategy is preferred to matching or contrasting. The denial of the prize they seek is within your grasp, whereas their response to your matching or contrasting behavior is not.

Disconnection of their behavior from the outcome can work immediately. It is something that *you* do, not them. It does not require their permission or acknowledgment. They may continue whatever behavior they choose, all to no effect, because you have determined that their behavior will not affect you.

The only threat to the success of a disconnection strategy is that you lose your resolve or, alas, have it removed by higher authority in whatever organization you operate.

HOW NOT TO STOP NEGATIVE BEHAVIOR

It is not uncommon for people who are negatively affected by the behavior of others, such as in an industrial dispute, unintentionally to give succor to those inflicting on them their negative behavior.

A strike disrupts normal business relationships—as indeed it is intended to do! A third party, badly affected by the strike, appears on television to tell the world how badly the strike affects them—lost orders, stymied investment, laid-off workers, competitive advantages handed to (foreign) companies, spoiled holidays, fretting children, despairing old folk, and such like. The blackest of pictures is intended to show just how bad the strikers are in continuing to hit the country's hard-pressed businesses.

The result: the strikers' resolve is increased, which is not what those commenting on the damaging affects of the strike intended.

Why? Because if the strikers' behavior had no effect, their resolve would weaken.

Therefore news that the strike is having a damaging effect confirms that their strike behavior is working! The greater the damage detailed, the better for the strikers' morale and the more likely they are to believe that their employer will concede in the dispute.

Interventions from above

Unhelpful interventions from "above" in a large organization are always a potential factor in the conduct of a dispute. Those in authority, but not involved, often take it on themselves to take stances that reconnect certain negative behaviors with the outcome, despite the sensible pursuit of disconnection strategies to separate them.

Include all viewpoints

Similarly, in a democracy where constitutional parties and terrorist organisations (extreme red behaviorists!) are competing for support, it is Canute-like to assert that only constitutional parties can discuss a political settlement—

on the grounds that "we cannot negotiate with terrorists". A settlement that does not embrace the political viewpoints of the terrorist organizations (unless they are militarily defeated first) will not endure.

To get an agreement for peace, the constitutional parties wind up negotiating with terrorists, which, ironically, gives pathetic credence ("without our Armalites we would never have got a seat at the peace talks") to the terrorists' appalling behavior and which democratic constitutionalists, quite rightly, abhor.

Far better, surely, to invite all organizations, constitutional or terrorist, to the talks, excluding nobody, so that terrorist routes to influence a solution are made redundant? Why take all the personal risks of being a terrorist, if your viewpoint can be expressed at the talks without having to be a terrorist?

Disconnecting behavior from the outcome has many applications. It is a matter of resolve. The more clearly you state that the other party's behavior will not affect the outcome and demonstrate that it doesn't (by not negatively over-reacting to their behavior), the more likely the terrorists will be to reduce the incidence of their outrageous behaviors.

If certain types of behavior arise from the alleged injustices of specific organizational or constitutional forms, then addressing these injustices should be the target, not outrage at those who believe they have a right to behave as criminals because of alleged injustices.

In the 1960s, the quickest way to settle a dispute at a manufacturing plant was to call an unofficial strike. Taking the dispute through official grievance procedures could take over 100 days, often much longer. A stoppage brought the dispute to the immediate attention of senior management, who usually did something about it to secure an early return to work. Those managements that didn't give in usually faced a messy strike, and then gave in. A very few fought it out to the bitter end.

In the circumstances, the growth of "wild-cat" strikes is fully explained, as is the steady loss of UK industry's

---

UNBELIEVABLE!

In South Africa recently, some unions called a one-day general strike to support union social (i.e., political) policy. Some political leaders and a few employers publicly claimed that the day's stoppage would "severely damage the South African economy".

Not surprisingly, the one-day strike went ahead.

Yet that same week, all of South African industry stopped for the official May Day holiday. It seemed incongruous to observers that a day's holiday that week would not have an effect but a day's partial strike would "severely damage" the economy.

Surely a better line for the Mandela government would have been to assert dispassionately that the strike was a "waste of time" because the government sympathized with the union's policy on the issue, and that losing a day's pay in pursuit of an objective that the union had already "won" meant that nobody would lose money but themselves?

---

competitiveness at the time and the eventual loss of a large slice of it by the 1980s.

Sadly, experience shows that behaviors "justified" by an injustice are easily used to pursue unjustifiable ends. A strike to raise low wages can be followed by strikes to raise already high wages that then bankrupts the company.

Your counter to red-style behavior is based on convincing the perpetrators—sometimes by announcing the principle openly, sometimes privately depending on circumstances and context—that whatever their behavior, whether legitimate (a right to strike) or not (nobody has a "right" to commit acts of terrorism in a parliamentary democracy), it will not affect the outcome.

Of course, to make your assertion credible, you must first convince yourself.

MERITS OR TRADE

If you are not going to allow the other party's behavior to affect the outcome, what *will* you allow to affect it?

In the extreme, a dispute could arise from an injury of some kind caused entirely by actions for which you have total responsibility. Whatever merits there are, none can be found for your side in the dispute. Bereft of any redeeming features at all, the dispute is wholly one-sided. In short, the merits of the case point conclusively in the other party's favor. In these circumstances, the merits of the case might suggest that you should settle the dispute to their benefit.

Merits, therefore, are one of the two main influences that determine the outcome of a dispute.

MERITS

Most disputes are not so clear cut—and those few that are clear cut are seldom admitted as such by the party that has the least grounds for disputing the remedy.

There tend to be merits on both sides, which is why there is a dispute both about the extent of the injuries shared by the parties and the relative balance of the merits each side uses to justify their version of the appropriate outcome.

Thus, for most disputes, merit alone is seldom a sufficient criterion for constructing a settlement. It plays a part in any settlement, if only because the parties who feel that their case has merits—as most people do—are seldom willing to forgo the influence of the merits of their case on the settlement.

Trade, or the exchange principle, is the other main influence on the outcome.

TRADE

Disputed merits can be mediated by a willingness to trade for an acceptable outcome. What you give up to the other side (your blue offer) reflects a consideration by you of the merits of *their* case, in exchange for what you insist on getting (your red requirement) from them in recognition by them of the merits of *your* case. Both comprise the purple conditional trade.

Purple trade is the kernel of a negotiation process as a means of resolving disputes.

The content of an agreed exchange can vary enormously and depends on all sorts of factors, some within, others outside, the negotiators' control, not least the skill with which they formulate their proposals for settlement.

My advice on the skills required for selecting a purple settlement will follow. For the moment it is essential that you understand just how different settlement by merits and purple trade is from settlement by submitting to red-style behaviors.

Trade v submission

Trade is decision making by mediating the parties' interests; submission is decision making through bullying.

Succumbing to bullying is a serious mistake, as is refusing to negotiate a settlement as some sort of a condign punishment for the past behaviors of those whom you oppose (and whom you may have good reasons to oppose).

People who commit criminal acts—and terrorism is criminal behavior—remain individually answerable within the rule of law for their crimes. But if you want a solution to the problems of terrorism, you must distinguish between behavioral acts that will perpetuate terrorism and those that will deliver a negotiated settlement. Justice is safest when it is not negotiable and peace is securer if it is not one-sided.

SUMMARY

Some, usually other, people are difficult. Their behavior is intimidatory in the extreme. The two most commonly recommended strategies to deal with difficult people is to match or contrast your behavior to theirs.

Matching involves behaving yourself in a way that is an intimidatory as the difficult negotiator, except that, supposedly, you are not really trying to be intimidatory, only appearing to be so. You intend only to show the other party that you too can be difficult and as soon as they recognize this for what it is, they are supposed to change their behavior and become less intimidatory themselves. Fine in theory, but hopeless in practice.

Most times, by matching their bullying behavior you provoke an escalation and they move from being merely difficult to being outright obnoxious. They try to out-intimidate you and you have a fight on your hands.

Contrasting involves behaving in the opposite manner to the other party's bullying, except that you are not really submitting at all. You only appear to be so and they are supposed to acknowledge this by changing from their intimidatory behavior into becoming reasonable. As before, fine in theory but hopeless in practice.

No one else can see inside your head. Your pretend behavior appears to be submissive and, therefore, it is submissive as far as they are concerned. Instead of dropping their intimidatory pressure they maintain it.

Both matching and contrasting are founded on a behavioral error—you are allowing somebody else's behavior to determine yours. You are reacting to them, so, in effect, they choose how you behave. They intend to determine the outcome of the negotiation.

For them there is a direct link between their behavior and the outcome they seek. Your task, instead, is to break the connection. They may behave how they choose but however they behave you will not allow it to affect the outcome.

You will allow only two factors to determine the outcome: the merits of their case (if there are any) and the principle of trading, or some combination of both.

If your case has no merits, candor about this presumably evident situation protects your long-term interests. Defending the indefensible damages longer-term relationships and personal credibility.

If you present your trades conditionally, the purple format protects your interests at all times.

You have no comment on the other party's difficult behavior. You will not let it "get to you". You resolve only to be influenced by the merits of the case or by a proposed negotiated trade, or some creative combination.

ANSWERS TO SELF-ASSESSMENT 7

1

(a) Retaliation only acts as a challenge to him—he is obviously not intimidating you enough. He will put on more pressure.

(b) Yes, but only if you are clear that his behavior will not affect your choice of the outcome. A waste of time if your reaction only makes you feel smug.

(c) Never! Do not reward bullies by giving into their intimidation.

2

(a) Merely contrasting her intimidatory behavior only convinces her that the behavior is working. She will put more pressure on you to give in. If you "snap" you will end up matching her behavior.

(b) Never! Do not reward bullies by giving in to their intimidation.

(c) Yes, but only if you are clear that her behavior will not affect your choice of the outcome. A waste of time if your reaction only makes you feel smug.

3

(a) Recommended by "tree-huggers", but apart from making you feel better it is unlikely to have much effect. Some bosses are "pigs" and maturity is about not letting other people's behavior get to you.

(b) Yes. Don't let other people's behavior determine how you behave.

(c) Keeping your "head down" is one solution, but it is difficult to sustain if you become fed up with pandering to his ego.

10 The Color Purple

1 Negotiators should:

   (a) Judge each issue on its merits?

   (b) Consider each issue in its context?

   (c) Link all issues to each other?

2 We cannot negotiate a mutually acceptable solution:

   (a) If we have the same preferences for the same things?

   (b) Unless we prefer the same things with different degrees of intensity?

   (c) Unless we prefer different things with different degrees of intensity?

   (d) Unless we prefer different things with the same degree of intensity?

3 For negotiation we must:

(a) Choose between being hard red or soft blue?

(b) Be hard red or soft blue to suit the circumstances?

(c) Fuse hard red and soft blue behavior?

*A*S we have already seen in this book, most people's attitudes to negotiation come in various shades of red or blue and, accordingly, most people display a mixture of red and blue behaviors when they negotiate. The color mix of their attitudes varies according to the situation they believe they are in when they negotiate, who they negotiate with and what they negotiate about.

Relationships exist in time—past, present and future. Each relationship has a history from the past (you feel a "debt" of some kind for past kindnesses or "badnesses"). It also has a present state (the degree of likely beneficial reciprocation between the parties) and future prospects (the likelihood of future benefits). These states of a relationship influence the acceptability of a proposed negotiated outcome.

RELATIONSHIPS

Where there is no history of a relationship—two strangers—and no expected future for one—a one-off transaction—the whole of the negotiation process exists solely in the present, though experiences in the past may influence a negotiator's attitudes to the kind of problems addressed by the one-off negotiation. In these circumstances a tendency to red biases in behavior predominates. This is, for instance, the normal situation faced by a price haggler.

When there is an emphasis on the expectations of the future of the relationship—future long-term sales, a future partnership (courting?)—blue biases in behavior tend to predominate. Certainly this corresponds to the behavior of sales negotiators—and courting couples!

When there is a previous relationship between the parties, their prevailing behavioral biases depend on the history of their relationship.

At the extreme, people with a long experience of each other's mendacity or violence are likely to be red biased in their behavior when they interact. Public examples of extreme red behavior in intractable disputes abound— Palestine Liberation Organization v Israel; republicans v unionists in Northern Ireland; divorcing couples, and such like.

People with a long experience of each other's beneficence, including delivering on promised obligations plus evidence of trustworthiness, are likely to be blue biased in their behavior.

Public examples do not abound of the behavior of people in strong partnerships who practice the unruffled resolution of disputes between friends, because they are usually less newsworthy than the other kind.

Where a dispute erupts between former friends that overwhelms their past relationships, it becomes newsworthy if it attracts salacious commentary. "Hell hath no fury like a partner scorned...", for example.

In each case, the negotiators' behavior is dependent on how they perceive the relationship (if there is one). If perceived relationships tend to guide current behaviors this means that the state of a relationship—including the lack of one—tends to entrench current behaviors.

The average negotiator, therefore, is a prisoner of their perceptions—they react rather than determining their negotiating behavior on the basis of their interests. This falls far short of what is required to give a negotiator a negotiating edge.

What can negotiators do when they do not wish to be the prisoners of their disappointments or unfullfillable hopes in their relationships but want, instead, to have more freedom in how they might choose to behave? This is a highly practical question for those who are trying to improve their negotiating performance.

MULTIPLE-ISSUE TRADES

In the price haggle there is a single issue. Most negotiations, however, involve multiple issues; some issues may be quantitative, others not.

When multiple issues are taken together as a package, the negotiating problem does not lend itself to a haggle. It is essential to trade across and between the multiple issues.

Of course, if the multiple issues are taken separately, one at a time and in isolation from each other, this forces you to haggle over each issue. Negotiators who fall into the trap of single-issue haggles severely constrain their opportunities for mutually beneficial trades, particularly when they combine this failure with reactive red or blue behavioral biases.

Relying on red positional warfare by playing a so-called hard game to force other negotiators to move from their declared positions, while resisting their pressure on you to do likewise, reduces your negotiation strategy to a series of separate red-style haggles, in which your tactical aim is to make the other party move more often, and in bigger steps, than you do.

Alternatively, resolute purple negotiators trade to a solution from their initial positions on the issues by trading movement on one or more issues in exchange for movement by the other negotiator on other issues.

Purple trades

While this is still a zero-sum outcome, like the red haggle, on individual issues (because what one negotiator gains the other loses), it is now a non-zero-sum outcome across *all* of the issues (because what one of them loses on some issues is compensated for by what they gain on others).

On some of the issues, purple negotiators move closer to their pre-planned limits, perhaps even beyond them, and on some other issues they remain closer to their opening positions. But the net sum of their traded movements across multiple issues defines the purple package bargain that, considering all of the circumstances, they are prepared to accept as a solution to their negotiating problem.

When—as is normal—the negotiators prioritize all of the negotiable issues differently, purple negotiators trade larger movements on their lower-priority issues for smaller movements on their higher-priority issues.

In principle, numerous possible purple solutions, comprised of various combinations of traded movements across the issues, are available. Purple trading is a safe and robust method for iterating towards possible solutions.

Why posture on positions, or follow strategies of forcing the decision by the lotteries of red posturing or blue submitting, when purple proposals for multiple exchanges are possible?

After training and with practice, purple trading by negotiation is an easily applied method of ensuring the exploration of potentially satisfactory outcomes.

RED DEMANDS VERSUS BLUE OFFERS

Whenever anybody makes **demands** on you without reciprocating with an **offer** of something that you want in exchange for what they want, they behave in a red manner.

RED DEMANDS

Red negotiators want something for nothing. Red demands are one-sided. The red negotiator demands only what they want and, if they think about it at all, they would probably argue in their defense that it is up to you to make clear what you want. Their red attitudes lead them to believe that if you fail to assert your requirements that is your lookout.

The red negotiator is unconcerned with you or your requirements and accepts no criticism of the one-sided nature of the deal they propose. It is not an exchange of something for something but an exchange of something for nothing—you get nothing, they get something.

But everything you ever want is in truth a red demand—because wanting something for ourselves comes before we realize that the best way to get what we

Exhibit 28   Red demands and blue offers

Red demands

"You will deposit an irrevocable performance bond of $2 million in a bank of our choice and subject only to our discretion on when it is drawn down."

"The copyright of all materials created for this project will be vested solely in our company."

"If we cancel the program at seven days' notice, no liability for cancellation fees will be entertained; if you cancel the program for any reason at any time, compensation for the inconvenience will be paid by your company to ourselves at our sole discretion as to the amount."

Blue offers

"OK, we will agree to two years' warranty."

"How about we pay all associated costs of the transfer?"

"We never make any claims to intellectual property rights."

---

want is to offer something in return to whoever has what we want. The baby's cry precedes the adult's offer to trade.

Though you might learn (eventually!) to accept that you will have to exchange something to get what you want, when you demand what you want by itself and on its own, what you want expresses the red side of your negotiating persona, because what you want is for yourself alone.

Demanding something for yourself without offering something in return is unlikely to endear you to the listener. You may feel comfortable with such an attitudinal stance (who cares about endearment?), but you are unlikely to get what you want if the person who has it also has the power to resist your demands.

As a negotiating stance against blue givers, one-sided red demands are effective. If, however, you are dealing with purple traders not blue givers, you are going to have to do something other than make one-way demands on the other party.

In contrast, when you offer something to somebody and fail to make a demand for something in return, you behave in a submissive blue manner.

BLUE OFFERS

Blue submissives give something for nothing, or for much less than they could expect to get for it if only they behaved differently. Often they feel they have no choice but to submit, because they are intimidated into doing so.

Blue offers are one-sided. They mirror the one-sided demands of the red negotiator.

Unassertive blue negotiators deliver to other people what they want at the cost of neglecting their own wants. But everything you ever offer to anybody else is a blue gift because learning to give is our first lesson in being "nice". Giving, socially and morally, is an advance on the selfish habit of taking, but it is only our first step in learning to trade.

Though you might hope that you will get something in exchange for giving the other party what they want, your one-way offer expresses the blue side of your negotiating persona.

Offering something to some other person may endear you to them and you may feel morally comfortable about this (doesn't an act of charitable giving make you feel better, if only momentarily?), but you are unlikely to get what you want in return, unless they are feeling beneficent. When they get something for nothing, they may not feel required to reciprocate—otherwise they did not get it for nothing!

As a negotiating attitudinal stance, blue give-aways are not efficient, unless you are dealing with another blue giver. If you aren't, because they are red players and you want something from them in return, you are going to have to do something more than offer them one-way free gifts.

Those negotiators who conform to the stereotypes of the "hard" or "soft" bargainer operate in a very narrow range of strategic behavior: the hard bargainer relies on somebody softer giving in, and the soft bargainer relies on somebody harder taking less.

If being "hard" or "soft" is all the choice negotiators have, it is sensible to play a different game. If you can't beat them and don't care to join them, it makes sense to play something different. Because the choices open to negotiators are wider than the dead ends of taking or giving, the remedy for red or blue behavior is **purple conditionality**.

PURPLE CONDITIONALITY

The situation of the negotiator faced with making singular red demands or unilateral blue offers is much like the situation of any person faced with a daily need to ingest the elements sodium and chlorine.

By themselves, sodium and chlorine are not safely ingestible, though without them both your body would be in trouble in a few weeks. Nature's way of assuring you of a supply of sodium and chlorine is through a compound of both, commonly known as table salt (sodium chloride), which is only safely digestible in small doses.

Likewise, your red wants can be combined with your blue offers into purple proposals, in a perfectly sound combination, known as the principle of purple conditionality.

Indeed, the purple format of proposals is the only safe way to make proposals in a negotiation and it is notably robust in all circumstances.

By linking your red demands to your blue offers, using the **If–then** format (Exhibit 29), you retain control of your proposal because the listener cannot have one part of it (your offer) without also accepting the other part (your condition).

If–then

Exhibit 29   The purple format of conditionality

What you want	What you offer in return
If you give me	*Then* I will give you
Your red side +	Your blue side

= Purple conditionality

The condition and the offer are inextricably bound together because your red condition is always linked by an If–Then proposal format to your blue offer.

It is not a question of being solely red or solely blue but of how they are joined together. You can be very red in your condition—you demand a lot from them—and stingy in your blue offer—you offer very little in return.

Or you can be only lightly red in your condition—you do not demand very much from the other party—while being very blue in your offer—you offer a great deal to them. Many shades of purple are possible and your chosen shade in any particular negotiation is a matter of predilection, choice and circumstance.

All manner of shades of red conditions and blue offers are possible—as many as there are shades of the colors red and blue, from the deepest of imperial purples to the palest of "whimpish" blue.

Resolute purple

Nothing in the purple formulation prescribes the content of what is acceptable as a proposal. However, it does firmly and resolutely prescribe that it must be presented as a conditional offer only.

If the other party accepts your offer but not your condition—which they are perfectly entitled to do—you must hold back what you offer until they propose to amend your condition on terms satisfactory to you.

Let there be no room for ambiguity: explicitly and resolutely, **if they reject your condition, they don't get your offer.**

If they reject the offer, you may amend the condition if it suits you to do so, by making it tougher in your favor in

Exhibit 30   A proposal exchange sequence

Lender: "If you were to improve the interest charge then I might consider lowering the security the bank requires."

Borrower: "By how much must I improve the interest rate?"

L: "At least 80 basis points."

B: "If you reduce the security level by returning $250,000 of my share certificates, then I might consider accepting a higher interest charge."

L: "How much higher?"

B: "45 basis points."

L: "If you made that 65 basis points, then I could return $180,000 of your share certificates."

B: "Make that $200,000 then I'll go to 68 basis points, and we have a deal."

(The usual wording between the statements has been omitted.)

exchange for making your offer more favorable to them.

You may also amend your condition or your offer and re-present your amended proposal for their consideration, or you can withdraw both condition and offer.

This resolute purple method sets out the boundaries for a deal, because any changes in your offer are inextricably tied together with changes in your conditions, and vice versa.

If the other party doesn't like your proposal, you can ask them for their suggestions and then debate what they offer to you and their conditions for your getting it. This way, using the red + blue = purple conditionality format (Exhibit 29), whenever you make any proposal in a negotiation you cannot be ambushed, nor will you be subject to creeping concession grabbing.

In summary, you get what you want on their terms, or they get what they want on your terms, or you both get some combination of what you both want on terms satisfactory to both of you.

The solution does not have to be an outcome from hell. Most negotiations provide solutions to disputes without the traumas associated with the stereotypical positional posturing alluded to by some critics of negotiation. Indeed, in practice most people produce negotiated outcomes that both parties can enthusiastically endorse and implement.

It's not all doom and gloom for negotiators out there!

HANDLING ALL BEHAVIORS

The purple conditionality principle allows for an economy of responses to any color of behavior that comes across the table, because you respond in an identical If–Then format to all of them.

This has a significant advantage. It does not require complex personality analyses, convoluted tactical ploys or high-tension risky choices.

Behavior is more reliable as a guide to a negotiator's intentions than any explanations for, or interpretations of, their attitudes and beliefs. Behavior tells you what the other negotiator is about.

If their behavior hides rather than reveals their game, your own purple behavior continues to protect you whatever they do.

When they exhibit an open red style of behavior, their one-way, exploitive intentions are fully revealed.

Where open red behavior causes discomfort for you, as can be the case with "difficult" negotiators, you neither match nor contrast. You do not allow your behavior to be determined by other people's behavior.

You respond on all occasions and in all circumstances with purple conditionality, saying, in effect:

"You will get absolutely nothing from me unless and until I get something from you."

For you it is a traded solution, not a one-way street.

It is the traded deal in the If–Then format that determines the acceptability of the proposed solution, not the state of the other party's behavior prior to presenting it.

And if they don't present it the If–Then format, you certainly will, perhaps by responding to their one-way deal—a demand only—with questions along "WIFM" lines—"What's in it for me?"

WIFM

If they don't satisfy you on WIFM, you must supply the answers yourself by reformulating their one-way proposals into purple conditional proposals and putting your price on what they reveal that they want.

Now, using the purple principle to deal with difficult negotiators is clear cut and I have experienced little resistance from practitioners when they are advised to respond in this manner. But purple conditionality does not just apply when dealing with difficult negotiators—it applies to all negotiators.

PURPLE CONDITIONALITY FOR ALL NEGOTIATORS

Not all red negotiators are open about their intentions. The difficult ones are easy to spot, but many red negotiators are not so obvious. They can be less overt, even chillingly cold and quietly spoken, than the all too obvious loud-mouths who bluster and attempt to dominate.

To the extent that their demeanor is sufficiently open to be noticed—and looking into the snake eyes of a quietly spoken red player is enough to disturb anyone—you must treat them, as you would their blustering cousins, as red-style negotiators.

Some red-style negotiators can be quietly devious (or, as we say in Scotland, sleekit!) and can successfully hide their red intentions—that's why they are devious.

These devious negotiators are among nature's cheats and scoundrels and, because they are accomplished liars, you mostly don't realize until it's too late the kind of behavior you were dealing with. You and your interests need protection from such people.

Some negotiators are not intentionally devious. At least, that is not what they set out to be. It just happens that circumstances arise in the negotiation where an opportunity to be quietly devious presents itself, and they can't help themselves. Like Oscar Wilde, they can resist everything except temptation.

Again, you and your interests need protection from these people and your protection comes from the consistent application of purple conditionality.

Protecting yourself

As you don't know for certain which people are the career cheats and which have simply found it unexpectedly worthwhile to park their conscience, you do not allow that false friend, appearances, a free rein over your behavior. That would be a sure-fire way to gain unwanted experience!

What you do instead is present and re-present all proposals—yours and theirs—in the If–Then purple conditional format. That immediately protects you from the devious.

You insist on trading with, not conceding to, that "nice and polite" negotiator who assured you that she believes in motherhood, apple pie and Santa Claus and claims that she helps little old ladies across the street.

Soft blue negotiators

What of the soft blue negotiator who gives rather than takes and is prey to red sharks of all kinds? This is the real test of your commitment to purple conditionality.

Think about the problem you have with red-style negotiators and ask why it is that they proliferate in most societies. We can discount moral failures and personality disorders, but something clearly encourages red behavior. That something has a great deal to do with the success of red-style behavior for certain people.

Bullying, for some people, mostly pays. Because enough people give in to intimidation, or are prone to being cheated, some negotiators commit to intimidatory red styles of behavior (open or devious) as their main approach.

Interestingly, the aggrieved victims of red behavior imitate those who successfully intimidated them (at least that is the most common explanation for being red that I hear from these people).

So, now you have a blue submissive across the table—a live one—and you must decide what to do.

If you are in a position to get something for nothing, can you resist the temptation? If you can't, you behave like a devious red, which makes you a devious red!

If you apply a little pressure to get more from the submissive, you behave like an overt red, which also makes you an overt red.

These behaviors do not only happen to someone else—they also happen to you.

I have asked thousands of negotiators if they have ever behaved in a red manner and I have never (yet) come across anybody who has denied that they have behaved red on occasion.

Everyone behaves red sometimes

Why? Because negotiating behaviors are not hard-wired into your brain. Your behavior is driven both by attitudinal predilection and circumstance and controlling it takes a great deal of practice.

The trained negotiator applies the purple conditionality principle to soft blue negotiators too. This behavior trains the soft blue negotiator in purple trading and serves your interests by reducing the number of soft blue negotiators who are vulnerable to the red play of others.

If you like, regard this as a "social service" on your part to all negotiators on your part.

The fewer soft blue negotiators there are, the harder it is for red players to flourish and, therefore, the fewer flourishing red players, the more opportunities you have for finding purple traded outcomes.

Lastly, and briefly, there are assertive blue negotiators who have learned to trade using purple conditionality.

Assertive blue negotiators

Meeting one of them is good news. The outcome is

going to be based on a traded exchange presented in the purple conditionality format.

Assertive purple negotiators recognize each other by their mutual insistence on conditionality. An assertive purple negotiator would not expect you to behave differently and the exchange of purple conditional proposals is how you both behave when negotiating.

So, by preference, If–Then purple conditionality dominates your negotiating behavior against all-comers.

As you are not required to change your behavior when dealing with either red or blue behavioral styles, and as these styles cover all behaviors found in negotiation, you can be confident that the consistent application of purple behavior copes with whatever behavior comes across the table.

If–Then purple conditionality dominates all forms of negotiating behavior, which is why so much emphasis must be placed on it by those who want to do better than average.

Continual practice leads to continual improvement and as you only have the one purple format to practice, you can quite rapidly reach a relatively high standard in proposing and bargaining.

SUMMARY

Red and blue behaviors are extremes and most negotiators exhibit various shades of red and blue in their negotiating behaviors in pursuit of their results.

Relationships also affect behavior, depending on the situation and the extent to which their intensity modifies the drive for pure results. The past history of a relationship fosters red attitudes when the relationship has had negative impacts on your interests, and blue attitudes when it has been beneficent.

Aspirations for the future of a relationship tend to foster blue attitudes, as seen in the normal behavior of trained sales negotiators.

When there is no past relationship and no expectation

of a future relationship, this situation tends to foster the red attitudes of suspicion and distrust, as is commonly found in haggling.

Negotiation is not merely a haggle written larger. Negotiation does not in most cases confine itself to a dispute over a single issue. Multi-issue bargaining is the norm, not the exception. Separating issues to treat them individually as haggles or keeping the issues linked to facilitate a trade is, however, the key strategic choice for your negotiating behavior.

Negotiation is possible because people have different preferences or priorities across a number of negotiable issues and, even when their initial positions show an identical preference ordering, an outcome can be negotiated from traded movements of varying distances from their initial opening positions towards their final positions.

The possible packages of movements across the issues can sufficiently compensate the parties who have moved, to produce a mutually agreed settlement, without forcing the negotiators to change their priorities.

Where negotiators have different priorities for the issues, they trade positions on lower-valued issues for movements by the other negotiator on higher-valued issues.

If the net sum of all traded movements improves someone's situation compared to the existing situation before they negotiate, they are likely to agree to a settlement, all other things being equal. If it doesn't, they are likely to decline to settle.

All demands are red in nature and all offers are blue. The purple conditionality principle requires that all proposals and bargains are stated in an If–Then format, ensuring that every iteration of movement is conditional.

If the condition is met then the offer is delivered. The two are inextricably linked—the other party can't have the offer without accepting the condition.

Purple conditionality handles all shades of behavior common to negotiation. Overt red, devious red, soft blue and assertive blue behavior styles are handled with the common proposing or bargaining format of If–Then:

Nobody, no matter how they behave, gets anything from you unless and until you get something from them.

ANSWERS TO SELF-ASSESSMENT 8

1

(a) No. Negotiating involves multiple issues.

(b) Same error as (1).

(c) Yes. Nothing is agreed until everything is agreed.

2

(a) Yes we can! We can trade movements on some issues for larger/smaller movements on others.

(b) No. We don't have to want the same things.

(c) No. We don't have to want different things.

(d) No. We don't have to have the same intensities of preference.

3

(a) No. That is a false choice.

(b) No. Sounds attractive but isn't.

(c) Yes, in the form of purple conditionality.

11 *Proposing*

1 A union leader interviewed on television made a passionate case that if only the management would return to the negotiation table and "show some flexibility", he had no doubt that the bitter strike "would be settled in a matter of hours". Did he mean that:

(a) The union was ready to make some concessions?

(b) The management must make concessions?

(c) If the management made some concessions then the union would too?

2 In an effort to conclude the negotiations, the seller offered to cut her prices by 10 percent and drop the pre-payment demand. Which statement would be most likely to achieve her objective?

(a) "OK. We'll cut our prices by 10 percent but we must be paid 30 days after delivery."

(b) "If we drop out prices by 10 percent and allow 30 days' credit, can you confirm the order of 1000 units?"

(c) "If you confirm the order of 1000 units, we will reduce prices by 10 percent and allow you 30 days' credit."

---

3 A relatively inexperienced negotiator wanted to make a proposal and played around with different wording. Which of the following was recommended by her boss?

(a) "If you agree to consider a warranty clause covering a shorter period, then we will accept liquidated damages of 5 percent."

(b) "If you agree to a warranty clause covering six months, then we will consider accepting some level of liquidated damages."

---

*I*N negotiation, language is everything. What you say and how you say it have a decisive impact on how it is received and to what it leads.

Language is crucial in the proposing and bargaining phases. Because they are in seamless contact with debate behavior (question a proposal and you return to debate; follow a signal and you move to proposing), care taken over the form, tone and content of your language distinguishes the skilled purple negotiator from the average red or blue negotiator.

Language is crucial

The language of pure **debate** is benignly interrogatory. You exchange information and seek to uncover the other party's interests, wants and positions and to disclose yours (without revealing, of course, how far you might move).

Ideally, the language of **proposing** is assertive as you define the terms of the exchange (what you require for what you might be prepared to offer). Of course, what happens in everyday practice can be a long way from the ideal. But the ideal is a benchmark. The consequences of sloppy language—and tone—when making or responding to proposals can be seen where the parties are unassertive and soft blue.

Many negotiators are unaware of the qualitative change in the degree of assertiveness which may be appropriate during a purple debate that leads towards a proposal and the degree that is required when making a purple proposal. Partly, this is because signaling rewards subtlety, not assertiveness, yet assertive language, not subtlety, is essential to the presentation of a proposal.

Degree of assertiveness

Exhibit 31   Examples of submissive proposals

"How about we make it 10 percent?"

"We'll make it 60:40 in your favor."

"No problem."

"If we uplift, can you pay some of our costs?"

"It'll be tough to meet that deadline but, OK, we'll give it a go."

"Phew ... can you at least feed our crews on their arrival?"

"I hope you can meet that deadline."

"We were hoping to include a liquidated damages clause."

It is very easy to slip from language like "it may be possible in some circumstances to circumvent the need for on-site inspection" (a purple signal) to "OK, we'll forgo on-site inspection" (a submissive blue attempt at a proposal). Signals have to be nursed and submissive language is inappropriate for transforming signals into assertive proposals.

Some people feel that switching from the softer tones of signaling to the more assertive tones of proposing is too abrupt a departure from the relative "sweetness and light" of constructive debate. At workshops, some negotiators admit to being reticent to make the switch. They feel that having cooled down a rough debate by subtle signaling, it is not a good idea to "heat" it up again by using what they see as the "harsher" language of assertive conditionality.

Yet, observation and experience show that submissive proposal language leads to poorer deals than are

Exhibit 32   Examples of assertive proposals

> "If you make it a 10 percent discount, then we will order in lots of 100,000."
>
> "If you agree to deduct our set-up costs from the gross, then we'll agree to a 60:40 split in the net profits in your favor."
>
> "If you pay our costs, then we could consider uplifting it ourselves."
>
> "If you pay our premium hourly overtime rates then we'll go for that deadline."
>
> "We require you to feed our crews on arrival."
>
> "If you meet that deadline then we can consider giving you the work."
>
> "If you include a liquidated damages clause then you are eligible to be awarded the contract."

necessary. Once submissive blue language becomes the norm, the blue proposer, like a supplicant, seeks the permission of the other party to formulate their own proposals. Sure, it can work, provided that the other negotiator is not exploitive of your submissive blue style. However, purple negotiating practice requires a more general applicability than only working if the other person, fortuitously, is of like blue style and outlook to you. Proposal language is always more effective if it is assertive and conditional.

Less assertive language includes asking **question-proposals** instead of making proposal statements. What should be stated as "If you ... Then I" becomes, usually without thinking, "If we ... will you?"

The effect of a question is to weaken the assertiveness of the proposal because it is akin to asking permission. It

Question-proposals

is more of a tentative plea and is usually treated as such. "Will you?" question-proposals might seem to be "nice" and courteous, but their impact is to invite a negative response like: "I'd love to, but I can't afford to", or another similar excuse.

Question-proposals originate in the error of presenting your offer before your condition, instead of always presenting your condition first and then your offer.

"If you" (your condition) should always precede your offer ("then I") because this ensures that you state the price (what they must do for you) before you state what you will do for them.

Try stating any proposal the other way round (telling them what you will do for them before telling them what you want them to do for you) and you will find that you slide from an intended statement to a question inadvertently. If the "I" comes before the "you" it is almost always bound to end up as a question.

"If I do this for you" leads inevitably to "Will you do this for me?"

True, you have a condition linked to an offer (which is correct) but they are linked as a question (which is incorrect). Of course, an offer linked to a condition, even if it is also a question, is better than an offer not linked to a condition. To avoid this error some care in your language is called for.

Negotiators who "wish", "hope", and "would like", mislead their listeners. If you would only "like" something to happen, it cannot be anything of great importance to you and it is likely to be treated as such by your listeners. This causes resentment when you hear their response.

When what you regard as crucial to your happiness is apparently not treated with the degree of seriousness you think it deserves, you have only yourself to blame because you buried it in overly unassertive language. The message you sent was not the one received and if the listener is only slightly more assertive than you, let alone outrageously red and aggressive, they will be inclined to demand a higher price for exchanging what you want from them.

Assertive purple negotiators use language that states clearly what they "need", "require", and "must have". You are not being aggressive by stating clearly what you want instead of merely hinting at it. You sound more confident because you are more confident and, because the message is clearer to your listeners, it is taken more seriously by them.

Some people say that assertive language is off-putting and alienates the listener. Having got the attention of someone, the last thing you need is to upset them! But almost anything can be said in a manner that rubs at least one listener up the wrong way.

Actors can demonstrate that anything can be said in any manner. I once listened to two famous actors reciting, in Shakespearean style, names and addresses randomly picked from a telephone directory. The entire audience, me included, fell about, tears streaming down our faces, in humorous ecstasy!

Haven't we all been angered at some time by somebody's mode of speech? And when they repeat what they said later, to deny they spoke brusquely, using a tone far removed from the one we heard, our denial of their innocence is as warm as our resentment at their fantasies.

Assertive language is an everyday, perfectly normal experience that is so familiar you probably never think about it. When shopping, for instance, you do not react negatively to the seller placing price tags on their goods. The tag tells you that if you want the item concerned, then you must pay the price stated on the tag. If you do, you can take the item home, otherwise it stays in the store (I ignore the legal semantics that a price tag is merely an offer to "treat").

I have never observed anybody in a store cringing in anger at "assertive" price tags on goods, though I have watched people boil over in irritation when the check-out clerk does a price check. The well-known reaction to half-hidden small print suggests that people do not like less than clear confirmation of what something will cost. What would they say if they had first to select items and then wait at the checkout for their prices to be attached?

Some soft blue sellers are embarrassed by their prices and try to steer clear of mentioning them. When forced to mention them, they wrap their replies in such mealy mouthed verbiage that they are embarrassed by the price they were hoping to get. Naturally, if you are embarrassed by your prices, red buyers might as well ease your embarrassment by offering to pay you less! This is what happens when you use unassertive language when proposing.

An assertive proposal is like a clearly written price tag—it tells the other party clearly what they must pay, if they want to acquire your goods. A purple proposal tells them what they must do (the condition) if they wish you to do something for them (the offer). Assertive language assists in identifying possible decisions you could make.

TENTATIVE PROPOSALS

You can negotiate how people behave but not what they believe.

Fights, arguments and debates cannot be negotiated. You cannot negotiate opinions, beliefs, emotions, feelings, principles, attitudes and "facts", though all of these play a part (sometimes too big a part!) in a negotiation discourse.

You can coerce people, for instance, into asserting that they have changed their opinions (dictatorships intimidate people into not expressing dissenting opinions at all), but as nobody can see inside anybody's heads, dictators can never be sure that your assertions are genuine (which accounts for their paranoia).

You can negotiate the express wording of a professed belief or policy, or accept the chosen wording by a system of voting, but this does not mean that you have changed your mind on what you believe—it may be prudent to accept the majority's wording, or you can join a schism (a not uncommon experience among sectarian "true believers").

SMALL ISSUES, BIG TROUBLE

- The Vietnam–United States peace talks became bogged down on the deceptively difficult issue of the shape of the table. The United States perceived that there were four parties in the talks—the North Vietnamese, the Vietcong, the South Vietnamese and the United States; the North Vietnamese saw two—themselves and the United States. A four-sided table was politically inappropriate as it mirrored US perceptions. Eventually a compromise was made and a round table was carried in, thus eliminating the issue of how many "sides" were involved.

- The Iraqi and Iranian delegations to the peace talks to end their war had a different problem. These talks were held under the auspices of the United Nations Secretary General. If the parties were to sit on opposite sides of the table then eye contact between them was inevitable and contrary to their cultural imperatives. The solution was to place two rectangular tables in a "V" shape so that the delegations would only have eye contact with the UN Secretary General, who sat at the "open mouth" end. In this way the delegations did not have to look at each other.

- When a group of social workers disputed with the management about a staff grading scheme, they met with the city's director of social work to negotiate a solution. But they adamantly refused to negotiate with him when he set out the room in the normal manner in which social workers facilitate disputes between troublesome "clients". These special seating arrangements are designed to remove the "confrontational" overtones of disputants facing each other across a table. In the social worker's model arrangements there are no tables, only low chairs, which are set out in a circle, with everybody able to see each other at a glance. The social workers on this occasion demanded that the room was changed for the negotiation with their boss, plus they demanded to sit behind a large table at normal height, with them on one side and the boss on the other. They "had come for a confrontation"(!) on a matter of great importance to them and they did not want what they described as their profession's "manipulative crap".

You can only negotiate proposals, preferably in the purple conditionality format, though you might get away with something slacker if the other negotiator is as careless as you are. Negotiations are about making decisions and proposals are the tentative content of a negotiated decision.

Indeed, until something is proposed, the negotiation proper has not begun. Preparation and debate are merely a prelude to the unique behavior that characterizes a negotiation. Up to then, your preparation and debate behavior is little different from what you would contribute to a review meeting or general discussion. Nothing really happens in negotiation until the parties become aware of the possible decisions that they could make.

Proposing is the crux of negotiation

This makes proposing the crux of negotiation. When you make and consider proposals you no longer merely debate a problem—you move towards a jointly agreed solution. This is why proposing and bargaining are distinct phases in the process.

Proposals are tentative solutions to the problem(s) that necessitate negotiated solutions. Proposals can be on fairly minor matters, such as the venue for the meeting, the duration of a session, the seating arrangements, the identities of the participants, even the arrangements for ventilation. In some contexts these minor matters have undue significance, though they may not be trivial to those involved at the time.

Proposals are exchanged both informally and formally. The former tend to be about the arrangements and timing of sessions (and adjournments), though they can be of substance too in "off-the-record corridor" discussions, while the latter tend to be on matters of substance and subject to myriad local conventions.

But the main characteristic of proposals is their **tentative** nature. This expresses itself in the language of a proposal and the extent to which the negotiators adhere to the language determines their effectiveness.

Observation and experience suggest that negotiators who take care with the way in which they propose do better than those who don't. Shambolic rambles that bury the contents of the proposal in verbiage and wandering *ad hoc* commentary both lose their impact. They invite disregard for your seriousness and are treated with appropriate derision. Given the importance of proposals, they should always be treated with due care and attention.

Proposals progress best by changing from outright vagueness towards increasing conditional specificity. They can be extremely tentative to begin with, becoming less tentative as they are amended by debate. Like signals— that most tender of hints at a proposal—they invite questioning and clarification. To that end, the purple format assists progress towards increasing conditional specificity.

Proposals consist of two elements—the condition plus the offer. Both can be couched vaguely and are best presented using an If–Then type of format:

If–Then proposals

"If you change your terms of business, then I could consider some amendments to our payment schedule."

This example illustrates a proposal that is vague both in its condition and in its offer. So far, the proposer has not specified what changes they want in the terms of business, nor have they specified what amendments they will consider in their payment schedule. It is a vague–vague proposal, because it is non-specific in the condition and in the offer.

A SHAMBOLIC RAMBLE

"Look, can't we get this settled quickly?—God knows, we've spent long enough on it already—is that the time?—I'm offering you five extra days of annual leave in place of five public holidays, though I'm quite prepared to change only three days, if you insist, but I don't see why you should—It's all the same to me, I don't get days off anyway—except for last Easter but that was only because my daughter got married on Easter Monday—cost a bloody fortune, I'll tell you—why dads have to pay for it all I don't know—Now your claims that I'm reducing your holidays are rubbish—I don't know where you got that idea from or who's stirring it up—I thought when Susan left we had got rid of our rumor monger and now she's got a baby she'll soon learn all about being inconvenienced by its demands on her time morning, noon and night—nor do I know where you get the time to print these leaflets telling such nonsense—I trust you are not using the company photocopier because it breaks down enough, thank you very much, without it being used on the few times it's working on union not company business—I couldn't get a board report printed last Friday—or was it Thursday?—anyway, these silly rumors spread like lighting—or is it wildfire?—and I spend more than enough time correcting the rumors with the facts which I've already spelled out to you endless times before—but as I said more than once I'll say it again—you will get the same number of days off as always and you can take them at any time throughout the year—except of course for Christmas, New Year and Easter Monday—which I would have thought was a great idea as it gives you flexibility—true it gives me flexibility too, but what's the point of getting a quid if there isn't also a quo?—fair's fair..."

Proposals can also be specific–vague, or specific in the condition but vague in the offer: "If you amended the penalty period from 14 to 7 days, then I could consider some amendments to our payment schedule."

This time the proposer has been specific about what they want (a reduction in the penalty period from 14 to 7 days) but they are still vague in their offer ("some" amendments), which they are only committed to "consider".

Being vague in the offer is a sure sign of a proposal.

Exhibit 33   Vague and specific proposal formats

Type	Example
Vague–vague	"If you could change the terms of business, then I could consider some amendments to our payment schedule."
Specific–vague	"If you amended the penalty period from 14 to 7 days, then I could consider some amendments to our payment schedule."

You don't have to follow a strict sequence, but observation suggests that effective negotiators do move cautiously from vagueness to specificity in their proposals. When a proposal is presented it is best to be vague because you do not know how close or how far you are from the settlement area. Jumping in with specific proposals—while not exactly outlawed—is needlessly hasty, particularly when what is proposed is influenced by the statements that each of you makes during the debate.

From vague to specific

By being tentative, you can test the water before you commit yourself. As each of you states your own proposals and amends the other's, a little vagueness smooths your deliberations.

It is essential that offers are always vague, though conditions can be either vague or specific.

Vagueness in the offer prevents ambush by the other

negotiator if, inadvertently, you go too far and become too specific. While this might seem a strange device, it is advisable. Over-shooting the other negotiator's expectations, or even their most ambitious wants, means you "pay" too much for what you want. If they grab your specific offer too eagerly you know you have gone too far. If they are careful not to appear too keen, they might use your overly generous offer to press for more ("always challenge the first offer!").

Sometimes the fear of offering too much inhibits and prolongs the negotiation, while trying to get back what you have thrown away is extremely difficult (if you are skillful enough to manage to reverse a specific offer, you might as well use your skill to avoid the error in the first place).

Between the errors of being too cautious and being overly generous, you should use vagueness in your offers, to keep open your room for maneuver until you are sure of the shape of the deal.

PURPLE RESPONSES TO A PROPOSAL

A common reaction to a proposal with which you disagree is to reject it, usually outright.

Red responses like "No way", "Never", "Out of the question", "You must be joking", "Are you serious?", and so on give a flavor of the politer forms of rejection.

Slamming the table, walking out and exchanging verbal abuse are also well-known reactions. Allowing for a little red "theater" in a negotiation is appropriate, but red theatrical behavior is time consuming and often counter-productive. In general, instant theatrical rejection is inappropriate, though not uncommon from red behaviorists.

It is far better to respond to proposals in a more positive manner, if only to welcome the fact that a proposal has been made. You do not have to agree with the contents of what they have proposed just because you welcome the fact that they have made a suggestion for a solution (assurance behavior). What has been proposed,

Exhibit 34   A vague proposal sequence

"We can't agree to that restrictive covenant."

"Why not?"

"Because as it stands it could put us out of business"

"Suppose we found another form of words, would that
      help?"

"Depends what words you include and exclude."

"OK, if you accept that you cannot build a similar
      exhibition display stand for any of our competitors
      for use in the greater Glasgow area for, say, 48
      months, then we would be prepared to consider
      commissioning you as the approved supplier for our
      exhibitions for this year."

"You will have to define what you mean by terms like
      'similar stand', 'our competitors', the 'greater
      Glasgow area', how firm your offer to 'consider' is
      and the scope of our being 'approved', and for what
      number of 'exhibitions' you are talking about. Also is
      it this calendar year or the next 12 months?"

(After some debate on these questions, a bargain is
      formulated.)

"If your list of identified competitors is accepted as
      being reasonable, and Glasgow means within the
      city boundary, and we are appointed sole supplier
      for all your exhibitions in the UK, there being not
      less than 14 of them in the next 12 months, then
      we will be prepared to build our new "Electra"
      model stand exclusively for your company for the
      same period of 12 months, and will give you first
      option to renew this arrangement for subsequent
      periods of one year at a time."

---

in principle, can be improved on, which is what you are
there for anyway.

The format of vagueness in a proposal makes instant
rejection—and instant acceptance—inappropriate. You can
hardly instantly accept something that is non-specific in
what it offers you. The other party's proposals will address

their interests before they address yours, and if they do address some of your interests at all, it will likely to be only in a partial manner, at least initially.

Your main task is to firm up their offer by questioning the vagueness of its content. What do they mean by "consider", "review", "look at again", "see what can be done", and such like? The extent to which they flesh out their meanings and make less vague the contents of their offer gives you valuable insights into their intentions.

How you verbalize your reaction to their proposal influences what happens next. Stamp on their proposal—or worse, impute malign motives to them for making one—in the usual red manner and you take the negotiations back to red argument and beyond. Some red negotiators believe in behaving this way and, if you have to deal with them, you may have to grin and bear it.

Some reputable trainers suggest that you "flinch" on receiving any proposal, presumably to convey, via your body language, that you consider that their proposal is too tough or not generous enough. Fair enough on occasion, but flinching every time you hear a proposal is bound to be as tiresome as it is predictable (and thereby discounted by those whom your flinching is supposed to impress).

It is much better for you to listen in silence to a proposal to make sure that you understand it (ask clarification questions!) and then consider the merits of its content before reacting.

Improving the offer

Is there anything in the proposal, either in the condition or the offer, that could be built on to make it more acceptable to you? Could you improve on the vagueness of their offer by making it more specific in some way to meet your requirements? Can you relax some aspects of their condition to make it more palatable to you? They expect you to do either or both, which is why they left the offer vague.

It's your job, not theirs, to improve their offer by amending or replacing what they have suggested and it is your job to challenge the conditions.

You may decide to make your own alternative proposal, probably consisting of some of what they included in theirs, but if not it's not a total calamity. If theirs is one-sided and off-track you might judge it better to start again with your version.

Research suggests, however, that too much reliance on instant counter-proposals is counter-productive because your negotiating partner feels aggrieved that you did not give their proposal proper consideration before coming back with your own. That's why asking questions about their proposal conveys a different and more acceptable message to the other party:

"Having given full consideration to what you have proposed, I want to make the following amendments to your proposal", or

"Having given full consideration to what you have proposed, I think that we could make more progress if we approach this problem from a different perspective, which is why I suggest the following..."

Alternative proposals that incorporate some parts of the other party's proposals are usually more acceptable than an entirely new proposal, but neither is as unhelpful as an outright instant rejection, especially if accompanied by the usual red theatricals.

Because some elements of the other negotiator's proposal are included, they have some claim to ownership of the joint decision that emerges from the negotiation. This is more palatable than having their work (biased towards their interests as it may be) apparently thrown out altogether. If your rejection is done without sensitive treatment and timing, you can set the negotiations back for some time.

PURPLE PACKAGING

The number of issues covered by a proposal can vary enormously, and the more issues included the less

WHO RUSHES LOSES

Two business partners were negotiating a separation of their interests—one wanted to retire and the other wanted to expand into new lines of work. Their lawyers proceeded through the contract to dissolve the partnership, clause by clause and line by line in their traditional manner.

They ended up with only one clause outstanding—the money!

As one partner was retiring, he wanted as much in settlement as he could get to fund his retirement. The other was continuing and he wanted as much capital as possible left in the business. But they had no scope for trading across clauses because their lawyers insisted that clauses that had been agreed, stayed agreed. The money was to be agreed on its merits alone (possible, perhaps, in an ideal world).

There was, however, an asymmetry in the partners' attitudes to time, which made their world less than ideal. The retiree was relaxed about the time taken for the negotiations because he only had to wait for his money (as he had enough to live on from his salary and savings he was in no hurry to settle). The other partner was frustrated because he could not start his new ventures until he had clear title to the business, so he was in a hurry to settle.

Time pressures won out. The partner remaining in the business exclaimed: "I am trying to run a business, not a seminar in negotiation tactics" and offered much more money than was justified or prudent to his erstwhile partner, who accepted the offer of a much larger amount than he had expected. He retired in affluence to read books; his erstwhile partner's books ran into difficulties, from the business being under-capitalized in a recession, and he went into receivership. The two lawyers took their usual (large) fees.

manageable they become. Keeping more than four or five issues linked together requires practice—link ten or twenty issues and you're in trouble. The alternative is to attempt to deal with them one at a time.

Draft contracts with multiple clauses are usually negotiated clause by clause. The attraction of this approach is that you can whip through a great deal of routine clauses fairly quickly, leaving more time for the "difficult" ones. In major tenders—several volumes long—linking is fraught with complexity. But the downside of separating the issues must be acknowledged and you should be alert to the difficulties that separation provokes.

Linking and separating

For a start, separating the clauses isolates potential tradables and prevents them being used to secure better deals on issues that are important to you. If all your movement is confined to one clause at a time only, you stand or fall on whatever you can extract from that clause. Instead, with some judicious linking, you could secure movement on this clause for agreeing to move on that other clause, which might be of particular significance to the other side though less so to you.

A compromise between the two approaches of linking and separating is possible: you could agree to run through the clauses individually and provisionally agree what can be routinely agreed (though regularly make it clear that "nothing is agreed until everything is agreed") and then package the outstanding clauses together. As these are usually the ones that are not open to easy agreement and they require more detailed bargaining, they can form the basis for a package deal.

In a recent construction contract, the bidder agreed to every clause except four: the formula for liquidated damages, the duration and scope of the warranty, the penalties for late delivery and, typically, the price structure of the project. This gave us, in effect, the possibility of striking a mini-deal, so we sought and got the four clauses treated together as a package. We also managed to re-open some minor clauses already provisionally agreed (commitments on inspection, delivery schedules, and the allowance for technical risk) because they manifestly assisted both sides in trading across all of them to get an acceptable agreement.

SUMMARY

Language in negotiation is everything. If you tend to behave in a red or blue style, then your proposal language reflects this. If soft blue, you tend to "hope", "wish", and "would like" this or that to happen. If red, you "insist", "demand" and "will have" this or that happen. Assertive blue or purple behaviorists prefer to "need", "require" and "must have" this or that happen.

Assertive language is essential in the purple proposal phase if you intend to influence the other negotiator to take seriously your requirements for a deal to be concluded.

When you make any demand on somebody without offering something in return you are in a red mode, just as you are in blue mode when you offer something to somebody and ask for nothing in return. By themselves, red and blue styles are unimpressive to negotiators.

Together, however, they form the purple assertive conditionality style, especially when expressed in an "If–Then" format:

"If you do this for me, then I will consider doing that for you."

Purple negotiators place their conditions before their offer. They make proposal statements, rather than ask proposal questions: "If you ... then I" not "If we ... will you?"

Proposals are tentative suggestions of possible solutions—they state what you expect them to do for you in exchange for what you will consider doing for them. They consist of your red condition (what you want) and your possible blue offer (what they want). Your condition is tied inextricably to your offer. They can't have one without the other.

Proposals consist of a vague or specific condition but always a vague offer. The best response to a proposal is to question the condition or the offer, or both.

Proposals should where possible be linked to avoid getting into a zero-sum, single-issue haggle. It is more productive to be able to trade across issues in a package deal. Generally, nothing is agreed until everything is agreed.

1

(a) Unlikely. In the public relations "war" during bitter strikes the union has to keep the spirits of the strikers high and convince the public, particularly where they are inconvenienced, that it is doing its very best to find a settlement, that it is open to positive ideas from the management and that only intransigence on the management's part is inexplicably holding up a return to work. Usually they mean what they say: a return to work is conditional on the management showing "flexibility", i.e., conceding the union's claim.

(b) Yes.

(c) Unlikely. If movement was possible if reciprocated the union would hardly use a public forum to send that message to the management. They would do so privately to avoid a public and, perhaps, negative response from the management, and to avoid alerting the strikers that the union was weakening.

2

(a) Deceptively OK, except that it is a unconditional offer requiring nothing to be offered in return by the buyer. A free-gift concession, not a trade.

(b) A question-proposal which is always weaker than a statement-proposal. It asks the buyer for what the seller wants (an order of 1000 units) after announcing to the buyer what the seller will concede (10 percent price cut and 30 days' credit).

(c) Yes, much better. The bargain is conditional and the condition (demand for an order for 1000 units) is stated first, followed by the offer (10 percent price cut and 30 days' credit).

3

(a) No. This is vague in the condition and specific in the offer. The other side only has to "consider"—what does "consider" mean?—a shorter warranty clause—how short is "short"?—but she is offering a 5 percent liquidated damages obligation. They can say "thank you very much" and give nothing at all in return.

(b) Yes. This is specific in the condition ("six months") but vague ("consider") in the offer. If they accept the condition, they still do not know what they are getting in return.

12 *Purple Bargaining*

1 How might the following proposals be amended to make them assertive?

   (a) "If we agreed to foreign rights, would you accept this on a licence-only basis?"

   (b) "Your fee is slightly more than I was expecting, so could we pay it in monthly installments?"

   (c) "Would it be OK if we used our own transport?"

2 How would you amend the following proposals into a bargain format?

   (a) "If you agree to some form of bonus, then we will raise productivity by 5 percent"

   (b) "If we secure and fence the site, will you expedite the purchase date by 90 days?"

   (c) "If we receive assurances, then we will pay $100,000 against your outstanding debts."

3 You are negotiating with an airline about freight costs from Heathrow to Kuala Lumpur, Malaysia. They propose a bargain: "If you guarantee a minimum of 2000 kilos a week, then we would bring our price down to $3 per kilo." Do you:

(a) Say "Yes"?

(b) Question either the offer or the condition?

(c) Say "No"?

*U*NLIKE proposals, bargains are anything but tentative. They are specific in both condition and offer. They state what the negotiator is prepared to settle on, leaving no room for ambiguity (if there were any ambiguity it would be too tentative for a bargain).

A bargain in this sense does not mean that it is a good deal, for no judgment is implied about its content. Stores offer "bargains" in their special sales and some people rush to get them, usually spending more than they intended and effectively saving less than they think. Buying a dress in a sale that only cost $200, against a normal price of $450, allegedly saves you $250, and that is as far as most people think about the transaction. But they could have saved themselves $450 by not buying the dress at all and have been even more deliriously happy at their savings.

A purple negotiator's bargain is different. It is the explicit behavior that concludes the negotiation, i.e., what they get for what they give. In Scotland, solicitors close a negotiation by announcing that "a bargain is concluded", and so it is in our meaning of the word, which is why I use it in the four-phase approach.

Bargains are specific in the If–Then conditional format, both in the condition and in the offer:

Bargains are specific

"If you pay $250,000 to Mr Green, then Mr Green will transfer his business known as 'Green & Son' to you."

It usually best to state your condition first—because then it is not forgotten—before you state your offer. While the other negotiator wants to hear both parts of the bargain, they are naturally most interested in what you offer to them.

If your conditions are outrageous, they might switch off listening to the rest of your bargain because what you require as a condition is judged to be against their own interests. They feel they must reject it out of hand because their red theatricals require public knee-jerk reactions. Interrupting a bargain in this manner is not advised because your interruption sours their attitude towards you before you have heard what they will offer.

Negotiators who are annoyed by interruptive reactions sometimes modify their intended bargains and make them even less generous than they were before they were interrupted.

Only inexperienced negotiators feel it necessary to show by interruption that they disagree with a bargain's conditions. They allege, when questioned, that they interrupt just in case their silence is thought by the speaker to somehow legitimize the content of what they are saying. Waiting until they finish to disabuse them of such hasty notions is surely only onerous for the grossly impatient.

Saying "No" to a bargain does not end the negotiation by any means. It might send you back to purple debate or, if handled poorly, it might start an red argument or a fight. But the negotiations will continue after anything other than a walk-out (definitely neither advised nor practiced by purple negotiators).

If you don't agree—can't agree—with a bargain statement, you must continue looking for a solution until it is abundantly clear to you both that a solution does not exist because the gaps are too great. Even then, it doesn't end the negotiation completely if the parties are bound to each other in some way and the alternatives (e.g., violence, prolonged civil or family unrest, endless strike action, legal sanctions, and so on) are unpalatable. In short, negotiations continue.

A negotiator who says "Yes" to a bargain closes the negotiation. There is nothing left to negotiate if agreement has been reached.

You then write up what has been agreed and the negotiation is over. (The above bargain with Mr Green is deliberately left extremely brief for presentation purposes only—I acknowledge that the transfer of a business for anything like $250,000 would require the written agreement to contain much more specific detail.)

The language of the bargain is conditional (If–Then, or similar wording) and the offers and conditions are specific in every detail. Leaving gaps in meaning is disastrous for implementation and long before a bargain is concluded, prudent negotiators will have exercised what is known as "due diligence" in examining every detail of the transaction and the probity of all commitments that have been asserted.

Due diligence

In major business transfers, due diligence is a lucrative source of fee income for accountants and solicitors (which is why it is also a lucrative source of damages when the professionals fail to give the transaction the diligence that it was due!).

NEGOTIATING A PURPLE BARGAIN

Not all bargains are acceptable.

Some bargains are proposed when negotiations commence and their non-acceptance in the exact form in which they are first offered is assumed. A negotiator may submit her detailed and specific proposal in correspondence to the other party before meeting with them to discuss what they propose. A company replying to a request for a proposal (RFP), a union making a demand for a wage increase, an insurance company responding to a claim, or a lawyer writing to a person who is deemed by their client to have caused them distress are all examples of negotiators opening with their bargain.

While bargaining is the fourth of the four phases, it by

no means has to wait until the other three phases are completed.

The four phases are not necessarily contiguous in time. The proposed bargain can come before the other phases in the sequence, but the act of concluding a bargain closes the negotiation (as does the final act of refusing to do a deal on the offered terms).

Bargaining can occur at any time

Because bargains are stated in specific terms it is normal that, whatever order they were proposed in, the stated bargain is either accepted or is subject to further negotiation.

You can ask questions of any aspect of the bargain: you may challenge the conditions—what they want from you—or their offer—what you get if you say "Yes". But because the bargain is stated in specific terms, some people find it a great deal easier to be more assertive in this phases than when they are tentatively proposing. When bargaining is undertaken towards the end of a negotiation, the "decision crisis" (as Anne Douglas pointedly described it) approaches with an edge of finality in its language.

The shape of the bargain emerges as the parties edge towards (or even away from) each other. Phrases are exchanged like: "So, what you are offering is..."; "OK, I get the picture..."; "Let me be clear, you want... x....for...y..."; "If I understand what you want ..."; "Here's how I see the deal..."; and "To sum up, in return for ..y...I'll agree to ...z..."

Negotiators have the choice of saying "Yes", or continuing to try to improve the bargain by changing the conditions or changing the offer. They usually do so somewhat speedily.

Negotiators may appear more alert and show this in their body language—often sitting up and leaning on to the table. Unlike in the proposal phase, negotiators in the bargaining phase tend to feel the pressure of time. The whole phase can move swiftly, with counter-bargains exchanged without a great deal of attention given to the proprieties of timely consideration of each other's suggestions.

Whereas instant counter-proposals are insensitive of the proposer's sensibilities in the proposal phase, counter-bargains are much more acceptable in the late bargaining phase—even mandatory when the deal is so close it would be pointless to drag out the final wording of the deal.

In amending proposals, you are still trying to influence the possible shape of the deal; in amending a bargain, you are specifying the explicit wording you prefer for the deal. There is much greater commitment in the late bargaining phases than there is when an early proposal is still sufficiently vague to permit wide-ranging discourse on its uncommitted content. Bargains are so specific that earlier commitments are embodied in its wording.

If a bargain is rejected, or not yet accepted, in the later stages of the phase, you can go back to the debate phase and explore what progress you can make on final details, or you can conclude that further progress is unpromising and you must now contemplate a failure to agree. You may postpone that conclusion until you are finally convinced that all the remaining gaps remain stubbornly unbridgeable.

BARGAINING LEVERAGE

In his models of competitive advantage, Michael Porter alludes to the twin bargaining powers of a firm's suppliers and its customers. These are red-style behavioral concepts.

Porter's discussion of the attributes of competitive power indicates that he intends it to mean the balance of competitive advantage in favor of one or other party in their transactions. If a supplier has the advantage in key elements of a company's value chain, and it dominates in its own markets, it will almost certainly have bargaining leverage over the customer. This means it will be able to exploit its bargaining leverage and earn higher returns than it would if it was a small supplier in the same market with no leverage.

Likewise, in some markets, customers dominate their

4:1 AGAINST IS A NEGOTIATING MOUNTAIN TO CLIMB

Harry sells specialized services to an insurance company. He was desperate to raise his fees because he was being squeezed by the rising costs of delivering his services and the insurance company's unremitting resistance to price increases (which in turn squeezed its profits).

After two unsuccessful attempts to raise his prices, Harry consulted an experienced negotiator to see if any light could be shed on his problem. He was asked: "What proportion of your supply of special services is accounted for by the insurance company?" Harry wasn't sure and said he would check (i.e., ask his assistant).

When he returned, he said it was exactly 20 percent. He was then asked: "What proportion of the insurance company's purchase of special services do you represent?" Again, Harry wasn't sure and said he would check (i.e., ask his assistant). When he returned, he said it was about 5 percent—as well as he (or more likely his assistant) could judge.

The negotiator commented that on these figures it was unlikely that Harry had much bargaining leverage on the insurance company. It could be different if the ratios were reversed.

---

suppliers—they can leverage lower unit prices, and therefore lower profits, on firms which have large market shares because of the nature of the product they sell or their competitive position within their market sector. Substitutes for their products, or the emergence of new technologies, can shift their bargaining leverage from that of near monopoly to near competitive anarchy.

In short, negotiators do not always have a neutral or benign environment in which to exercise their skills. There is a world of difference between having a queue of customers six deep and a mile long, all clamoring for your services, and needing something like a Hubble telescope to catch sight of your next customer.

People can grasp the stark facts of bargaining leverage—even people who can't spell Bob backwards give fairly shrewd assessments of who has and who dreams about having bargaining leverage.

Bargaining leverage

When you believe that the leverage works in your favor, your behavior is going to be bullish red. You are going to make red demands and demand red bargains. It has nothing to do with sentiment, nor with being fair. If the market swings in your favor, you will push for better deals, which means one-way deals in your favor. When it swings against you—as it surely will—you will have to accept worse deals: still one-way, but this time not your way!

Red behavior predominates in these situations. If you're the only game in town you decide the ante; if they are, they decide. And it doesn't take long to shift your attitudes of what is "fair", once the temptations of opportunity waft their message across your bank balance.

TENDERS

Tenders are the most common red bargaining system in business. Many reasons are advanced for tenders.

Probity, not value for money, is the main excuse in the public sector. (However, tendering adds anything up 40 percent to total costs of government purchases. If you want to find an expensive way of doing anything, get the government to pay for it!)

Market testing is the main excuse in the private sector. But the real reason for making buying decisions through tenders is that it exerts to the utmost the red buyer's leverage on vulnerable sellers.

In a tender, the seller prices their offer to supply goods or services to the buyer's specifications. They make their decisions on the basis of the invitation to tender (ITT) documentation, knowing that the rules preclude them from negotiating on what they are supplying or the price they are seeking.

Apart from the information they can glean from the

DESPERATE NEEDS NEED DESPERATE REMEDIES

A developer over-reached herself in a slower than expected speculation on land rezoning. She needed cash more than she was cautious about who she got it from.

She wanted $100,000 yesterday. She offered to take a second mortgage on a building she owned. An investor, always on the lookout for asset-rich people in need of cash, looked over her books and the property and proposed: "If you will pledge your property and give some other collateral, as the building is already mortgaged and the equity in it is insufficient to cover a loan, then I will consider advancing you $100,000 immediately." Reluctantly, she added some land she owned as collateral, which was due, she said, for re-zoning for development, as security for the mortgage.

She knew it wasn't a good deal but felt that she had no choice as she needed to pay $75,000 to a creditor immediately. She also wanted $25,000 for "expenses" in connection with the rezoning of the land. So she said "Yes". The investor said he had some "minor details to examine more closely".

The minor details proved troublesome. Until the remaining units were let, the property was below 60 percent occupied, so the investor reduced the amount he would lend from $100,000 to $80,000 with the balance paid over to her when 90 percent of the units were let. The developer said "No", none too politely, and he said he had a plane to catch in 40 minutes, which he could just do if he left immediately. She became agitated, angry and abusive, but she eventually said "Yes".

He noted that she had local taxes of $20,000 due over the coming year on her rent income and demanded that she pay the taxes monthly direct to him, so that he was assured that there would be no chance of the city seizing the property to cover her tax debt (the city having precedence over other debtors). She said "No" and he said he had a plane to catch, and having missed the earlier flight, he could catch the next one. After more tantrums, she said "Yes".

He gambled she would get the rezoning but would also go bust; she gambled she could stave off a collapse. He made money whatever happened; she risked her assets.

(Adapted from J. R. Ringer (1974) *Winning Through Intimidation*, Fawcett Crest, New York)

documents, or from experience of the business sector, they bid blind. It is meant to be a "one-shot" bid, with their "best price" to the fore. It's "quick-kill", not "hold back".

In theory, there is no room for price padding, if it's going to be a quick-kill decision. Sealed-bid tenders remove the seller's influence from the outcome once they seal their bid in its envelope. (I am keeping strictly to the theory of the bid here, and not diverting into its many variations—and lapses of "clean" conduct—that are found in practice.)

The buyers consider the bids and select the one most favorable to their interests. They are in a perfect position to exercise a red choice if you think about it. They are safe from charges of exploiting bargaining leverage because, after all, the sellers voluntarily submitted their bids, obviously quite happy with their prices and with the terms of the tender, and the buyer is only choosing from what was voluntarily offered. As it's an arm's-length transaction, there is nothing personal in it. If sellers aren't happy with the terms of the ITT they need not tender.

It doesn't always end there in practice.

Buyers "reserve the right to accept or reject any or all proposals and to negotiate for appropriate modifications". In some sectors, post-tender negotiations are mandatory, with the ITT being used as a pre-qualifying process to select a short list of possible suppliers.

The greater the value of the supplied services, the more it costs a bidder to prepare their tender, and the higher the tendering costs the more pressure there is on the remaining bidders to comply with the buyer's (often late) demands.

The costs of tendering can be enormous. Teams of estimators and tender specialists can cost hundreds of thousands, none of which may be recovered in a failed tender. The alternative to compliance is to waste their cost of tendering to get to this stage, hence the maximum pressure is felt on their pricing and their costs.

Because the costs of failed tenders must be absorbed—otherwise bidders over a run of tenders would go bust—they spread these costs across the prices of their successful bids. Buyers pay more than it costs for a service, because successful bids include the cost of selecting suppliers by tender. This raises the costs of supply, and by encouraging multiple suppliers of the same services and the costly management of drawn-out tender processes, there is a great deal of duplication in the administration of the purchasing function.

Some red buyers use a phoney tender system to force gullible sellers into reducing their prices, often below a level that is sensible for them. They use the red buyer's bargaining leverage in a tender process to great effect.

The buyer invites tenders for the supply of some specified good or service. In the tender they tighten quality, service levels and other controls to any degree that they think they can get away with. They sit on the tenders until they get calls from bidders asking about progress, or they ring them after a while. The buyer refuses adamantly to give any information about who else has tendered or how far anybody is above the price that they are looking for. All they tell bidders is that their "price is too high" and that it must come down if they are to win an order.

Some (sensible) sellers will drop out at this, not being willing (or able?) to cut their prices. Others (foolish?) rebid. The buyer repeats the process as many times as necessary, including, in an exhibition of ultimate redness, allowing the last remaining (and desperate) seller to bid against themselves under the illusion that they are still bidding against the others! Typically, red buyers defending this behavior assert that it is up to the seller at what price they rebid and it is not the proper concern of the buyer to tell them how to run their business.

PURPLE RELATIONSHIP BARGAINING

Bargaining doesn't have to be a one-way street.

A school of negotiating has developed that prefers to judge the outcome of a negotiation on the extent to which it strengthens the relationship between the parties, rather than the extent to which it serves only one side's interests. Broadly, this is a purple approach, but not one based on soft blue naivety.

The tensions between a results or a relationship orientation in negotiating have been studied for some time.

The **results** orientation is solely concerned with how the outcome rewards the red player with the measure of success to which they aspire. "What's the score?", they ask. "Am I winning?", they muse. Given their goal, their behavior is driven by a need to do whatever is necessary for them to be seen to "win"—or to "get the job done", as American football coaches put it.

Results

The **relationship** orientation is concerned with the development of the relationship between the negotiators. The measure of success is how close the parties manage to integrate their interests. "What can I do for you that makes it profitable for both of us?", they ask. "Are we succeeding?", they muse. Given their goal, their purple behavior is driven by a need to do whatever helps them to succeed together.

Relationships

Blue relationship orientations are self-defeating if applied solely by one party and not the other. They end up as classic blue submissive surrenders, driven by illusions that being "nice" for its own sake makes you and everybody you deal with "better persons".

Extreme blue players are rare, for apart from the question of their ability to sustain a sacrifice of resources for little or nothing in return. Extreme blue players, of the unilateral variety, do not endure through the brutish course of the events they encounter.

Fortunately, most negotiators are neither extreme red results nor extreme blue relationship oriented—they are mainly a mixture of both. They may predominate in one orientation over the other as they mix their orientations to suit their attitudes and experience. Left to themselves, unaware and untrained, they tend to red or blue to some degree.

Both playing blue

Purple relationship bargaining is not about discovering one's predilections and then, so to speak, coming out of the blue closet! The red–blue game shows that playing blue is not enough—it can be treacherous territory for the albeit well-intentioned player—and without considerable effort to align one's blueness with somebody else's blueness, playing blue in isolation from other people's behaviour is naive. For you to benefit from playing blue, the other party has to play blue too!

How do we arrive at such a happy state? Not without difficulty.

Remember, the somewhat dismal conclusions of the dilemma game (only 8 percent make choices that allow them to achieve a "win–win" outcome) are valid for people who play the game for the first time. Many players afterwards complain that if they had been told to play for a joint maximum in points they would have played differently. Therefore training, and personal experience of the consequences of a failure to reap the benefits of joint maximization, can raise the percentage of joint maximizing outcomes dramatically.

It is a similar thought that drives an increasing number of negotiators to look to purple relationship, instead of red results only, bargaining. But unlike a pure switch between the orientations—either all one or all the other—purple relationship bargaining must produce high results

---

A NEW START?

A producer of biochemical products was approached by one of its suppliers with a proposition that they set up an exclusive supply deal. In return for becoming the sole supplier—eliminating four other competing suppliers—it would open its books to show the unit costs and profits of the products it supplied, provided its customer did likewise and showed its revenue and profits from selling the products that resulted. It would also enter into jointly funded R&D of the products it supplied, sharing any patents that arose from this work.

---

as well as strong relationships.

If it did not produce at least as good a set of results as pure red results bargaining, purple relationship bargaining would be competed out of sight.

Advocates of purple relationship bargaining—or "supplier partnering"—claim that by reorienting bargaining partners, they can achieve impressive gains for both sides.

Mutual gains can best be achieved by bargaining in a conditional format in the developing relationship ("If you open your books, we'll open ours"). It is necessary to get away from one-way streets—red or blue—to both-way streets, or purple conditional bargaining. This lays the proper foundations for full and open relationship bargaining, in which the presumption of mutual trust and mutual servicing of each other's interests is underscored by their behaviors and not just by their mission statements.

Mutual gains

Partnering relationships reject tendering among large numbers of competitors and carefully select one supplier as a sole partner. Then they jointly examine ways in which the unit costs of supply are to be reduced, with both parties working together to improve design and delivery.

An interesting development in purple relationship bargaining is the introduction of the idea of replacing all-

Coopetition

out competition against everybody (in the Porter mold) with selective **coopetition** with suppliers and customers. (The new word coopetition, was formed by merging cooperation with competition.)

Instead of viewing everybody as a competitor, certain people with whom we do business are seen to be complementors, because the business strategies that increase their success increase our success too.

Treating complementors as if they are in a competitive power relationship with us, as in Porter's model, is inadequate as a strategy. Customers and suppliers are not competitors—the other people who supply our competitors or who are the other customers of our suppliers are our competitors. Therefore a purple negotiating relationship with our customers and our suppliers must have a different basis to the one we have with our competitors.

Coopetition creates what Nalebuf and Brandenburger call a **value net**. Complementors add value to your product. Thus, Netscape software bundled with a brand of computer hardware enhances the value of both products, and makes Netscape and that computer brand complementors.

Competitors reduce the value of your product—if a competitor sells its product to your potential customers, they value your product less because they already have a product that substitutes for yours.

Coopetition creates barriers to entry to your markets by your competitors. These barriers are higher because they are raised by your customers, not by you.

Customers who feel that they are pushed around or exploited react by seeking alternatives or protect themselves by keeping several suppliers of the same product on short leashes in case one of them grows too complacent at having all of their business. It's back to trust and vulnerability.

Coopetition changes the perspectives of business partners. It changes their negotiating behaviors too. There are mutual rewards from revealing costs, profits and market plans, normally kept commercially confidential from each other. Major dependencies of suppliers and their customers become a source of strength instead of a cause for concern about vulnerability.

Reassessing former models of competition through the value net of coopetition changes the negotiating relationships between you and your customers and suppliers. Using bargaining leverage to raise your profits from suppliers or customers may not be in your interests after all.

CLOSING THE NEGOTIATION

We negotiate in order to make a decision and then we implement the decision.

Management is about implementing decisions, not permanently negotiating them. So all decisions have a finite life: a finite time to make them and a finite time to implement them (if it doesn't matter when a decision is made or implemented, you might as well not waste time making it). This necessitates the use of **closing** behaviors to end the decision-making phases of the negotiation process and to commence the decision-implementing phases of management.

The most obvious way to end decision making by negotiation is for the parties to agree—they both say "Yes" to the bargain as it stands. If one of them says "No", they either continue searching for a solution or they terminate the negotiation.

There are several devices for precipitating the decision to agree or not to agree. These closes can be briefly outlined in ascending order of relative difficulty. Your use of them may not follow the exact formulations I have outlined, but their broad features are sufficiently distinct for you to recognize and apply them when you feel that circumstances warrant their use.

The most common bargaining close is the **summary** close. Here you simply summarize what is proposed, beginning with the details of your conditions, followed by

Summary close

the details of your offer (or in some formulations of the summary bargain, the details of your conditions are interspersed with the details of your offer because, for clarity, it is sometimes clearer to link two corresponding elements directly). Then you ask for their agreement.

If the summarized bargain is as they understand it to be and it is agreeable to them, they say "Yes". If some points need further discussion and these are sorted out to their satisfaction, they will then say "Yes". In both cases the summary of the bargain closes the negotiation. It is a simple and natural way to conclude a negotiation and it fits in neatly with the final and essential formality of agreeing what is agreed.

Adjournment close

In more complex negotiations, or in some simpler ones, where there remains some marginal differences, the **adjournment** close is appropriate. This gives the other side time and space to ponder the terms of what is on offer. By adjourning to consider the final agreement, there is an expectation that they will return with an acceptance of the bargain. If they do, they say "Yes" to the deal and the negotiation is over. If they say "No", or wish to discuss some other issues, the negotiation continues until both say "Yes" or they conclude that there is no prospect of a successful outcome.

Unions withdraw to consult with their members; managers retire to consult with their boards; peace makers adjourn to take instructions from their governments, and so on. In these contexts, the negotiators are ruled by the organizational arrangements within which they must operate.

Adjourning opens the possibility of the non-participants overturning their negotiators' recommendations and giving instructions to reject parts or all of the proposed bargain. This is the price paid for not having principals present who have the authority to settle without further reference. On the other hand, in representative negotiations that require reference back to those with the final authority, this is the only way in which these parties can negotiate.

There is no point resisting what is not resistible. The

one thing you can do as a negotiator in these contexts is to persuade (or require) that the other side makes positive recommendations about the proposed bargain when it reports back to its constituents.

Of course, not being present at their report-back sessions, you have no way of knowing if they do so with alacrity, or if they just go through the motions of doing so. Making a recommendation in a dead-pan tone, or without any enthusiasm ("damning with faint praise"), is contrary to the spirit of agreeing to their making a positive recommendation.

Sensing the mood of a report-back meeting, or being forewarned about the contrary views of a board, can provoke a swift and prudent adjustment in attitude in the most hardy of negotiators and can change their commitment to deliver what they promised to you before they adjourned. In my experience, however, most people who undertake a personal commitment to recommend something positively to their members or board usually do so.

Where the other party has reservations, or anticipates them being expressed at the report-back sessions, they usually raise them while you are still together, presumably in search of some relief from their concerns. This gives an opportunity to consider using the **traded small movement** close.

Traded small movement close

You can use the traded small movement close there and then, or decide to use it when the other party returns with their reservations more insistently stated because they are backed by a recent mandate.

The traded small movement close refers to a small movement because it is only sensible to make a small adjustment at this late stage in the negotiation. To agree to move at this time on some significant issue would be counter-productive.

Large movements near the end of a negotiation send the wrong signal—if you move on a major issue or make a large movement on an issue at this time, why should the other party consider that your room for significant movement on other issues is over? They might as well keep pushing to see how far you will move on every issue.

So to be credible, any movement at the close must be small relative to movement experienced at the beginning of a negotiation, and it must only be on a relatively minor aspect of the deal. People still pushing for large movement this late in the proceedings are not close to agreement anyway.

The movement must be traded and not merely conceded.

You offer to move on the small issue at the request of the other negotiator in return for something that would be to your benefit. That is why it is a useful device to secure their positive recommendation for the agreement in exchange for meeting in some limited way on their remaining concerns. Of course, they can manipulate these sorts of concessions out of you, but provided that you pay attention and continue to be alert to the danger of making important breaches on major issues, or of making small movements on issues that have major implications for you down the track, you can contain the danger. This is not easy near the end of long and tiring negotiations in uncomfortable and stressful surroundings and with the distractions of the increasing euphoria you begin to feel now that the end is in sight.

Final offer closes   One area of confusion in closing is the vexed question of so-called **final offers**, or "take-it-or-leave-it" closes.

Usually, the biggest problem with final offer closes is that they ain't. They are sometimes sprung too early and are bereft of credibility. Naive negotiators use them, almost from the start. They present their bargain and exclaim that this is "my final offer".

Only slightly worse is the equally silly question in response to a first, or early, proposal: "Is that your final offer?" It's a silly question because, if you think about it, the likely answer you'll get is not the one you want.

You want the other person to respond with something like: "Of course it's not my final offer. If you don't like it, I've several more in my bag for you to consider." Your chances of getting this reply are as close to zero as you can get. They are more likely to answer: "Yes, it is my final offer".

How can they answer otherwise? You boxed them into a corner by asking them a silly question. If they did answer in the way you dream about—it would have to be a dream because reality isn't remotely like that—how would you react? You'd do the obvious and ask to see their other offers, which is why you don't get the answer you think you want.

As you won't get the answer you want and won't like the answer you get, my advice is not to ask silly questions in the first place!

Claiming your bargain to be a final offer when it isn't is certainly silly. Your assertions about final offers notwithstanding, the point of negotiating is to arrive at a jointly agreed, not unilaterally asserted, final offer (the bargain). Experience shows that unilateral final offers are seldom agreed. They provoke resentment if credible, and derision if not.

A final offer precludes negotiation on it and, if it doesn't, it isn't a final offer. Unless you are seriously determined to do without an agreement on mutually acceptable terms and are prepared to live with the consequences, you are advised to take great care before trying final offer closes.

Telling the other party to "take it or leave it", using any form of words you like, may lead them to leave it. If you can do without the deal, fine, but if you can't, or prefer not to, it's not such a wise close on your part. Ultimatum closes are products of your emotionalism, frustration and above all inexperience. It will damage your credibility to make "final offers" and then continue negotiating.

I heard one recently, when a relatively small sum of $12,500 in compensation was declared to be a "final offer" (this in a negotiation with a gross value of $1.4 million). The lead negotiator had declared privately beforehand that he "would not under any circumstances pay more than $12,500", because he considered it to be "too generous" already (it was his money!).

The other negotiator looked incredulously at him when he heard the "final offer" close. I knew what was coming next—the lead negotiator was asked if he was serious and if he would jeopardise the entire $1.4 million deal for $12,500? He was also asked to reconsider his "final offer" during an adjournment. Following the adjournment and after further negotiations, his "final offer" proved to be only a "final offer but three", because they settled the compensation at $31,500.

Observing this predictable outcome—I was not conducting the negotiation because he insisted on doing so himself—I noted that once his credibility collapsed, following his silly "final offer" close, he handed the initiative over to the other side. Clearly they didn't make silly mistakes about "final offers".

SUMMARY

Bargains are explicit, not tentative, proposals because they state the specific solutions on which a negotiator is prepared to settle. If they are accepted, then the negotiation part is over, and the negotiators only have to agree what has been agreed.

Bargains are best stated in an "If–Then" format with the conditions stated first, followed by the offer. Both conditions and offer must be specified, leaving no room for ambiguity.

Bargains may be rejected, but a more effective response (unless there are major issues and interests left unaddressed) is to question those aspects on which you have reservations and to offer a counter-bargain expressing your specific alternative.

Red bargaining is institutionalized in the tendering system. It appears "fair" to sellers but it maximizes buyers' pressure on them. In effect the buyer says: "If you comply with my terms and do not pad your prices, then I might consider your offer." The seller feels compelled to put in a "compliant" tender (accepting all the buyer's terms, even onerous ones) and to trim their prices, leaving no room to trade, if pushed to do so later. They rely totally on the buyer, and their own imagination, for information about the state of the competition (if there is any!).

The costs of failed tenders—and they can be very large sums—must be spread as overheads in the prices of the successful tenders, thus increasing the unit cost of supply.

The alternative of purple relationship bargaining, or partnering, has come into vogue recently. This removes tensions between a red results or a blue relationship orientation.

To be considered successful, purple relationship bargaining must produce results at least as good as red or blue bargaining and the relationship must serve the interests of both parties.

The buyer carefully selects only a few suppliers— preferably one for each service in place of dozens—on the basis of experience of their working methods and products.

The relationship develops from explicit conditional bargaining (purple conditionality) to implicit relationship bargaining, in which each party is totally open about costings, profit margins, research and development, and the sharing of cost savings from collaboration.

The recent development of the concept of coopetition could prove a fruitful extension of relationship bargaining by wedding it to business strategy.

Negotiations can be closed by several helpful devices such as the summary close, the adjournment close, and the traded small movement close.

Less helpful closes, such as the "final offer" close, are not advised. They can precipitate a failure to agree when there was still scope for agreement.

When parties agree, they should "agree what they have agreed" before they separate because this avoids difficulties later. Even unintentional misunderstandings engender mistrust.

RECOMMENDED READING

John A Carlisle and Robert C Parker (1989) *Beyond Negotiation: Redeeming Customer-supplier Relationships*, Chichester, John Wiley.

P D V Marsh (198) *Contract Negotiation Handbook*, Chapter 4, Aldershot, Gower.

Barry J Nalebuff and Adam M Brandenburger (1996) *Co-opetition*, London, HarperCollins.

Michael E Porter (1980) *Competitive Strategy: Techniques for Analyzing Industries and Competitors*, pp 24–32, New York, Free Press.

Neil Rackham, Lawrence Friedman & Richard Ruff (1996) *Getting Partnering Right: How Market Leaders Are Creating Long-Term Competitive Advantage*, New York, McGraw-Hill

ANSWERS TO SELF-ASSESSMENT 10

1
(a) "If you accepted it on a license-only basis, then we would agree to foreign rights."

(b) "If we can pay in monthly installments, then we might accept your fee."

(c) "Would it be OK if we used our own transport?"

2
(a) "If you agree to a 20 percent bonus, then we will raise productivity by 5 five percent."

(b) "If you expedite the purchase date by 90 days, then we will secure and fence the site."

(c) "If we receive the appropriate assurances as detailed in our letter of 12 August, then we will pay $100,000 against your outstanding debts."

3
(a) Only if the deal is acceptable because a "Yes" to a bargain closes the negotiation.

(b) Certainly, if either or both are not yet satisfactory for you.

(c) Only if the deal is unacceptable. Probably best to try (b) first, just in case their answers clarify some aspect of the condition and the offer and signal possibilities of further flexibility. Merely saying "No" does not help progress your interests.

13 Rational Problem Solving: An Alternative?

1 Isaac and Mustafa are negotiating a business deal but cannot agree on the terms. It is getting quite heated. Should they:

   (a) Go their separate ways?

   (b) Ask a facilitator to assist them?

   (c) Continue negotiating?

2 A tenant is stressed to find out that his landlord wants to increase the rent on his apartment. Should he:

   (a) Initiate legal proceedings?

   (b) Report her to a Rent Control Board?

   (c) Offer to keep quiet about her greedy intentions, provided that she reduces the rent immediately and pays compensation for the stress she has caused?

Roger Fisher and William Ury, two academics at Harvard University, produced a book in 1981 called *Getting to Yes: Negotiating Agreement Without Giving In*. This has had a profound effect on the theory and practice of dispute resolution from a rational problem-solving perspective. In this chapter I will consider the main characteristics of this approach and how it differs from the approach of purple conditionality which I advocate in this book.

PRINCIPLED NEGOTIATION

Principled negotiation is an alternative to the red behavior which manifests itself whenever bargaining over **positions** is undertaken. The goal, say Fisher and Ury, should instead be an agreement that is "wise", "efficient", and "good for the relationship".

People should be separated from the problem with which the negotiation is concerned by being "soft" on the people and "hard" on the problem. A wise agreement, like justice, is blind. It judges issues on their merits. There is no tension between "trusting" and "distrusting" because reaching agreement is independent of the degree of interpersonal trust.

Principled negotiators are concerned with **interests**. They accept the need to "meet the legitimate interests of each side to the extent possible" by "resolving conflicting interests fairly".

They invent **options for mutual gain**—as many as are feasible—through brainstorming and postpone judgment on the options until these can be discussed.

Last, the resolution of the problem is by reasoning, not coercion. This is achieved by agreeing on an "**objective standard**" or criterion against which the proposed solutions are tested. Principled negotiators "yield to principle, not to pressure".

Principled negotiation has proved attractive to people disillusioned with the everyday practice of negotiation—its adversarial biases, emotional content and the deals decided by who has the most power and not by who has the best case. Although principled negotiation provides powerful insights, it has not swept the board of negotiation practice. It is worth examining why.

RATIONALITY AND IRRATIONALITY

The theory of rational decision making is intellectually unchallengeable. Studies show the stark consequences of avoidable irrational errors made by negotiators.

However, the irony is that bitter disputes do not occur because people are opposed to rationality in decision making. People enter into disputes because they believe that they are rational and others are irrational.

"Rational expectations"

When a decision that is extremely important to your interests is to be made by somebody else, and what you do depends on your "rational expectations" of what that person will do, you are vulnerable to their, perhaps imperfect, rationality. When you are frustrated by that rationality you react with simmering (sometimes boiling) hostility.

Experiments show that highly motivated rational individuals, when interacting in pairs, can make incompatible choices, even when they have the same evidence and data (consider the prisoner's dilemma). When the stakes are high—somebody gets killed, for example—the outcome can be tragically personal. Fortunately, when pairwise rationality fails, it's mainly just irritating.

HARD OR SOFT?

Positional bargaining

Positional bargainers adopt a position and defend it at all costs, until forced to shift to a new position which they defend until forced to shift again. If both negotiators shift their positions enough times, they might reach an agreement. If either digs in too deep for too long, the other might get disheartened before they reach an agreement.

Hard and soft games are alternative ways of dealing with a negotiator who does not shift their position quickly enough. The soft negotiator attempts to close the gap between positions by moving towards the hard bargainer, and the hard negotiator attempts to achieve the same end by forcing the soft(er) bargainer to move towards them.

Two soft negotiators collapse towards each other; two hard bargainers provoke a deadlock. As principled negotiation denies that there is a third option (purple trading, for instance), it is necessary to "change the game" altogether.

This is a credible, but false, formulation of the bargaining problem. The language that reflects this erroneous view of the process is endemic in the common discourse of negotiators. They talk about "making concessions", "conceding", "giving up this or that", and "concession making", as if this accurately describes what negotiation is about. It is very easy to slip into the behavior which this language implies.

This view disregards the essentials of multilateral **trading** behavior. Negotiators who make one-way concessions, whether through yielding to pressure or through a futile search for the goodwill of a "hard" negotiator, move by unilaterally conceding, not trading. It is not necessary to choose between being hard or soft, it is only necessary to change your behavior and practice purple trading.

Purple trading is the way forward

A BRIEF CRITIQUE OF PRINCIPLED NEGOTIATION

The case for deciding on the basis of merit ("yield to principle, not to pressure") may be seen as overwhelming, although it is difficult to apply when your version of the merits of your case varies from somebody else's.

Fisher and Ury illustrate positional bargaining by alluding to a dispute between two people, one of whom says: "I'm not going to give in. If you want to go to the movies with me, it's *The Maltese Falcon* or nothing." But what are they bargaining about? It's not positional bargaining: it's positional posturing by ultimatum.

Positional posturing

They advocate "focusing on interests not positions", as if positions are the problem. Posturing over positions *is* a problem, but bargaining over them is not. Focusing on interests to the exclusion of considering positions is not wise. Interests are our motivation for negotiating. They are why we want something in this or that form.

It is unquestionably sensible that interests should be explored and understood. However, it is not wise to exclude issues and positions. Issues are the agenda items of the negotiation and find their expression, usually as quantities or forms of words, in ranges of positions.

Interests are not negotiable

You cannot reach a settlement to a negotiation solely by focusing on interests. Indeed, interests are not negotiable. Each person unilaterally decides on their own interests and nobody has a veto on which interests you are permitted and which you must abandon. You negotiate on your positions on the issues that you believe will deliver your interests.

There is a range of positions that are acceptable to you on a particular negotiable issue, commencing with your entry position and moving through a range to an exit position, beyond which you prefer not to go. You reach an acceptable solution by trading along and between the ranges each person holds on the issues. This is the workaday activity of negotiating.

Fisher and Ury recommend that principled negotiators move from "interests to concrete options". By this they must mean that negotiators consider their positions—for what is a position if not a "concrete option"?

They suggest that principled negotiators think in terms of "illustrative suggestions", and assert that:

> Much of what positional bargainers hope to achieve with an opening position can be accomplished equally well with an illustrative suggestion that generously takes care of your interests.

Note the language: an "illustrative suggestion" (a proposal?) that "generously" (an opening position?) addresses your interests—or, in other words, your opening position!

And they describe (approvingly) an "illustrative suggestion" from a baseball player's agent, who suggests (proposes?) that his client be offered "$250,000 and a five-year contract" (a bargain?). From my considerable experience of agents negotiating with football clubs, I fail to see how the "illustrative suggestions" of a principled negotiator are any different from how players' agents propose their positional bargains.

Fisher and Ury's insistence on applying objective criteria *appears* to be a rational alternative to the sometimes messy exchanges of positional bargaining. On examination, however, the search for objective criteria is found wanting.

OBJECTIVE CRITERIA

In legal processes where the principle of applying objective criteria (the law) is endemic, the parties do not have to agree on what constitutes appropriate criteria or on whether they apply in the particular circumstances in which they prosecute or defend. That is for the judge and jury to decide. In contrast in negotiation, a mainly private process, there is no set notion of what constitutes objective criteria.

Consider two positional bargainers searching for a solution. Naturally, they prefer their own solutions to someone else's. Only uninvolved third parties, immune to the consequences of the eventual decision, are (possibly) indifferent as to which solution is chosen.

If negotiations were only conducted by the uninvolved, rational choice decisions could prevail. But people who feel aggrieved don't hand over their disputes to third parties. In some cases this might be feasible—public policy controversies, perhaps—but in the vast majority of negotiations it would not. Arbitration or mediation is normally a last, not a first, resort of those in dispute.

A rationale

If by objective criteria we mean that a solution should have some rationale behind it, few would quarrel with that as an ideal prescription. Negotiators already agree with the sentiments of rationality by their evident habits of justifying their stances by reference to some coherent, and in their view compelling, logic. This does not resolve the dispute on its own, of course, because competing "rational" solutions to the same problem are presented— this is why we negotiate!

The dispute over criteria—with each side believing that

their own selection is truly "objective"—is every bit as controversial as the decision that the criteria support. Insisting on objective criteria does not remove the dispute, nor the pressure (not just intimidatory pressure but also pressures of time, saving face, culture, politics, and so on). Insisting on objective criteria merely shifts the dispute to other levels.

THE ORIGINS OF PRINCIPLED NEGOTIATION

Three sources can be identified for the origins of the prescriptions of principled negotiation.

First, it is a rational decision model, with its theoretical roots in the individual decision models of Nobel Prize-winning economists Herbert Simon and Milton Friedman.

Second, its conceptual roots lie in critiques, written by Roger Fisher, of US foreign policy and practice during the Cold War.

Third, the methodology is rooted in mediation processes and is dependent on third-party intervention by facilitators.

Negotiators have to negotiate in the world in which they operate. For the foreseeable future, principled negotiation will remain a minority activity, confined to mediators and facilitators in public dispute processes and international conferences. This is not so depressing a conclusion as it may imply. Principled negotiation is actually a misnomer. It is not about negotiation as most people understand and practice it. It is a mechanism for rational joint problem solving that, in common with all methods of decision making, is applicable in certain circumstances but not others.

RECOMMENDED READING

M. H. Bazerman & M. A. Neale (1992) *Negotiating Rationally*, New York, Free Press.

Roger Fisher and William Ury (1981) *Getting to Yes: Negotiating Agreement Without Giving In*, Houghton Mifflin, Boston.

M. A. Neale & M. H. Bazerman (1991) *Cognition and Rationality in Negotiation*, New York, Free Press.

T. C. Schelling (1960) *The Strategy of Conflict*, Cambridge, Mass., Harvard University Press.

ANSWERS TO SELF-ASSESSMENT 11

1

(a) Perhaps, but how do you know that they have fully explored all the possibilities? Don't judge negotiations by their noise.

(b) How did she get into the question? Is there a pool of facilitators ready and waiting which we don't know about?

(c) Yes. Early rhetoric in a negotiation is to be expected. Both Isaac and Mustafa should know that and probably won't thank you for giving in so easily if you chose (b), and may wonder about who is to pay for the "facilitator" if you introduce one without their asking for one. Most parties to a negotiation prefer to handle their own affairs.

2

(a) Perhaps not, as this keeps makes it public and it could sour relationships, plus it costs money.

(b) What Rent Control Board? There just happens to be one in your city? How convenient!

(c) Not advised on its own because what the tenant is proposing smacks of blackmail, which, if it doesn't work and he then chooses (a), the landlord's lawyers will focus on the attempted "blackmail" as their reason for not correcting the "oversight" of their rent increase.

14 The New Negotiating Edge

YOU now have the necessary behavioral tools to acquire and sustain a new edge in most, if not all, of the negotiations in which you are likely to be a player.

To benefit from your new negotiating edge, you do not have to deal only with people who recognize red, blue or purple behaviors. Nor are you limited to those who realize that there is a process common to all negotiations, no matter with whom they negotiate, what is at stake, which cultures the participants are from or what interests they have in common or which conflict.

The edge lies in your awareness of how people negotiate the world over.

Start with behavior

The behavioral approach starts from how people behave, consciously or unconsciously, whatever their level of understanding of what they are doing or why they are behaving in this or that way.

Your behavioral edge comes from being aware of the common process (conveniently summarized as four phases: **prepare**, **debate**, **propose** and **bargain**) and being able to practice those behaviors that have been shown to work most effectively in the appropriate phase.

Simultaneously, you will seek to reduce (eliminating them altogether is probably a utopian ambition for most of us) the incidence of those behaviors that have been shown to be ineffective, even dysfunctional, in their contribution to securing acceptable settlements.

Most untrained negotiators behave for much of their time as **red** players because they are heavily tainted with varying shades of aggressive, competitive, and untrusting interpretations or expressions of the role of negotiation in decision making

They behave in a red style because they mistakenly believe that red behavior is the way to get the best results. In doing so, they sacrifice the potential gains they could get from developing their relationship with those able to help them achieve their results.

Other negotiators behave as if the only option for them is to behave in a **blue** style because this seems to be the only course of action open to them if they wish to avoid contamination by those with red intentions and with whom, for various reasons, they believe they must sustain a relationship.

Blue players ignore the evidence of experience (always a dangerous folly for a negotiator) and are too trusting, too guileless, and too often candidates for the status of "lambs to the slaughter".

Red behaviorists welcome blue behavior in those with whom they negotiate. That is their life mission: to intimidate their way to getting what they want—without, if possible, having to trade anything to benefit those from whom they aim to get what they want for (next to) nothing.

The **purple** behaviorist, however, does not imitate the red style of negotiating behavior just because everybody else seems to behave that way. Nor do they submit to red-style behavior by giving in. They are interested in *both* results and the relationship and know that both objectives are closely linked to how they behave during the process and in the quality of the outcome.

Purple behaviorists see negotiation as a **trade**: they

seek to get what they want from those who want to get something from them. They fuse their red demands (what they want) with their blue offers (what the other party wants) in a conditional purple format: "If you give me what I want, *then* I can give you this amount of what you want."

How much is traded in exchange for what each party wants is decided by the universal process of negotiating. Each can withhold their consent—each has a veto, in this sense. What they agree to—if they agree—they voluntarily consent to because they always have the option of doing without what they want from that party. In the event that they exercise their veto, they either must find somebody else, or do without what they want altogether, or find some other means of acquiring it other than by negotiation.

PREPARE

In **preparation**, you seek to identify your **interests**—those motivations that drive you to seek this or that solution to some problem you want addressed, such as your wanting more money, more resources, less hassle, less pollution, further promotion, continuing peace, swifter redress, more freedom for yourself, less freedom for somebody else, and so on through the endless list of potential wants to which any one of us might aspire in a lifetime.

If you see negotiation as a means to get you what you want, irrespective of the wants of the other party, you are thinking in a red manner and will probably disregard any consideration of the other party's interests. This is a profound mistake, but none the less common for being so.

The imperatives of interest-based bargaining were recognized by Adam Smith over two centuries ago: the surest way to serve your own interests by getting what you want from somebody else is to serve their interests too. Serving the other party's interests by offering what you have that they want, in exchange for what they have that you want, is the foundation of the purple approach.

From their interests, the purple negotiator identifies the negotiable **issues** that could address their problem(s)—these form your negotiation agenda. Some issues are of greater importance to you than others. Achieving them will contribute more to your satisfaction with the potential outcomes than achieving others. Therefore, you **prioritize** the issues, either implicitly or explicitly.

The simplest priority ranking you can use is to allocate the issues into high priority (those wants that you must get if you are to do a deal at all), medium priority (those wants that you regard as important to the overall deal but not in themselves deal breakers), and low priority (those wants that would be good to get, but they do not constitute deal breakers—though they may be of higher priority to the other party).

For each of the issues you identify positions along a **range** of possible solutions, from where you enter the negotiation dialog (your **entry** position) to where you intend, on the basis of what you know, to exit (your **exit** position). Your negotiation range on each issue is a matter of predilection and circumstance, including the time that you have available to negotiate on any particular occasion.

The range for each issue can be relatively large (you enter "high" but you are prepared to settle "low") or relatively narrow (you enter not very far from where you decide you must settle). Negotiation is an art not a science, so your choice of negotiation ranges will depend on what is credible or defensible and on your beliefs about the other negotiator's expectations.

DEBATE

The largest proportion of time taken up by face-to-face negotiation sessions is accounted for by **debate**.

Red and blue debate behaviors complement each other: the red arguer intimidates the blue submissive by various forms of destructive debate (blocking, attacking, blaming, threatening, and demanding "one-way street" decisions). The blue submissive is intimidated and coerced into disregarding (or at least downplaying) their own interests.

When two red behaviorists clash the outcome is a

product of their adversarial and confrontational manners, often accompanied by sanctions and other coercive and threatening behaviors.

Purple debate behavior builds on purple preparation. It is predicated on the assumption that the other party is in legitimate pursuit of their interests and that identifying the other party's interests requires the negotiator to engage in purple behavior, such as asking **questions** and listening carefully to the answers; **listening** to statements and views about how the other party sees the problem and what solutions they prefer; being able to **summarize** their views neutrally to check for understanding; **signaling** and responding to the other party's signals to encourage a willingness to consider movement (negotiation is the management of movement); and generally on conducting your own behavior in a constructive—but firm—manner.

PROPOSE

Nothing really happens in negotiation until the parties discuss **proposals**, which are **tentative** suggestions of what might constitute a solution. Red proposals are "one-way streets" that take no account of the other party's requirements. Blue proposals are also one-way streets but are offers to settle on the other party's terms without a requirement—though there may be a hope—that their own wishes are met.

As a purple negotiator you state your proposals in the purple **If–Then** format. This sharpens your edge because you fuse both your red **demands** (what you want) with your blue **offers** (what you will give them in return). You use assertive language, but always temper red demands with the palliative of being prepared to consider making a blue offer.

Moreover, you eschew negotiating on a piecemeal basis, such as taking each issue on its own and settling it before moving to another issue. The purple negotiator prefers to **link** issues together and to construct package deals, where "nothing is agreed until everything is agreed". This does not preclude your reaching provisional agreement on individual issues—doing so can be a

confidence-building measure—but the purple negotiator
seeks to link even "settled" issues, if by so doing it creates
possibilities for movement on issues where the parties are
temporarily deadlocked or in difficulties.

Where proposals are tentative, bargains are **specific**. The
parties know the terms of the deal in the bargaining phase
and bargains that are expressed in the If–Then format do
better than those expressed otherwise. The **condition**
specifies what is wanted and the **offer** specifies what will
be given in exchange. There is no ambiguity in the bargain,
though it is still open to further negotiation should that be
necessary.

BARGAIN

    However, if the bargain is acceptable and both parties
say "Yes", the negotiation is over. It remains for you to
record what has been agreed and then to implement it.

    If the bargain is unacceptable, the receiving party can
seek to amend it, either in its condition or in its offer. You
could state your price for accepting the other party's
conditions or specify your conditions for accepting their
offer or, of course, specify some combination of changes to
both their conditions and their offer.

    If necessary this can involve returning to debate (asking
questions, listening, etc.) or to each side floating tentative
suggestions (proposals) of how the bargain could be made
more acceptable.

    The purple negotiator is able to work backwards and
forwards through the phases in any order as required.

    You have the confidence and the skills to do so
because you understand both the way in which the
process of negotiation is structured and the way in which
purple behavioral skills are integrated into each phase.

The next thing for you to do is seek opportunities to
practice your new negotiating edge. Practice makes for
proficiency, as can be seen in the difference between
those negotiators who are excellent and those who are
only of average proficiency.

PRACTICE

    The excellent negotiator always gets the basics right

and the average negotiator often gets them wrong—while those below average seldom do anything right.

You can start practicing right away. Select individual skills and practice them three or four times until they become part of your repertoire and so automatic that you do not have to think terribly hard about applying them.

Some people when introduced to the behavioral skills of negotiating treat them as if they are too simple to be applied by someone doing important work. They go off in search of an "advanced" skills course, without having undertaken the necessary practice to ensure that they are proficient in the "basics".

This is unfortunate, because there are no advanced skills as such. The four phases and the behavioral skills to which you have been exposed in this book are all the skills that you need to negotiate in any circumstances.

True, there are simple or routine negotiating circumstances and complex and highly complex negotiating circumstances. But the behavioral negotiating skills required are no different in any set of circumstances, because it is the circumstances that are more complex, not the skills.

And in any case, if you do not have the basic skills of negotiation up to an excellent level of proficiency, it is difficult to see what you will gain from seeking so-called advanced skills.

Interestingly, in this regard, when Martina Navratilova asked Billy Jean King to coach her in preparation for her seventh Wimbledon final, she was astonished to find her new coach and friend (herself many times Wimbledon champion) asking her to explain how to play tennis, starting with how to hold the racket and how to serve a ball. In time Navratilova realized just how important it was for a highly proficient and experienced player such as herself to go back to the basics of what the game is about, so that she could apply her undoubtedly great proficiency in the more complex circumstances of yet another championship final.

You can do yourself the same favor that King did for

Navratilova by practicing everything from the beginning until you are a lot better than "good enough". And when you are better than "good enough", what's holding you back from becoming (and staying) excellent?

This final self-assessment is in the form of a short examination in negotiation. If you would like your answers to be assessed by the author and wish to receive a set of model answers, please send them (typed if possible!) to the address at the end of the self-assessment.

It is best if you give evidence of your understanding using relevant examples, especially from your own experience or from observations of negotiating problems in the media. Answers heavily contaminated with non-relevant material (no matter how accurate the non-relevant material) will undermine confidence in your ability to answer the question.

PART 1: FASHION TRADE CASE
Read the following short case and then answer the questions as if you were giving advice as a negotiator to the company:

Top Class Fashions, based in Hong Kong, are due to have a meeting with Swift Holdings, a European client, with whom their current turnover is $15 million (when the relationship started five years ago, Top Class produced clothes to Swift's designs and the turnover was $5 million). Top Class has intimated by e-mail that they will be looking for a 9.5 percent increase in price, effective next month.

Recent productivity improvements at Top Class dampened down cost increases to only 5.5 percent during the past year and they also gained from a 3.5 percent windfall foreign exchange movement. This year Top Class invested heavily in a new plant in mainland China and need to expand sales by volume and revenue to pay for the borrowing costs and to justify the growth in capacity.

Swift Holdings have already expressed their doubts about price rises while there is uncertainty about exchange rate movements in Europe and the short term prospects for the Euro. While the recession is over in the UK, it is still a problem in other European countries. The most Swift is prepared to consider is a price rise of 3 percent.

They have informed Top Class that they have a new range of clothing designs ready for release, worth initially about $1 million a year and growing thereafter, in addition to their current ranges, and they intend to place this order following the meeting, either with Top Class or with another manufacturer in Thailand.

They also have a problem to bring to the meeting concerning a shipment of 10,000 pairs of jeans which Swift has rejected because of "poor stitching". These jeans cost Swift $20 a pair (cost, insurance and freight from Hong Kong plus UK inspection and packing) and they normally retail in Europe at $60. Shipping them back to Hong

Kong would cost $30,000, or they could be disposed of below cost in the secondary "imperfect" market.

Top Class asks your advice in the form of the following questions:

1   What are our interests and why?
2   How would you rank our priorities?
3   What should we propose about the rejected jeans?
4   What pricing proposal might we put to Swift?

Each answer is worth up to 10 marks (total = 40 marks).

PART 2: ESSAY QUESTIONS
Please select *three* questions to answer. Each answer is worth up to 20 marks (total marks = 60). Essay answers should contain between 500 and 800 words only.

1 Why do most people interpret their objectives in the red–blue dilemma game as obliging them to play red in the opening round?

2 In what ways might signaling behavior help move a negotiation forward?

3 Why is a proposal not a bargain?

4 How does the negotiator's surplus assist in understanding the dynamics of a negotiation?

5 Why are the distinctions between interests, issues, and positions important in negotiation?

6 Faced with a difficult red behaviorist, how might you behave?

Send your answers to:

> Negotiate Limited
> 99 Caiyside
> Edinburgh EH10 7HR
> Scotland
> UK
> Tel: +44 (0)131 445 7571
> Fax: +44 (0)131 445 7572

If resident in the UK, please enclose a stamped addressed envelope for the same amount it costs to send your answers.

If resident elsewhere, please enclose an addressed envelope and International Postal Coupons to the same value as it costs to send your answers.

Please allow 30 days for processing.

Appendix:
Rules for the Red–Blue
Dilemma Game

Players are divided into pairs.

Each participant takes two pieces of paper about the size of a credit or business card. On one of these pieces they write the letter R (for red) and on the other the letter B (for blue).

Players will always commence each round of the game with their own two pieces of paper and they always make a private and independent choice as to which of the two pieces of paper, "red" or "blue", to play.

There are 10 rounds in the dilemma game. Each round consists of each player independently selecting one of their pieces of paper marked either R or B, a selection which they reveal to each other simultaneously.

The round is scored depending on which combination of red and/or blue the players have independently chosen and simultaneously revealed. All three possible combinations of red and blue produce a score (positive or negative). The three possible combinations produce the following scores:

Blue and Blue	+ 4 points each
Red and Red	− 4 points each
Red and Blue	+ 8 points to the player who played red
	− 8 points to the player who played blue

The objective of each player is to maximize their positive score over 10 rounds.

Note: do not elaborate on this objective. Deflect questions on what it means, otherwise you might inadvertently influence how the participants play the game.

For example, they often ask if it is their combined or their individual scores that they must maximize. Tell them they must interpret the objective themselves. And make no comments on how the objective can be interpreted.

Remind the players that they must play every round under the same rules— their partner must not be able to see which color they are playing before they have revealed their choice.

MORE ON HOW TO PLAY THE DILEMMA GAME

The 10 rounds in the game are divided into three sessions:

Session I

Rounds 1 to 4, before and during which no discussion between the players is permitted. They meet, independently select their choices for round 1 and then simultaneously reveal their choices to each other.

They note their scores from the three possible combinations of red and blue and continue to play silently through rounds 2, 3, and 4.

Break: After round 4, the players may discuss for 5 minutes what has happened so far, what they might wish to do for the next four rounds, and how they might coordinate their play.

Rounds 5 through 8 are played in exactly the same manner as for rounds 1 to 4, i.e., players independently choose which color to play, simultaneously reveal their plays and maintain silence while playing.

Whatever they might have agreed, the "agreement" is unenforceable, i.e., either player may defect on what they agreed and in consequence play differently. But each round must be played under the rules—i.e., unlike golf shots, no round is assumed to have been played, it must *be* played.

Break: After round 8, the players have another discussion, again seeking agreement on how they might play rounds 9 and 10. Their discussions, and willingness to reach agreement are influenced by what they experienced in rounds 1 to 8. Again, after five minutes they must recommence playing with or without agreement.

There are two rounds left (9 and 10). For these two rounds the scores double, positively or negatively. Thus, the combination of blue and blue produces a score of +8 each; red and red produces a score of –8 each, and the combination red and blue produces a score of +16 to the player who played red and –16 to the player who played blue.

End: At the end of the 10 rounds, each player adds their scores for each round to produce their total for the game.

Source: *The Negotiate Trainer's Manual* (1996) Edinburgh, Session 11, pp 6–9.

Session 2

Session 3

NEGOTIATE LIMITED

ex bona fide negotiari

Negotiate is an Edinburgh-based international consultancy that specializes in negotiation skills training and negotiation consultancy.

Negotiate supplies books, videos, and training materials on negotiation in English and 11 other languages.

Negotiate licenced trainers deliver training workshops and seminars in Europe, South Africa, South Asia, and Australia.

For details of our negotiation products and licence opportunities, hit our Web site:

http://www.negotiate.co.uk

Dr Gavin Kennedy may be contacted by e-mail at:

gavin@neg1.demon.co.uk

Negotiate is always interested in hearing from practicing negotiators and negotiation trainers who wish to discuss any aspect of negotiation skills, policy or strategy.

Contact us at:

Negotiate Limited
99 Caiyside
Edinburgh EH10 7HR
Scotland UK

Tel: +44 (0)131 445 7571
Fax: +44 (0)131 445 7572